BENJAMIN FRANKLIN AND HIS GODS

Benjamin Franklin and His Gods

KERRY S. WALTERS

UNIVERSITY OF ILLINOIS PRESS
URBANA AND CHICAGO

Manufactured in the United States of America
1 2 3 4 5 C P 6 5 4 3

This book is printed on acid-free paper.

Library of Congress Cataloging-in-Publication Data

Walters, Kerry S.
Benjamin Franklin and his gods / Kerry S. Walters.
p. cm.
Includes bibliographical references (p.) and index.
ISBN 0-252-02433-8 (acid-free paper) / ISBN 978-0-252-02433-7
ISBN 0-252-06739-8 (pbk. : acid-free paper) / ISBN 978-0-252-06739-6
1. Franklin, Benjamin, 1706-1790—Religion.
2. Statesmen—United States—Biography.
I. Title.
E302.6.F8 W27 1999
973.3'092—ddc21
[B] 98-9068
CIP

For Edwin and Cynthia Johnson,

Friends of Liberal Learning;

and for

Jim Pickering,

in memoriam

En chaque Religion il y a des choses essentielles, & il y a d'autres qui ne sont que des Formes & des Modes; Comme un pain de Sucre qui peut-etre enveloppé en Papier brun ou blanc ou bleu, & lié avec ficelle de chanvre ou de laine, rouge ou jaune; c'est toujours le Sucre qui est la chose essentielle.

—Franklin to Mme Brillon, April 1781

Contents

Acknowledgments

THAT EXTRAORDINARY MAN of letters C. S. Lewis was asked midpoint in his career to contribute a volume to the Oxford History of English Literature series. Lewis agreed but struggled with the book and a bad conscience for an unseemly number of years before he finally delivered the manuscript. During the uncomfortable interval, he grew accustomed to referring to the work in progress as his "OHELL book."

I know how he felt. I started thinking about and writing this book one summer over ten years ago in the Williams College library. Two other books and a handful of essays somehow got in the way, and several times the manuscript found itself temporarily shelved because I needed either more time to think through Franklin's writings or a vacation from them. As the seasons came and went I began to refer to the work in progress as my "Ye Gods!" book. I wasn't sure it would ever see the light of day.

But it has, and several people have helped me along the way. A final, much-needed incentive was provided by James Campbell when he kindly invited me to read a paper on Franklin's religion at the 1995 annual meeting of the Society for the Advancement of American Philosophy. I profited greatly from the feedback of the session's participants. I am grateful to them, as I am also grateful to Peter Hare, who subsequently invited me to publish the paper "A Note on Benjamin Franklin and the Gods" in the *Transactions of the Charles S. Peirce Society* 31 (Fall 1995). Douglas Candland of Bucknell University, one of the few authentic renaissance persons I have ever met, also prodded me at a time when I especially needed prodding. My thanks to him. The library staffs at Williams College, Harvard Divinity School, Bucknell University, and Gettysburg College were gracious and helpful. My students also served as patient and responsive sounding boards for my endless discourses on Franklin and Enlightenment religion.

I am immensely grateful for the careful eye and sensitive ear of my editor, Carol Bolton Betts. I am also indebted to the anonymous reader for the University of Illinois Press who offered insightful observations about an earlier version of this book. Factual inaccuracies or misinterpretations are, of course, my sole responsibility.

In this book I disagree, sometimes quite radically, with the earlier interpretation of Franklin's religion defended by Alfred Owen Aldridge in his book *Benjamin Franklin and Nature's God.* In spite of the differences in our interpretations, however, I am indebted more to Aldridge for my understanding of Franklin in particular and early American thought in general than to any other person. If I have managed to say anything worth reading in this book, it is because I have stood on the shoulders of a giant, and I take great pleasure in publicly acknowledging just how much I owe him.

This book is dedicated to three people who have meant much to liberal learning in this country and to me personally. The humanities, along with their tradition of civil discourse, humane tolerance, and reflective wonderment, have fallen on hard times lately. Ed and Cynthia Johnson are working diligently to preserve that tradition, as did my mentor and colleague Jim Pickering. I thank them for their contributions and their friendship.

Jonah and Kim, as usual, have kept me sane by slowing me down and helping me not to take myself so seriously. Old Ben Franklin would've gotten a kick out of both of them.

Benjamin Franklin and His Gods

Introduction: In Search of Franklin's Religion

BENJAMIN FRANKLIN wrote both too much and too little about his religious convictions. His reflections on things divine are voluminous, but scattered in time as well as unsystematic in presentation. These two qualities account for the difficulty in pinning down his religious beliefs. In the first place, the sheer bulk of Franklin's work makes the task of sifting through it a formidable one. Franklin was a tireless scribbler for close to seventy of his eighty-four years, and his multitudinous writings on God, religion, and morality must be gleaned from far-flung sources. These range from private memoranda and correspondence to short journalistic pieces, from an early metaphysical treatise (the only one he ever published) to the later, sometimes disingenuous recollections in his *Autobiography,* from correspondence intended for public perusal to letters written only for the eyes of his intimates.[1] Second, the lack of systemization in these various musings often so perplexes the hapless reader that he or she is apt to reach the disheartened conclusion that there is simply no core of consistency, no unifying theme, to the bewildering patchwork of Franklin's religious thought. Too much to assimilate readily, too little obvious cohesion to facilitate interpretation: these are the twin hurdles any interpreter of Franklin's reflections on religion must leap.

Partly because of the disorganization and daunting volume of Franklin's religious writings, partly from the frustration even the most patient of readers experiences in trying to decipher them, and partly because of the natural inclination to impose coherent patterns on unsystematic texts, there is a great temptation to make sense of Franklin's religious thought by stamping it with a template of the reader's own preference. The temptation is understandable. The possibility that there may be no system in the religious belief of a thinker as methodical as Franklin is difficult to accept. Consequently, the commentator sometimes unwittingly forces the issue by feeding the texts around the spindle of his own pet theory and then weaving an interpretive fabric that appeals to those passages that support it and ignores those that don't.

Within certain limits, a contrived reading of Franklin (or anyone else, for that matter) is inevitable. All of us are acutely aware these days of just how difficult it is to capture the "inherent" meaning of a text. But there is also a real danger in conceptual templating. It runs the risk of trivializing the actual ambiguities, inconsistencies, dead ends, and retrenchments that may be present in a work, and which reflect an essential ambivalence in the mind of the author. A Procrustean reading that lops off or stretches recalcitrant texts in order to make them fit interpretive beds results in monolithic readings of what might in fact be kaleidoscopic complexity. It also risks refracting the text through an interpretive prism largely the reader's own.

Unfortunately, this is precisely the modus operandi many commentators on Franklin's religious beliefs have adopted. In working their way through his sometimes baffling remarks on God, religion, and ethics, they've arrived at cohesive but artificial patterns by stamping his writings with any number of templates. This strategy, predictably, has produced a startling divergence of judgment about Franklin's religious thought. Some commentators read him as a profound albeit unorthodox Christian. Others see him as an infidel, indifferent if not outrightly hostile to religious sentiment. Some applaud him as a religious thinker far ahead of his time, while others deplore the shallow expediency they discern in his perspective. The spectrum of interpretations runs from hagiography to vilification.

The eighteenth-century Abbé Fauchet, for example, paid Franklin the backhanded compliment in 1790 of calling him "the philosopher par excellence of protestantism."[2] Less equivocally, James Parton in the mid-nineteenth century claimed that Franklin was "the consummate Christian" of his day. "Indeed," Parton gushed, "I do not know who, of any time, has exhibited more of the spirit of Christ. Like Christ, he lived among a host of narrow and intolerant sects without quarreling with any of them. Like Christ, he subordinated opinions and observances to conduct and feelings. He was tolerant of everything but intolerance, and made some charitable allowance even for that."[3]

But attempts such as these to elevate Franklin to the status of Christian prophet reflect the minority opinion. Much more prevalent is the contrary one that he was a disbeliever in Christianity—or, what often amounted to the same thing in the judgment of eighteenth-century minds, an out-and-out atheist. John Adams sneered that Franklin properly belonged to the ranks of "Atheists, Deists, and Libertines."[4] William Robertson, principal of the University of Edinburgh, more judiciously wrote in 1765 that "of all the Sciences the only in which I suspect he is not perfectly sound" is theology.[5] Joseph Priestley grudgingly allowed that Franklin believed "in the Being of a God and a particular providence," but he deplored the fact that Franklin's pernicious denial of a future state unhappily "made many Deists."[6] An American commentator in 1796 wrote that Franklin displayed a marked "indifference about religion," and he went on to remind his readers that such a charge was hardly surprising: "It is well known that the doctor believed *nothing*. . . . all the world knew that this great man disbelieved Christianity."[7] The Abbé Flamarene, less conflicted than his colleague Fauchet, concurred with this assessment. He reported with grim satisfaction that France's freethinkers had given Franklin their imprimatur on religious matters after concluding that "he had none [religious belief] of his own . . . , none at all."[8] Flamarene's appraisal was obviously shared by many of his countrymen, since they bestowed on Franklin the rather dubious distinction of listing him in the 1800 *Dictionnaire des athées anciens et modernes.*[9] Moreover, Ernest Renan, hardly a paragon of Christian orthodoxy himself, later echoed the judgment by branding Franklin as that type of worldly and materialistic man "beyond whom there are none in the world more atheistic."[10] A twentieth-century commentator agrees with Renan's sentiment by attributing to Franklin an "inability or at best unwillingness to partake of deep spiritual experience" and concludes that he was "nonreligious."[11] And another, in contrasting the "Franklinian [religious] dream" with the "Emersonian" one, determines that the former is a "self-validating materialism . . . ignorant of the inner, positive meaning of the freedom it posits as its end, and is in fact complacently blind with respect to any positive moral values or genuinely spiritual sense of human life."[12]

Any number of other purple encomiums and condemnations of Franklin the religious thinker could be cited, but the pattern would hold. Some commentators read him as a deeply religious, even orthodox, thinker. Others examine the same texts and conclude that Franklin had no religious sensibility or, if he did, it was at best shallowly conventional. As I suggested earlier, Franklin wrote both too much and too little about his religious thought. This almost invariably seduces unwary readers into filtering his work through their own preconceptions, and consequently discordant and even contradictory interpretations arise. In short, most commentators on Franklin's religion concur on the presence of the trees but disagree as to the lay of the forest.

Although efforts to come to grips with Franklin's religious thought often reveal more about the commentator than Franklin, some unsuccessful attempts illuminate, although dimly and indirectly, certain key features of his position. The trees are there for anyone to see, even if their precise pattern tends to be obfuscated by their density and range. Two twentieth-century analyses of Franklin's religion in particular unwittingly shed some light on the lay of the forest, and even though neither succeeds in charting its exact boundaries, an examination of them is instructive. Each in its own way points to an interpretive path to follow as well as dead ends to avoid. One comes from the deliciously vitriolic pen of D. H. Lawrence. The other is from the much more temperate hand of Alfred Owen Aldridge.

In a famous essay from his 1933 *Studies in Classic American Literature,* Lawrence brutally denounces Franklin's religious and moral thought as nothing more than a smug brief for bourgeois, marketplace values. Franklin, Lawrence insists, confused the rich glow of true interiority with the sparkling tinsel of silver dollars. His concept of God is a sickeningly pedestrian one: a divine Bookkeeper in a respectably boring business suit who mandates standards of behavior that justify a shallowly utilitarian approach to religion and morals. The highest form of veneration humans can bestow on this deity is worldly activity that leads to commercial and social success. As Lawrence poisonously says, "God is the supreme servant of men who want to get on, to *produce.* Providence. The provider. The heavenly storekeeper. The everlasting Wanamaker. And this is all the God the grandsons of the Pilgrim Fathers had left. Aloft on a pillar of dollars."[13]

This concept of the deity as a sort of celestial Entrepreneur who makes humans in his own cigar-chewing image and is gratified by their "reverent" pursuit of worldly success may have comforted the eighteenth-century merchant anxious for a divine nod of approval at his wheeling and dealing. But it's hardly an appropriate way to think about either God or what it means to be a person. Neither human nor divine nature can be captured by such a crudely self-serving model that oversimplifies as much as it offends. The "soul of man is a vast forest," insists Lawrence, but "all Benjamin intended was a neat back garden" laid out in mathematically precise rows of religious and moral bromides.[14] Do this, and one is happy, wealthy, and wise. Do that, and one wins worldly success as well as spiritual dividends from the heavenly stockbroker.

Lawrence refuses to be seduced by such a simplistic and smug perspective. "I'm not going to be turned into a virtuous little automaton as Benjamin would have me," he tells us. "I'm really not just an automatic piano with a moral Benjamin getting tunes out of me."[15] Instead, Lawrence declares that he will exult in the complexity and ambiguity that is his birthright, a richness of depth unplumbed by Franklin's prudential maxims. In one of the most striking passages of his essay, he counters what he sees as Franklin's shopkeeper mentality with his own defiant credo, taking it as a more authentic statement of the human spirit than Benjamin's "neat back garden."

"I believe," says Lawrence,

> That I am I.
> That my soul is a dark forest.
> That my known self will never be more than a little clearing in the forest.
> That gods, strange gods, come forth from the forest into the clearing of my known self, and then go back.
> That I must have the courage to let them come and go.
> That I will never let mankind put anything over me, but that I will try always to recognize and submit to the gods in me and the gods in other men and women.[16]

Lawrence's evaluation of Franklin's religious sensibility is remarkably illuminating, but not at all in the way he intended. There is nothing original or insightful about his accusation that Franklin reduced the religious and moral life to the level of a self-congratulatory championing of bourgeois values. Others before and since Lawrence have made similar charges, in spite of the fact, as I will argue in subsequent chapters, that they are unfounded. Instead, what is illuminating in Lawrence's essay is the credo he espouses in defiance of what he reads as poor Benjamin's shopkeeper spirituality. Lawrence would have been quite dumbfounded to discover that the credo he took as his own comes closer to capturing the heart of Franklin's religious thought than the stereotype he so entertainingly savages. Contrary to the caricature accepted by Lawrence and others, Franklin the religious thinker never deceived himself about either the nature of self-insight or the knowledge of God. He saw the two as quicksilverish, ineluctable, essentially elusive. For all his cheerleading rhetoric about worldly success, hard work, and the promise of reason, it's clear from his writings that he came to distrust simplistic and easy solutions as much as did Lawrence—particularly when it came to foundational questions about human nature, values, and religious belief.

To be human, the mature Franklin believed, is an often frightening business. It is to be torn between conflicting existential poles—reason and passion, virtue and vice, energy and lassitude, dogmatism and incredulity, faith and anxiety. Consequently, the individual must be on guard, continuously searching for a modus vivendi by which to balance them. His *Autobiography*'s famous program for the habituation of virtue, ridiculed by Lawrence as a "player piano" brainwashing, is precisely just such a strategy, aiming as it does to lighten the soul's darkness by training the individual to reconcile tensions between the poles. Self-discipline, Franklin believed, could widen the clearing a bit but never completely fell the murky forest of the self. There would always be impenetrable regions. Contrary to Lawrence, there is little of the tradesman's shallow smugness in Franklin's reflections on either the human condition or religious belief, in spite of his own distastefully jingoistic posturing as the prophet of economic success.

Moreover, the central theme in Franklin's religious thought, one he arrived at as early as 1728 in a manuscript entitled "Articles of Belief and Acts of Religion," is that there are as many "gods" that "come forth" from the self's forest as there are sects and religions—and, indeed, worshippers—and that the sincere seeker of religious truth must be willing to let these "strange gods" emerge as well as intrepid enough to allow them to "go back" when their time has passed. This doctrine, the key to understanding Franklin's religion, I call "theistic perspectivism." It served as the foundation of his reflections on God and personal devotion as well as his belief that a habituation to virtue is a necessary apprenticeship for the religious life. Moreover, it also explains Franklin's lifelong advocacy of universal tolerance when it comes to religious persuasion and his resolve, to use Lawrence's words, "never [to] let mankind put anything over" on him while at the same time trying "always to recognize and submit to the gods . . . in other men and women."

Lawrence's essay on Franklin's religious sensibility, then, unwittingly comes close to the truth. Although the Jungian imagery in Lawrence's credo is obviously foreign to the eighteenth-century Franklin, the spirit of its tenets is not. For Franklin, religion was not a simple matter of rule-bound worldly behavior, nor was his concept of the deity shallowly (or at least solely) intended as a cosmic justification for the values and aspirations of his class. Instead, Franklin's religious position was predicated on an awed appreciation of the often murky depth of the self's yearning for self-knowledge and ultimate meaning, and his awareness that authentic spiritual inquiry is as diverse in approach as the "gods" who emerge from the soul's "dark forest." That Lawrence missed this point can be attributed to at least two factors: he focused exclusively on Franklin's autobiographical remarks on religion and morality, and he read the pattern of Franklin's religious writings through a template, namely, his own disgust at anything that smacked of middle-class complacency. Since Franklin was claimed by the received wisdom of Lawrence's day as *the* champion of bourgeois industriousness, Lawrence hastily concluded that Franklin himself must have advocated a congruent spirit in religious and ethical matters. This is true to a certain extent, but not as much as Lawrence presumed.

Equally illuminating but nonetheless incorrect in its reading of Franklin's religion is Alfred Owen Aldridge's study *Benjamin Franklin and Nature's God* (1967). Aldridge's evaluation is more sympathetic and judicious than Lawrence's. Although he agrees that Franklin "used social utility as the final measure of the value of belief and conduct,"[17] Aldridge does not repeat the charge that Franklin's God is nothing more than a heavenly prototype of the man of business. His study also has the advantage of examining Franklin's religious beliefs developmentally, tracing the permutations of his thought throughout his entire life rather than focusing, as Lawrence did, on a single text.[18] Finally, Aldridge correctly sees Franklin's discussion of "gods" as the central theme in the various stages of his religious exploration.

But for all its value, Aldridge's study, like Lawrence's before it, is flawed. Aldridge comes close to discerning the actual pattern of Franklin's religion, but the interpretive model he imposes on the pertinent texts ultimately distorts both their message and intent. There are two ways in which Aldridge goes wrong, and both of them are instructive.

First, although he is correct in arguing that Franklin's religion must be examined from a developmental perspective, Aldridge misunderstands the terms of this development. His interpretation has it that Franklin journeyed "intellectually the entire distance from atheism to polytheism."[19] But this claim, when weighed against Franklin's writings, simply doesn't hold up. Although the young Franklin drifted for a period into a dogmatic mechanism that reified God to the metaphysically distant status of a First Cause, he never slipped over the edge into outright atheism. Even at the enthusiastic high point of his naturalism, Franklin unequivocally expressed his belief in the existence of a Supreme Architect that establishes and ultimately sustains the system of physical laws that define and govern reality.

In addition, the conclusion that Franklin came to espouse polytheism is likewise incorrect. Aldridge bases his case primarily on Franklin's 1728 "Articles of Belief," which Franklin wrote as a guide for his personal devotion. In this manuscript as well as in a few later texts, Franklin rather cryptically refers to subordinate or "lesser" gods that "create and rule" the heavenly bodies. Taking him at his word, Aldridge interprets these and similar locutions as indicating that Franklin believed in the literal existence of a plurality of actual deities, and moreover sees this as the key to grasping his overall religious orientation. As I will demonstrate in this book, Franklin's scattered remarks about the "gods" *are* essential to understanding his religious thought. To this extent, Aldridge's reading is correct. But it is an error to presume that they point to a literal polytheism. Such a conclusion is as philosophically bizarre as it is textually unwarranted. It makes much more sense to interpret Franklin's talk about "gods" as a groping effort to formulate the doctrine of theistic perspectivism. Perspectivism, not polytheism, is the key to Franklin's religious thought. Aldridge comes close to this insight but is unable to follow it through because of his literalistic reading of the pertinent texts. Like Lawrence, he has stumbled onto the right path without realizing it.

Second, in spite of his efforts to examine Franklin's religious convictions from a developmental perspective, Aldridge slips into a false systemization of his thought that attributes a uniformity to it that the textual evidence belies. It is quite true that there are a few themes that recur in Franklin's reflections on God, religion, and ethics; his doctrine of theistic perspectivism is the most obvious of them. To that extent, it is appropriate to speak of a continuity in his religious belief. But a close examination of Franklin's writings also reveals a deep-seated ambivalence when it comes to religious questions, a tension between the orthodox tenets of American Calvinism and the rationalistic ones of the Enlightenment that Franklin never managed to resolve. At times his religious thought leans toward one end of this spectrum, at times toward the other. He himself was aware of the dissonance, and his doctrine of theistic perspectivism in fact can be seen as an attempt to reach a happy compromise between two poles. Ironically, however, the strategy exacerbated rather than mitigated the tension, and Franklin's religious beliefs continued until his death to waver between Calvinist and Enlightenment allegiances.

Consequently, it is too simple to claim, as Aldridge does, that Franklin's mature religious thought is polytheistic, albeit with an eighteenth-century deistic twist. Franklin was not a polytheist, and although he was clearly more sympathetic to the Enlightenment's religion of nature than to Calvinism's religion of revelation, the essential ambivalence of his convictions resists a straightforward label. Like many and perhaps most persons, Franklin was a man who struggled, sometimes successfully but more often not, to construct a religious worldview out of disparate raw materials. To ignore the dissonance that such an attempt inevitably bred is to oversystematize and hence distort the nature of his religious journey.

The examples of Lawrence and Aldridge, as I suggested earlier, are instructive for the explorer of Franklin's religious convictions. Both of them come close to the truth, but for the wrong reasons. Lawrence accepts the caricature of Franklin as the high priest of marketplace religion, and in so doing fails to see that Franklin's religious intuitions in fact are better expressed by Lawrence's own credo. This flawed appraisal warns us against focusing on a single text such as the *Autobiography* for our information about Franklin's religion, and also suggests a more fruitful mode of interpretation, one that Lawrence himself failed to recognize. Aldridge correctly sees that Franklin's religious thought is developmental rather than monolithic, and he equally soundly focuses on Franklin's discussions of "gods" as the key to understanding his position. But he fails to follow either of these insights to their ultimate conclusions. He errs in assuming that Franklin went through a youthful atheistic stage, too literalistically interprets Franklin's talk about "gods" as an endorsement of polytheism, and ultimately forgets his own developmental approach by imposing a false unity on Franklin's religious beliefs, thereby ignoring their essential ambivalence. Lawrence and Aldridge each caught a glimpse of the lay of Franklin's religious forest but were unable to perceive fully the richness of its dimensions. Each in his own way blazed valuable interpretive trails; but Lawrence could not discern his, and Aldridge failed to follow the one he laid out.

This book defends an interpretation of Franklin's religious thought that resists a facilely disjunctive reading of him as either atheist or conventional Christian and avoids the potentially fecund but ultimately false starts of Lawrence and Aldridge. At no stage of his religious development can Franklin be called an atheist. Nor is it the case that he was a Christian, orthodox or otherwise, although there are obvious elements in his religious perspective that are remnants from his Calvinist background.

Instead, Franklin is best described as a man intensely concerned with religious questions who borrowed from both the Christian and the Enlightenment traditions in his struggle to come to terms with his own hunger for God and self-knowledge. The result was neither a simpleminded eclecticism nor a systematic theology. Although Franklin attempted to marry disparate elements from Calvinism on the one hand and deism on the other, he never rested content with a mechanical conjunction of the two. Rather, he sought a unifying principle that would serve as a catalyst for their synthesis, an organic bond that would absorb without duplicating features of both. He was ultimately unsuccessful in this endeavor, partly because the project was impossible to pull off, partly because Franklin himself balked at dogmatic assertions of religious truth.

His reluctance to settle on a "definitive" creed—even one written by himself—is partly attributable to his empiricist orientation. From first to last, Franklin endorsed an experimental approach to both religious and secular knowledge, insisting that all proposed solutions are contingent, subject to subsequent reexamination and reformulation. But his refusal to dogmatize or indulge in theological systematics is also attributable to the very unifying principle he arrived at in his 1728 "Articles of Belief." This principle—his theistic perspectivism—is the great insight of his career as a religious thinker.

I will discuss Franklin's great insight in some detail in chapter 3. But since I've mentioned it several times thus far, and because it is the central heuristic of this study, I owe the reader a preliminary account here. Briefly, Franklin's doctrine of theistic perspectivism rests on three propositions: first, that God exists; second, that God's nature is inaccessible to human reason or emotion; third, that humans therefore symbolically represent God to themselves in such a way as to establish some sort of contact with the divine.

Franklin was too much a child of the Enlightenment to doubt the existence of God as First Cause, the aloof and impersonal Originator and Sustainer of law-bound physical reality. But he was also too much a child of the Christian ethos to derive comfort from such a distant First Cause. For Franklin, the human spirit naturally yearns for a point of contact with the divine. Individuals need to know—or at least believe—that God is a personal, loving, caring deity who concerns himself with their fears, aspirations, and concerns. Yet the deistic God of nature, whose necessary existence is demonstrable through the light of reason, cannot meet these needs. He (or, more accurately, "it") is as remote as the stars, and just as cold. Reason cannot fully fathom its nature, creeds cannot describe it, imagination cannot picture it nor emotions touch it. But humans, driven by their hunger for a personal encounter with the divine, have learned to compensate. They indirectly approach the frigidly austere deity by representing it in images and terms to which they can more easily relate. They elaborate theological, ethical, and devotional doctrine by humanizing, if you will, the Ground of being that in itself is inaccessibly nonhuman. These anthropomorphized conceptions of the divine serve as the foci for personal adoration as well as sectarian theologizing. Franklin refers to them as "lesser" or "subordinate" gods, intermediaries that bridge the gulf between God and humans.

But these gods do not exist in the way that the First Cause does. The latter is actual, dependent on nothing external to itself for its being. The subordinate gods, on the other hand, are human projections, faltering attempts to represent the deity to finite minds in such a way as to overcome, at least to some extent, the alienating distance between them. These representations are historically and culturally bound—hence my uniform use of the lower case in referring to them. They are, in other words, "perspectives," which derive their specific characters from particular places and times. Even though conventional worshippers are unaware of the perspectival nature of their gods, thinking them to be accurate depictions of the divine, none of the perspectives can be regarded as definitive or explicitly descriptive. Instead, they are metaphorical and prescriptive in nature. They are contingent attempts to capture the ineluctable, to define the indefinable, through the invocation of symbols and analogies drawn from the natural and cultural realms. They serve as guides for behavior and standards of excellence to be striven for. Different religious traditions, as well as particular sects within each tradition, endorse perspectives that vary in detail and nuance, but all of them share certain fundamental insights and similar goals: the establishment of some type of communion with the ineffable First Cause, the moral improvement of humankind, and the infusion of meaning into individual lives. All religious perspectives, then, insofar as they aim at the same end, contain the potential for both instruction and edification. Not all of them are equally reflective or salutary, but none of them is totally false.

Franklin arrived at the great insight of theistic perspectivism while still a young man, but it is clear from his writings that the path leading to it was neither short nor easy. Raised in a pious Presbyterian household on a diet of prayer, worship, and Calvinist texts, he early on began to suffer from religious doubts that unsettled both himself and his family. His parents' consternation over their son's budding apostasy is revealed in letters he later sent them in which he rather awkwardly tried to dispel their fears.[20] His own confusion and search for a reawakening of his boyish piety is evidenced by the fact that he devoured a number of antideist tracts while in his early teens. It is difficult to imagine why even as precocious a boy as young Benjamin would have plowed his way through such formidable theological tomes unless he was at least partly seeking an antidote to his own doctrinal confusion.

As sometimes happens, his voracious efforts to convince himself of the truth of his religious tradition backfired, and the antideist polemics on which he rested his hopes had the unanticipated consequence of persuading him, at the tender age of fifteen, of the religion of nature's truth. Like most adolescent conversions, this one was relatively unreflective. Franklin seems to have grasped hold of Enlightenment deism out of defiance of his parents and their religion as much as from sympathy with its principles. Fired with an enthusiasm for this newly found but uncritical faith, he fell into a facile mechanism whose logic forced him to deny the existence of good and evil, reject the possibility of human free will, and posit a God infinitely distant from and unconcerned with human lives or affairs. But this early religious dogmatism—the only one to which Franklin ever succumbed—quickly soured. Its abstractly sterile worldview, although possessing a certain pristine aesthetic appeal, increasingly disappointed Franklin's emotional need for a more intimate relation with the deity. In addition, he eventually realized that the mere metaphysical denial of good and evil, regardless of how logically impeccable it might be, could not gainsay their palpable presence in the world.

Franklin's initially enthusiastic defense of dogmatic mechanism drove him into a speculative fly-bottle, occasioning confusion and despair that steadily eroded his confidence in his immaculate system. Recognizing that a Newtonian-inspired deism was spiritually impoverished, but unable either rationally or emotionally to return to the orthodoxy of his boyhood, he was at loose ends for a few years, intellectually adrift and emotionally buffeted by a series of personal crises. His great insight of 1728 provided him with a way out of his theological and existential impasse. The solution he arrived at—his doctrine of theistic perspectivism—enabled him to escape from the mechanistically sterile cosmos into which he had drifted without falling back into a Calvinist worldview whose central tenets he found unacceptable. Theistic perspectivism satisfied his reason by admitting the existence of an impassable and unknowable First Cause, but it also salvaged his emotional need for a personal relationship with a benevolent and loving deity by positing the symbolic reality of more approachable gods.

Franklin's great insight served as the nucleus around which his subsequent religious worldview revolved. As already suggested, it provided him with what he took to be the unifying principle in religious inquiry for which he had been searching. It explained why different sects and traditions envisioned God in a multiplicity of doctrinal ways and at the same time asserted the presence of a core of belief common to all. It underlay the universal tolerance that became a staple of Franklin's religion by granting that there are many legitimate paths to the divine, and that each of them, in its own perspectival attempt to grasp the unknowable, contains grains of truth and insight. Finally, it tied into Franklin's concern with the cultivation and practice of virtue by forging a link between ethics and religion. Religious perspectives may employ different metaphors in their efforts to represent what Paul Tillich later would designate the "God above gods," but all of them agreed, in Franklin's estimation, on the essential role of virtue in the religious life. In elaborating his almost mathematical program for the habituation of virtue, Franklin went to great pains to ensure that it would be palatable to persons from any—or no—religious background. As he tells us in the *Autobiography,* "tho' my Scheme was not wholly without Religion there was in it no Mark of any of the distinguishing Tenets of any particular Sect.—I had purposely avoided them; for being fully persuaded of the Utility and Excellency of my Method, and that it might be serviceable to People in all Religions, I would not have any thing in it that should prejudice it."[21]

This concern to design an ethical model inoffensive to sectarian doctrine does not reflect, as Franklin's critics have often concluded, either a cynical expediency on his part or a disdainful rejection of any relationship between ethics and religious belief. On the contrary, Franklin's desire to avoid semblances of "distinguishing Tenets of any particular Sect" is an indication of his sensitivity to the diversity of religious orientations, a sensitivity born from his theistic perspectivism. The manner in which different traditions envision God is perspectival and therefore an issue that no single theological model can legitimately claim to exhaust. But ethical precepts, derived as they are from an examination of human nature as well as the system of natural laws ordained by the divine First Cause, can be ecumenically agreed on. Individuals of all faiths can profit from the cultivation of virtue, because such an endeavor helps to achieve a healthy equilibrium between the existential polarities definitive of the human condition. Such an accomplishment is pleasing to any of the perspectival gods because it is conducive to the well-being of the race. In habituating oneself to virtue, then, one pleases and honors the gods of all traditions.

I claimed earlier that Franklin saw his perspectivism as that religious touchstone which could not only make sense of the diversity of doctrinal belief but also serve as a catalyst to reconcile the dissonant tendencies in his own religious thought. That dissonance, it will be recalled, was spawned from his sometimes awkward efforts to marry certain tenets of Calvinist theology with the deistic assumptions of Enlightenment rationalism. But his conviction that all human attempts to conceptualize God and divine workings are necessarily metaphorical did not succeed in ameliorating the ambivalences in his own religious beliefs. In fact, it actually exacerbated them. Theistic perspectives by their very nature are not descriptions of objective reality and hence cannot legitimately be appraised in terms of how well they correspond to "objective" facts. But this doesn't imply that there is no standard of appraisal by which to sound them. They are properly evaluated, at least in Franklin's judgment, on two separate counts: their utility in bestowing meaning to an individual's life and encouraging him or her to pursue virtue, and their internal coherence. The divine may be representable only in terms of symbolic and metaphorical expressions, but the standard of coherency demands that such expressions, when taken together, form a consistent picture. Theistic perspectives that attempt to incorporate inconsistent or even contradictory claims are immediately suspect from both a conceptual and a normative standpoint.

Their incoherence offends human reason and thus demands blind and intolerant fidelity.

But this is a point Franklin lost sight of when it came to *his* theistic perspective. He seems to have mistakenly assumed that, in his own case, theistic perspectivism's claim that many doctrinal paths lead to God also implied that a single perspective could accommodate discordant symbolizations of the divine. Consequently, the ambivalence in his religious thought originally bred by his divided loyalties to Calvinism and deism gradually became less disturbing to him personally, although just as glaring when examined from an external viewpoint. Franklin's great insight, in short, provided him with not so much an intellectual tool by which to marry rationalism and Calvinism as an excuse to allow the two tendencies to coexist in an uneasy and ultimately incompatible union. As a consequence, the very principle by which he hoped to ameliorate his ambivalence ultimately institutionalized it.

Theistic perspectivism and religious ambivalence, then, are the two underlying connective themes in Franklin's religious thought as a whole. This is not to agree with Aldridge that there is a uniformity to Franklin's various musings on God, values, and religion that brings them together into a harmonious system. It is to say more modestly that in spite of Franklin's nonsystematic reflections on religion, two features are discernible that explain his general orientation as well as his many inconsistencies.

In the chapters that follow, I explore the dimensions of Franklin's religious thought by focusing on his theistic perspectivism as well as the religious ambivalence that runs through his various attempts to come to an understanding of things divine. This work, then, is neither history nor biography proper. Instead, it is an attempt to reconstruct and critically appraise the development and substance of Franklin's religious beliefs. Chapter 1 sets the stage by examining the worldview clash between American Calvinism and Enlightenment rationalism in which Franklin was caught. As we shall see, a good deal of the ambivalence in his religious thought can be traced to the confusing religious climate generated by this sometimes bitter confrontation in eighteenth-century America. Chapter 2 analyzes Franklin's early attempt to escape his Calvinist background by wholeheartedly embracing mechanism. It examines the forbiddingly sterile metaphysics of this early stage in his religious development, as well as the reasons for his eventual rejection of its conclusions and method. Chapter 3, the book's keystone, examines in some detail the great insight of theistic perspectivism that after 1728 served as the conceptual loom on which Franklin wove the fabric of his religious thought. Chapter 4 explores the ambivalence that remained in Franklin's religion even after the great insight by examining his uneasy attempts to reconcile the Calvinist-based doctrine of special providences with deism's desupernaturalized version. Franklin's insistence that the cultivation of virtue is the noblest form of religious worship, as well as his rather Lawrencean appraisal of the human condition as a constant battle between deep-seated and opposing psychophysical drives, is treated in chapter 5. Besides religion, no other single area of Franklin's thought has been more misunderstood than his reflections on ethics. As will be seen, his moral system is neither crudely utilitarian nor simplistically behavioristic. Instead, it is a sophisticated attempt to ground ethics on a naturalistic foundation as well as to show the crucial role of virtue in the achievement of spiritual growth, not just worldly success. The intent as well as the message of Franklin's ethical reflections cannot be fully appreciated without recognizing both the influence of Calvinist thought on them and their relationship to his great insight. Finally, in chapter 6, I explore the sectarian tolerance that is such a crucial element in Franklin's religious thought by showing that it is the practical corollary of theistic perspectivism's claim that there are many legitimate doctrinal and theological paths to God.

My analysis of Franklin's religious thought is based primarily on two strategies. First, I have tried to avoid imposing my own templates on his texts, instead starting from scratch and following his ideas where they led me. This effort to let Franklin speak for himself has prevented me, I hope, from forcing his more recalcitrant texts onto a Procrustean interpretive bed, and the result is that the portrait of his religion that emerges is less uniform and systematic, and perhaps less elegant as well, than the ones painted by previous commentators. This makes for a reading that may not be as nicely tied up as earlier ones; but it does, I believe, more accurately capture the spirit as well as the letter of Franklin's religion.

Still, for all his ambivalence and occasional inconsistency, there is a thematic undercurrent running through all of Franklin's religious writings after 1728: his doctrine of theistic perspectivism. Although never explicitly analyzed nor developed by Franklin himself, his tantalizing allusions to "gods" recur often enough to be seen as the conceptual glass through which he examined religious matters. Consequently, my second strategy in this study is to make sense of Franklin's writings on religion by fleshing out the nature and implications of theistic perspectivism in a way he did not. I have done so, however, by once again following his lead, refining the model he provided instead of imposing one of my own. I have tried not to create but to reconstitute, following clues, sources, and inferred motives with a detective's rather than a novelist's eye.

My claim that theistic perspectivism is the interpretive key to unlocking Franklin's religious thought is based, then, on a close scrutiny of his own words and a fresh rethinking of their significance. The strategy seems to work: most of the otherwise baffling pieces of his religious puzzle fall into place when measured against the standards suggested by his great insight. Most, but not all. Again, Franklin was not a systematic theologian. Nor did he always consistently follow the directions indicated by his theistic perspectivism. Consequently, there are corners of his religious forest that inevitably resist the cartographer's attempts to chart them. But a judicious use of the interpretive compass of theistic perspectivism provides us with as detailed a map of the Franklinian woods as we are likely to get. It not only sheds light on a remarkable man's lifelong quest for God and spiritual growth. It also quite possibly aids us in taking a few steps down the pathways of our own murky forests.

1 Between Worlds

BENJAMIN FRANKLIN was always a great admirer of the *Spectator* essays. He discovered an odd volume of them while still in his midteens and read it over and over with much delight.[1] The easy elegance of the writing enchanted him, and he took it as a model for his own prose. But the ideas expressed by Addison and Steele seized him as well, introducing him to a whole new world of liberal thinking that permanently influenced him.[2]

The young Franklin would have run across a tale in one of the essays that portended the course of his own religious journey. The story is Addison's retelling of an ancient Greek legend. Dionysius, tyrant of Syracuse, summons the poet Simonides and, in the philosophically innocent way of a potentate too accustomed to getting what he wants, orders him to define God. Simonides requests a day to think the matter over. But "when the Day was expired, he desired two Days; and afterwards, instead of returning his Answer, demanded still double the Time to consider of it. This great Poet and Philosopher, the more he contemplated the nature of the Deity, found that he waded but the more out of his Depth; and that he lost himself in the Thought, instead of finding an End of it."[3]

The tale is generally instructive because it warns against the foolishness of presuming that the riddle of God can be readily cracked by human reason and casually tossed into the metaphysical "outbox." But its message that initial religious certitude frequently gives way to a more confused but also more profound appreciation of the mystery of things divine also reflects the direction Franklin's own religious convictions took. As a boy he uncritically accepted the highly charged tradition of New England Calvinism into which he was born. Following a period of adolescent rebellion, he just as uncritically slid into a starkly lifeless deism. In both instances, he presumed he needed but a day to figure out how to answer the God question. In the first case, the religion of the Puritans supplied all the answers; in the second, Newton did. But after these two brief moments of youthful certainty, Franklin found himself increasingly perplexed by the God puzzle until, like Simonides, he realized he would never be able to think his way through it. His allegiance was too irreversibly split between the god of his Calvinist fathers and the god of his Enlightenment mentors to allow for a comfortable resolution. This religious ambivalence would remain with him for the rest of his life.

Franklin eventually made a conscious resolve to accept the ambiguity. He even elaborated a justification for it, namely, his theory that all religious beliefs are merely provisional, or perspectival. But justifications such as this one, although pleasing to the intellect, are notoriously difficult to incorporate into one's lived experience in a satisfactory way. Although Franklin tried to read his and others' religious beliefs through the theoretical lens of perspectivism, in actuality he often forgot to do so. Thus ambiguity rides on ambiguity in his lifelong search for God. There is first the ambiguity inherent in religious belief itself. Then there's the added ambiguity birthed by the frequency with which Franklin overlooked his own intellectual conviction that religious beliefs are always just perspectives, albeit functionally crucial ones.[4]

Franklin came by his ambivalence honestly. Although caution should be exercised in appealing to the dictum that "the child is father to the man," it's often quite helpful in trying to understand the origins of mature religious belief. Franklin came of age in a religious environment that itself was ambiguous. The unreconciled (indeed, unreconcilable) tendencies in his own religious convictions reflect the dissonance of the wider religious climate in which he was raised. Franklin's formative years were spent caught between two religious and intellectual worldviews battling one another for primacy: the aging and rather weary one of North American Calvinist orthodoxy, and the younger and more energetic one of Enlightenment liberalism. Tugged at by both, alternately drawn toward and repulsed by first one and then the other, his later religious ambivalence was almost guaranteed.

Boston at the beginning of the eighteenth century, the Boston into which Franklin was born, held some eight thousand souls, most of whom, so contemporary Calvinist divines feared, were hopelessly unregenerate.[5] Many of the city's clergy—and not just those in the conservative Mather camp—shook their heads sadly at the perceived ungodliness of their fellow Bostonians. In spite of continuous warnings from the pulpit (not to mention more ominous ones in the forms of epidemics, violent death, and natural disasters), and notwithstanding a series of laws enacted in the previous century to enforce obedience to at least the letter if not the spirit of God's law, Bostonians had wandered deeply into the thickets of sin.[6] Increase Mather of North Church expressed the concerns of many of his fellow pastors when he lamented that the "first Generation of Christians in New-England is in a manner off the stage, and there is another and more sinful generation risen up in their stead."[7] The conviction that the third generation of New England Calvinists had fallen away from the sanctity of their Puritan forebears was a continuous refrain in sermons and pamphlets of the period. John Winthrop's hope seventy years earlier was that the faithful would consider themselves "a City upon a hill," an example to all. But he had also made clear that there was a certain price exacted for the honor of being a living example. "The eyes of all people are upon us. Soe that if we shall deal falsely with our God in this work we have undertaken, and so cause him to withdraw his present help from us, we shall be made a story and a by-word throughout the world." Even worse, Winthrop warned, "we shall open the mouths of enemies to speak evil of the ways of God. . . . We shall shame the faces of many of God's worthy servants."[8] In the minds of many eighteenth-century Boston divines, Winthrop's worse fears had finally become real. Their sermons were liberally sprinkled with pointed reminders of God's habit of turning his back on apostate nations.

Nor was it just the divines who worried about Boston's spiritual health. John Dunton, a roving bookseller, spent ten months in Boston in the 1680s and later wrote a scathing account of the town's moral laxness and religious hypocrisy. While acknowledging that some of its citizens were "as sincere a Pious and truly Religious People . . . as is any where in the Whole World to be found," he also lamented that many more no longer walked in the steps of their "Pious Fore-fathers" yet "retain a form of Godliness, and make a strict Profession of the out-side of Religion, tho' they never knew what the Power of Godliness was." These hypocrites were so addicted to sin that even Boston's "Laws for Reformation of Manners," though "very severe," were little regarded.[9]

Of course each generation of Boston divines thought its flock less holy than earlier ones. Increase Mather longed for the lost purity of the first Puritans while his son Cotton in turn made unflattering comparisons between his own wicked generation and his father's more righteous one. Probably the good old days of strict Puritan rectitude were partly mythic. Even Cotton Mather implied as much, although perhaps not realizing what he was giving away, in his *Magnalia Christi Americana* (1702). He tells the story of a second-generation minister who, when he reminded a settlement in the "North-East regions" that its mission was to plant the wilderness, was sharply told by one of his listeners that the settlement's mission, on the contrary, was to catch fish.[10] Anecdotes such as this suggest that the veneration of first- and second-generation Calvinists was not entirely justified. Still, the conviction that eighteenth-century Boston had fallen persisted, and there was some truth to it. Religious standards *had* loosened over the years, nudging New England Calvinism, for better or for worse, away from a strictly orthodox reading of covenantal theology.

The theology of the first-generation Puritans revolved around the "Five Points" hammered out by Calvinist theologians at the Synod of Dort in 1618–19. Following the teachings of John Calvin, the synod proclaimed that God has chosen from the beginning of time who would be saved and damned; that Christ's sacrifice guarantees the salvation of some—the "elect"—but not all; that the depravity of humans since the Fall precludes their working out their own salvation; and that those elected by God for salvation are powerless to resist the divine gift and incapable of a subsequent repudiation of it. These five points captured Calvin's conviction of the absolute sovereignty of God and the total dependence of humans, and at the same time threw a gauntlet in the face of more liberal theological foes, particularly the Arminians. Persons are born in sin, depraved in both rational and moral faculties, and utterly incapable of healing themselves. Justice would require that all be condemned to everlasting hell, for all are incapable of honoring the covenant of works originally offered to Adam by God. But God is merciful as well as just and through Christ's atoning self-sacrifice offers a new covenant, this time one of grace. Christ's death cancels the sins of the elect. It is a freely bestowed gift, even if one the recipient is incapable of refusing.

On the American shore, the Calvinist ethos tended to focus on the fallen state of humans, relentlessly hammering home the ubiquity of sin. The faithful were enjoined in countless sermons, pamphlets, and books to exercise humility and engage in continuous self-examination in order to come to a full appreciation of the depths of their wickedness. Although salvation could never be earned, the self-loathing that arose from the recognition of one's own corruption drove the repentant believer to Christ and prepared him, if he was one of the elect, to receive grace.

The harsh scheme of salvation preached by New England Calvinism not only bred an almost unbearable sense of unworthiness in many of its adherents; it also institutionally legitimated a rigid and increasingly resented distinction between elected and nonelected souls. Only those fortunate individuals especially chosen by God to be regenerated through divine grace were eligible for full church membership. Only they were worthy to participate in the Lord's Supper. Inevitably the distinction between elect and nonelect created a hierarchical division within the church that many congregants and clergy came to see as hazardously contrary to Christian fellowship.

The second half of the seventeenth century gave rise to a number of revolts against the harshness and exclusivity of the traditional New England theology. In 1662, for example, the "Half-Way Covenant" struck at tradition by permitting the children of unregenerated (and presumably nonelected) church members to be baptized. The only conditions were that the "outward"-membered parents had to assent to the faith and conform their behavior to God's Word. The "Brattle Street Rebellion" of 1698, led by the liberal religionists John Leverett and William and Thomas Brattle, represented a further step away from the gloomy theology of self-examination and self-loathing. Believing the "*particular Forms,* and modes of Worship, or Discipline" less essential than the "*weighty matters* of the Gospel," a group of dissatisfied Boston clergy and laypersons founded the independent Brattle Street Church. They repudiated the customary public confession, abandoned tests for saving grace, and opened up communion to all who wished to partake. And at the turn of the century, Solomon Stoddard of Northampton proposed in his *Doctrine of Instituted Churches* the inflammatory notion that the Lord's Supper was not primarily a privilege reserved for the elect but rather a means of salvation for all.[11]

These reforms not only helped to ameliorate the rigor of traditional Calvinist doctrine. They also tended to chip away at the moral and social power of the clergy. Throughout the seventeenth century and even into the next, Calvinist divines enjoyed incredible authority in towns and villages along the New England coast as well as in the hinterlands. They defined the morphology of conversion and hence were all-important in judging whether or not an experience of regeneration was genuine. They served as secondary vehicles of grace because they preached the Word, thereby communicating the ways of God and extending the divine invitation to corrupt humans. They were the moral watchdogs of their communities, scourging the wicked and encouraging good works. And they were frequently the most learned men of their day, trained in classical and biblical languages, initially in England and then at

Harvard, and well read in reform theology. Nor were their intellectual interests limited to biblical exegesis or theological speculation. John Wilson scribbled verse, John Cotton wrote a business manual for Boston's early entrepreneurs, and both Increase and Cotton Mather were fascinated by natural philosophy. But the easing of the doctrinal importance of election in the latter half of the seventeenth century lessened the importance of the clerics in the scheme of salvation, and the arrival of the New Learning from England at the start of the eighteenth century accelerated the erosion of their moral and intellectual authority.[12]

The New Learning, a generic title for the "enlightened" way of regarding humans and their world born from the writings of luminaries such as Francis Bacon, Isaac Newton, and John Locke, presented a major challenge to New England orthodoxy, and Boston was ripe for it. Boston had always been a bookish town. The first bookseller set up shop as early as 1637; by 1690 the demand for books was so great that over twenty stores competed with one another. In the first two decades of the next century at least sixteen new booksellers popped up. In 1638 Stephen Day established a press in Cambridge; by the turn of the century, Boston was second only to London in the British Empire as a publishing center. Books imported from England or printed domestically flowed through the town and surrounding areas. True, more than half of them dealt with religious subjects, but many books of divinity printed in the final quarter of the seventeenth century reflected a theological liberalism inspired by the New Learning.[13] By the 1720s, Harvard's curriculum included the study of so many liberal religionists that Cotton Mather, who was not unsympathetic to the New Learning, thundered that the college's young scholars were reading books from "Satan's Library."[14]

Other branches of the diabolic library were established throughout the colonies in quick order. In 1714, while a student at Yale, Samuel Johnson eagerly plowed into the recently acquired Jeremy Dummer collection of New Learning volumes and devoured Descartes, Boyle, Locke, and Newton, along with the deists Anthony Collins and Lord Bolingbroke—this in spite of warnings to stay away from such authors lest they corrupt his religion.[15] By 1722 the influence of the New Learning was so pervasive that James Blair, president of William and Mary, somewhat apprehensively assured Virginians that the college had thus far managed to ward off the contagion of deism and atheism afflicting so many other schools.[16] (William and Mary proved not to be immune after all. By the end of the century, its students had earned a notorious reputation for outspoken infidelity.) In 1732, Jonathan Dickinson, alarmed at the threat of the New Learning to orthodoxy, published *The Reasonableness of Christianity* to convince youthful apostates that revealed religion was not incompatible with reason. Three years later, Philadelphia's *American Weekly Museum* lamented the fact that the rise of religious skepticism had poisoned so many young minds.[17] In the same year and in the same town, the Presbyterian minister Samuel Hemphill was convicted of "downright Deism" and ousted from his pulpit.[18]

There was good reason for the concern expressed by these and other orthodox Christians that the New Learning encouraged infidelity. The worldview it defended was remarkably hostile to the one endorsed by traditional Calvinism. Newton and his numerous popularizers (including that staple of colonial households, the almanac) convinced eighteenth-century readers that the physical order was a vast machine ruled by inexorable natural laws. Moreover, the Newtonian system so convinced many of them that secondary causes sufficiently explained natural phenomena that appeals to divine intervention were increasingly viewed as unnecessary and aesthetically sloppy. Inspired by the apparent reign of secondary causation in the physical realm, other thinkers quickly extended its explanatory sufficiency to all areas of human inquiry, including political economy, psychology, and history.[19] The orthodox conviction that God constantly and personally supervised the natural order receded into the background, taking with it the doctrines of special providences and miraculous intervention, both mainstays of traditional Calvinist preaching.

Locke argued in his *Essay Concerning Human Understanding,* a book in vogue in the colonies, that human reason was capable of discovering truths not only about its own operations but also about the lawlike universe it surveyed. He also implied with his doctrine of the tabula rasa that human nature, if not innately good, was at least neutrally plastic, and this in turn suggested that under the right conditions both the individual and society were perfectible. This optimism sat uneasily with a Calvinist ethos founded squarely on the twin assumptions that human reason was irretrievably depraved and that the human soul was incapable of freeing itself from corruption. It also further marginalized belief in the absolute sovereignty of God by eliminating the need for regenerative grace.[20]

Closely linked to the New Learning's trivialization of the traditional Calvinist doctrine of sin was its insistence that virtue was the most appropriate expression of religious belief. Locke as well as a number of other liberal Christians, such as Samuel Clarke (1675–1729), George Cheyne (1671–1743), John Tillotson (1630–94), and William Wollaston (1659–1724), not to mention outright deists like John Toland (1670–1722) and Anthony Collins (1676–1729), defended this view. The deity desired not fear and self-loathing so much as the rational pursuit of good works. The highest form of worship was imitation of the supremely good and rational Creator, and how better to do that than by exercising reason and virtue? The confidence that humans were indeed capable of genuinely good works, and that God exulted in them, was an additional assault on the Calvinist doctrines of human depravity and divine sovereignty. It also flew in the face of the Synod of Dort's repudiation of the Arminian "heresy" that humans are capable of participating in their own salvation, for it was clear to liberal religionists that regeneration depended at least in part on virtuous behavior, and virtue was a choice.

The arrival of the New Learning on the American scene, then, represented a major challenge to the entrenched Calvinist worldview, which already uneasily saw itself slipping away from the doctrinal purity of the first-generation founders. Some welcomed it as a much-needed antidote to religious chauvinism and became outright deists, either for a period or permanently.[21] Many others, horrified by what they saw as its incitement to infidelity, dug in their heels and branded the New Learning the New Antichrist. Still others, caught between the two worlds of Calvinism and Enlightenment, attracted by both and unwilling to forsake either, tried to marry the two. Committed to the tenets of their cradle Calvinism but excited by the flood of British books that expounded the new worldview, they struggled to remain faithful to the covenant of grace while searching for ways to accommodate it to Newton and Locke.[22] Nor were all who attempted this rapprochement liberal religionists. In the Boston of Franklin's youth, the tense effort to marry the two worldviews is nowhere better illustrated than by the intellectual and religious life of Cotton Mather.

Mather came by his fascination with the New Learning from his father and his father's cronies. Beginning in the spring of 1683, Increase and his friends founded a "private philosophical society" that met biweekly to add to the "stores of natural history." Amateur astronomers and meteorologists as well as some of Boston's most reputable physicians were members of the society.[23] Cotton, twenty years old at the time, sat in on many of its meetings. Before long he was observing the weather, speculating on the causes and cures of illness, peering through microscopes, and deluging the Royal Society with meticulously recorded accounts of New England's natural phenomena. The voluminous correspondence finally paid off in 1714 when the society's fellows, either through genuine admiration or sheer exhaustion, elected him an American member.

Mather welcomed the New Learning as providing rational grounds for belief in an all-powerful and benevolent deity. Unlike his more timid co-religionists, part of him was convinced that the Newtonian worldview could only strengthen human appreciation for the necessity of a rational and benevolent

Creator. As he wrote in *The Christian Philosopher* (1721), his most sustained attempt to marry Calvinism and the New Learning, "A BEING that must be *superior* to *Matter,* even the *Creator* and *Governor* of all *Matter* is every where so conspicuous that there can be nothing more *monstrous* than *to deny the God that is above.*" Thus "*Atheism* is now for ever chased and hissed out of the World, every thing in the World concurs to a Sentence of *Banishment* upon it."[24] Earlier in *Reasonable Religion* (1700), he reiterated the Enlightenment conviction that to live rationally would be to live religiously, and he consistently concluded that sin is a violence against the principles of reason. It was only a short step from this to the equally enlightened but dangerously heterodox thesis that a rational person's worship *was* the practice of virtue, and Mather came perilously close to defending it in his 1710 *Bonifacius: An Essay upon the Good.*[25]

Yet it would be an error to suppose that Mather, for all his enthusiasm over the New Learning, renounced the religion of his fathers. Jeremiads alternate with cool descriptions of natural phenomena throughout his writings. Just two years after his 1700 defense of rational religion, he thunders against the depravity of humans in general and his fellow Bostonians in particular: "If the Almighty God should from Heaven Rain down upon the Town an *horrible Tempest* of Thunderbolts, Cities *which he overthrew in his Anger, and repented not,* it would be no more than our unrepented Sins deserve."[26] The same man who in *Bonifacius* wrote favorably of a religious sensibility that expressed itself in the practice of virtue railed eleven years later in his diary against a shallow "Religion of Pues" that confused morality with piety and which "seems to be now the chief Religion of . . . a proud, vain, formal People."[27] The same natural philosopher who proudly trumpeted his membership in the Royal Society could also shrilly condemn Harvard's collection of New Learning volumes as diabolical. And even in *The Christian Philosopher,* dispassionate descriptions of physical phenomena such as earthquakes or the destructive fury of locusts suddenly give way not to tempered reflections on the immutable laws of a rational universe but to breathless sermons on human wickedness and divine retribution.[28]

As demonstrated by Mather's ambivalence, the clash of worldviews that defined the intellectual and religious climate of turn-of-the-century Boston was in no way ameliorated by attempts to wed the two. If anything, such efforts served only to underscore their incompatibility. Individuals who refused either to endorse or reject the New Learning uncritically, but who instead strived for a rational rapprochement between it and traditional Calvinism, found themselves caught between worlds, tugged this way and that, intermingling the vocabulary of Newton and Calvin, fearing Jehovah's fury and contemplating the rational placidity of the First Cause, deploring their own utter depravity even as they struggled for self-improvement. It is only natural that the period's religious ambiguity gave rise to a schizophrenic conception of God that nervously wavered between the deity as abstract Prime Mover and as personal Heavenly Father.[29] This is the dilemma Cotton Mather and many others wrestled with, and it defined the religious climate in which Franklin came of age.[30]

Benjamin Franklin's parents, Josiah and Abiah, lived across the street from and attended Boston's Old South Church.[31] By the time Benjamin was born in 1706, his parents had been covenanted members of the church for twelve years, two of the relatively few people in Boston entitled to feast at the Lord's Supper. Josiah was a person who took his religion seriously (as, presumably, was Abiah; we know almost nothing of her, although Mather in his *Magnalia Christi Americana* praises her father, Peter Folger, as a "godly learned Englishman"). He attended meeting on a regular basis, occasionally led closing prayers and congregational singing, hosted midweek prayer meetings at his Milk Street home, and ran for deacon at least once (he came in a distant last).[32] Like many other Bostonians of the day, Josiah was literate. He even owned a small library, which, in keeping with his piety, "consisted chiefly of Books in polemic Divinity." There was also a Plutarch's *Lives,* a copy of Daniel Defoe's *An Essay upon Projects,* and another of Cotton Mather's *Bonifacius.*[33]

Josiah comes across in his son's memoirs as an earnest man, a doer of good works who would have made Cotton Mather proud. He was meticulously honest in his business dealings. His discretion and judgment were such that "leading People . . . consulted him for his Opinion in Affairs of the Town or of the Church he belong'd to and show'd a good deal of Respect for his Judgment and Advice." He did his best to encourage virtue and high thoughts in his children, instructing them both by example and word. Nor was he above a bit of fun, frequently singing and playing the violin—but only "Psalm Tunes"—with the family at day's end.[34]

Benjamin's recollections of his father mellowed with time. There is no reason to doubt that he genuinely respected Josiah, but it's also clear that he soon felt somewhat constricted by the older man's conscientious virtue and religious intensity. There are occasional undercurrents of resentment in Franklin's descriptions of his father that suggest how he must have been first bemused and then irritated by his parent's almost unbelievable rectitude. Josiah, he tells us, early on exposed him to sundry "religious Impressions," and brought him up "piously in the Dissenting Way." But Franklin doesn't intend this description to be complimentary, since he immediately adds that he was scarcely fifteen before he rejected Josiah's piety.[35] Elsewhere, in describing the early days of his apprenticeship to brother James, he recalls how he studied in the printshop on Sundays, "evading as much as I could the common Attendance on publick Worship, *which my Father used to exact of me when I was under his Care*" (my emphasis). He tellingly adds: "And which I still thought a Duty," a confession that reveals his religious ambivalence even at this early age.[36] Franklin's reluctance to attend meeting was understandable. Even though Joseph Sewall's sermons at Old South likely reflected to some extent the growing influence of the New Learning, they were still filled with sufficient Calvinist fire-and-brimstone to set young Benjamin's teeth on edge and to turn church attendance into a grudging duty.[37]

Franklin also seems to have resented the fact that his father's library was limited mainly to works of "polemic Divinity," feeling later that he would have better profited if "more proper Books" had fallen his way.[38] Moreover, one has to wonder whether Franklin carried with him a sense of betrayal because of his father's decision to pull him back from a life of study. As early as he could recall, Franklin had been an avid reader, devouring every book he came across. This so impressed his parents that Josiah determined to "Tithe" him "to the Service of the Church," and accordingly sent him to school. But in less than a year, Josiah changed his mind and put the ten-year-old to work in the family tallow business. Josiah excused his decision on the grounds that he couldn't afford a college education and that he worried about its practicality—"Reasons," Franklin notes, that Josiah "gave to his Friends in my Hearing." This final curious note suggests that in Franklin's eyes Josiah's excuses for placing his son in trade were flimsy, that Josiah himself sensed as much, and that he tried to convince himself otherwise by loudly and frequently indulging in public explanations (public confession, after all, was an important feature of the piously dissenting way).[39]

Early on, then, Franklin's relationship with both his father and his father's religion soured. Although as an adult he always spoke of Josiah with respect, he visited his father's house only three times after he left Boston for Philadelphia (this was in 1723; Josiah died in 1744).[40] In later years he was much less respectful of his father's religion. But the dreary tomes of polemical divinity and the general Calvinist ethos of early eighteenth-century Boston left their mark on him. He would revisit the tenets of his youthful religious upbringing, albeit unwillingly and at times unknowingly, much more frequently than the house on Milk Street. Suckled as he was at the covenant of grace, he never quite succeeded in purging it from his system.

Benjamin stayed in Josiah's shop for two years, but unenthusiastically and resentfully. Relations between father and son must have suffered from the youth's dissatisfaction. Josiah eventually realized that he would lose the headstrong boy if he did not do something about the situation; Benjamin already had threatened on several occasions to run away to sea. At last, inspired by his son's "bookish inclination," Josiah resolved to make a printer of him. In 1718, when Franklin was twelve years old, he was indentured to his brother James, already a master printer.

It was now that Franklin's genuine education began. It was fortunate for his intellectual development that his father had decided against making a clergyman of him. Harvard's curriculum during these years had little to offer that stimulated or expanded the mind, while Franklin's autodidactic reading program, started in earnest during his apprenticeship with James, was both broad and profound. He frequently stayed up nights reading borrowed books. He doggedly honed his arithmetical skills, practiced composition, scribbled a few juvenile verses, studied grammar and the Socratic method of debate that he had picked up from Xenophon, and, inspired by Thomas Tryon's *The Way to Health,* experimented with vegetarianism. Benjamin proved himself every bit as zealous in his studies as his father was in his religious observances, a comparison the youth probably would have scorned.

Five authors in particular so impressed him during this period that he took pains years later to pay tribute to them in his *Autobiography.* Their influence on his religious development was deep and abiding. They helped him articulate his intellectual disagreements with Calvinism and pointed him in an alternate direction.

The first author was Joseph Addison. As already mentioned, the youthful Franklin ran across an "odd Volume of the Spectator," read it repeatedly, and became a lifelong admirer of both its style and ideas.

Addison's *Spectator* essays (and, later, his other writings) influenced Franklin in a number of ways. Most important, they introduced him to the New Learning, albeit in an indirect, secondhand fashion. Addison was especially taken with Locke, and the philosopher's insistence on the sufficiency of reason, as well as his distrust of religious enthusiasm, is evident throughout the essays.[41] Like most of the educated men of his day, Addison was also impressed by Shaftesbury's claim that morality, not terrified self-loathing, is the heart of true religion. As Addison says at one point, "there is nothing which strengthens Faith more than Morality. Faith and Morality naturally produce each other."[42] Devouring the *Spectator* as he did, and in the process imbibing the liberal spirit of the New Learning, Franklin was already familiar with and sympathetic to the arguments of thinkers such as Locke and Shaftesbury when he tackled them firsthand a bit later.

The apprentice who plunged headlong into Addison's works was clearly an angry young man, quick to dispute, as he admits, with everyone on just about any topic. Authority of all kinds seemed to rankle him. His father, the church, the properly pious people of Boston, Harvard scholars, the wealthy: all were grist for his mill. His disdain for vested authority and social propriety wasn't merely an idiosyncrasy. Many of his Boston contemporaries, likewise fed up with what they perceived as undeserved clerical privilege (and egged on to a large extent by the angry journalist James Franklin), were beginning to question the traditionally almost untouchable authority of the Calvinist hegemony. The resentment had taken an ugly turn. In 1717, for example, just a couple of years before Franklin discovered Addison, members of Old South were horrified one Sunday morning to find this inscription tacked on the church door:

> Good people, within this House, this very day,
> A canting Crew will meet to fast and pray.
> Just as the miser fasts with greedy mind, to spare;
> So the glutton fasts, to eat a greater share.
> But the sower-headed Presbyterians, to seem more holy,
> And their Canting Minister to punish sinfull foley.

Cotton Mather shortly thereafter declared Boston a town in the possession of Satan, which of course only escalated the tension. In rebelling against the religious establishment's moral authority, then, young Franklin was in part riding the wave of a widespread disaffection.[43]

Addison appealed to Franklin's rebellious side. He too was a great smasher of idols, and in his essays he frequently poked fun at the class snobbery of British society. Also a strong champion of self-improvement, he frequently voiced both convictions in words that couldn't have failed to inspire young Franklin: "The Mind that lies fallow but a single Day, sprouts up in Follies that are only to be killed by a constant and assiduous Culture. It was said of *Socrates*, that he brought Philosophy down from Heaven, to inhabit among Men; and I shall be ambitious to have it said of me, that I have brought Philosophy out of Closets and Libraries, Schools and Colleges, to dwell in Clubs and Assemblies, at Tea-Tables, and in Coffee-Houses."[44] Passages such as this were music to Franklin's ears. Like all autodidacts, he was insecure about his learning and jealously suspicious of formally educated scholars—a wariness he would later reveal in his Dogood letters.[45] Addison reassured him that a noncolleged printer's apprentice could become another Socrates.

The liberalism Franklin absorbed from Addison's words was both real and enduring. But the essays probably reinforced the young man's religious ambivalence as well. Addison was genuinely committed to the New Learning, but he was no deist. Instead, he was a liberal Christian. Consequently, one predictably encounters in his essays that curious incompatibility often found in the works of other eighteenth-century thinkers with mixed allegiances to both Enlightenment naturalism and Christian theism. The ambiguity in Addison born from this conflict was not as apparent as in the writings, for example, of Cotton Mather, and so probably escaped Benjamin's conscious notice at the time. But he could hardly have failed to absorb it in his obsessive readings of *The Spectator.*

Two books that Franklin carefully studied some time after he had discovered Addison also influenced him profoundly. One was *The Art of Thinking,* commonly known as the "Port Royal Logic" (1662). The other was Locke's *Essay Concerning Human Understanding* (1690).

The Port Royal Logic, written by Antoine Arnauld (1612–94) and Pierre Nicole (1625–95), was probably the most influential book of logic from the year of its publication until the end of the nineteenth century. It went through sixty-three French editions and ten English ones by 1881 and was adopted as a standard text at both Cambridge and Oxford.

The Art of Thinking is more than simply a handbook in logic. It is also a sophisticated compendium of grammar, linguistic analysis, epistemology, and metaphysics. The authors relied heavily on Aristotelian logic, but they were also committed Cartesians who sought to present a convincing case for Descartes's rationalist account of knowledge. Consequently, they agreed with their master that the empiricist dictum "Nihil est in intellectu quod non prius in sensu" was not only absurd (as Descartes demonstrated in the second of his meditations) but also "as contrary to religion as to true philosophy."[46]

Now, there is very little here with which a budding empiricist such as Franklin could sympathize. The puzzle immediately arises, then, why he specifically mentioned the Port Royal Logic in his memoirs. What did he find so important in his boyish perusal of a seventeenth-century apology for Cartesianism that he recalled it fondly years later?

The likeliest answers to this question are first, method, and second, an intellectual justification for the skepticism toward which he was moving at this time in his life. Franklin was always bothered by what he considered his lack of order. As an untutored youth plowing his way through complicated books, he felt strongly the lack of critical skills that could enable him to separate wheat from chaff. Moreover, he probably had become convinced, partly through observation of his pious relatives and acquaintances, partly through his reading of Addison's liberal criticisms of religious enthusiasm, that most humans are capable of egregious self-deception, and that it is the wise person who avoids this danger by cultivating clarity and orderliness in his thinking. The authors of the Port Royal Logic agreed. "Because the mind sometimes lets itself be misled by false glimmers when it does not pay enough attention," they wrote, "and because clearly some things are known only by long and difficult examination, it would certainly be useful to have rules for conducting oneself so as to make the search for truth both faster and easier."[47] Arnauld and Nicole promised that the logical techniques spelled out in their book would provide those rules. Franklin, anxious for an antidote to superstition, eagerly clutched at that promise while remaining unmoved by Cartesian rationalism. The Port Royal lessons stayed with him, and he became a lifelong advocate (although not always a practitioner) of methodical thinking. He sought a method for attaining virtue, defended religious toleration on the grounds that unmethodical "false glimmers" are all too frequent when it comes to theological convictions, employed a deductive, almost geometrical method in his only metaphysical publication—perhaps the Port Royal logic had left some slight Cartesian traces after all—and ultimately hit upon a method that explained without dissolving the diversity of religious claims.[48]

The Art of Thinking impressed Franklin with the importance of methodically scrutinizing arguments and ideas. John Locke's philosophical investigations into the "original, certainty, and extent of *human knowledge,* together with the grounds and degrees of *belief, opinion,* and *assent,*" underscored the lesson by reassuring him that the mind was capable of testing and, when necessary, correcting its judgments about the nature of the world, knowledge, and religious claims.[49] Moreover, Locke's analysis was untainted by the Cartesian biases that cluttered Arnauld and Nicole's account of the mind. In demonstrating that there are uniform and rational laws of the mind analogous to physical ones, Locke, evidently to Franklin's grateful satisfaction, undercut the Calvinist distrust of reason once and for all. Locke's book was well known in the colonies, but an ardently admiring Franklin made it more so by constant and sometimes hagiographic references to it in his journalistic writings. As he says in *Poor Richard's Almanac* for 1748, for example, Locke is "the Newton of the Microcosm," having made the internal world his own just as Newton claimed the outer one. "His book on the *Human Understanding,* shows it."[50]

In examining the origin and reliability of reason, Locke necessarily also took on the thorny issue of its relationship to revelation. Although Franklin had encountered Locke's general conclusions in Addison's essays, reading them straight from the master's pen must have been a particularly liberating experience for the young rebel. Locke argued that no new simple idea can be conveyed by revelation, since simple ideas originate in sensory experience and revelation by definition is extrasensory. Thus he effectively denied (without actually coming out and saying it) that revelation offers new insights into the nature of reality. But he left no doubt about his position when he went on to insist that no claim allegedly derived from revelation can be admitted that is contrary to the dictates of reason. If the orderly physical realm is indeed a reflection of the rational nature of its Creator, then both random physical events and irrational divine interventions are equally impossible.

These are chilling conclusions for religionists accustomed to thinking of God in terms of absolute sovereignty, but Locke insisted that there is no protection from the excesses of religious enthusiasm if reason is not employed as a barometer in the realm of faith. "*Reason,*" he wrote, "must be our last Judge and Guide in every Thing." "Perswasion," or intensity of belief, is simply not enough: "Good Men are Men still, liable to Mistakes, and are sometimes warmly engaged in Errors, which they take for divine Truths, shining in their Minds with the clearest Light."[51] These were incendiary ideas for a young man searching for a way out of his religious upbringing, challenging as they do the trustworthiness of subjective experiences such as regeneration that were so central to the New England scheme of salvation. Franklin would later paraphrase them at the conclusion of his 1725 treatise on natural religion.[52]

Franklin tells us in the *Autobiography* that the straw that broke the back of his fidelity to the religion of his fathers was his discovery of the works of Lord Shaftesbury and Anthony Collins. Both were deists, Shaftesbury slyly so and Collins explicitly; both rejected the liberal Christianity of Locke as too mild and compromising. Their minimalist natural religion struck Franklin as the logical conclusion of the New Learning's twin analyses of human reason and physical reality, and logical conclusions, rather than enthusiastic outpourings, were everything for the young man who had devoured the Port Royal Logic. When coupled with "some Books against Deism [that] fell into my Hands," which, he said, "wrought an Effect on me quite contrary to what was intended," Franklin became a thoroughgoing deist by the time he was fifteen.[53]

Anthony Ashley Cooper, Third Earl of Shaftesbury (1671–1713), made it his life's mission to attack and demolish revealed religion. An even more committed foe of enthusiasm than Locke, he insisted that "*Reason* and *sound Sense*" are the only proper arbiters in religious disputes because they are "sedate, cool, and impartial; free of every byassing Passion, every giddy Vapour, or melancholy Fume."[54] In the absence of sound sense, religious fervor encourages beliefs that no rational man could possibly take seriously: miracles that beg the question of God's existence, putative revelations that are nonsensical or wicked, prophecies that clearly are not fulfilled. Moreover, it breeds and legitimizes intolerance and persecution.

Religious enthusiasts generally cannot be reached through rational discourse, and it would be improper to resort, as they do, to threats of violence. Therefore, concludes Shaftesbury, bantery and ridicule are the best weapons against them: "GOOD HUMOUR is not only the best Security against *Enthusiasm,* but the best Foundation of *Piety* and *true Religion.*" "True Religion," in other words, consists in a rather urbane nod of the head toward an impersonal, distant First Cause and a sophisticated chuckle at the quaint superstitions of sectarians. In the final analysis, Shaftesbury's deism is a religion for worldly gentlemen who insist on good taste and moderation in their spiritual beliefs as in everything else.[55]

The young Franklin, already of a satiric turn of mind, must have enjoyed reading the witty, teasing Shaftesbury, even if the latter's natural religion seemed a rather insipid thing to his rebellious eye. The aristocratic freethinker, true to his conviction that laughter was the best weapon against religion, was a master of irony and innuendo. In the various treatises that comprise his *Characteristics,* the volume Franklin read as a teen, Shaftesbury deliberately speaks ill of deism, accusing it of being a disguised form of atheism, and claims to be a Christian of unimpeachable orthodoxy. While it is quite true that some of his beliefs are compatible with Christianity, it is also clear that his ironic attacks on scripture as well as his contemptuous treatment of supernaturalism place him squarely in the deistic camp, and that his self-described commitment to Christianity is actually a ruse. Certainly Shaftesbury was viewed as an infidel by many eighteenth-century readers who agreed with Alexander Pope's conclusion that the *Characteristics* had done more harm to revealed religion than any or even all other skeptical works.

If Shaftesbury was the gently mocking philosopher-nobleman, Anthony Collins (1676–1729) was a two-fisted streetfighter. Although he wrote several blustery defenses of deism, the one Franklin most likely read as a youth was the *Discourse on Free-Thinking.* The volume raised a tremendous storm when it appeared in 1713. At least twenty responses to it appeared in London within a year of its publication. One can imagine Franklin's excitement when he finally got a copy of it in his hands.

Collins actually said nothing that hadn't already been defended by earlier British deists. The difference was the pugnacious way in which he made his case. The *Discourse* rested basically on two claims: first, that all religious debate ought to be conducted in the spirit of free inquiry, without any fear of legal or social sanctions; second, that the inevitable conclusions of such unafraid debate will be that supernaturalism is irrational and ought to be abandoned. In support of his first point, he assembles a long list of historical figures, beginning with Socrates, he claims as allies in the historical struggle for free religious inquiry. In defense of his claim that supernaturalism is irrational, he more rigorously focuses on a sustained and at times fiery criticism of scripture. He asserts that the Bible is self-contradictory, impractical, fraudulent, and plagiaristic, many of its alleged miracle accounts having been stolen from pagan religions.[56] He also pressed a bitter anticlericalism, claiming that although the "layman wants to know the truth, a priest desires to have him of his opinion." Charges like this would later inspire American deists such as Thomas Paine and Elihu Palmer in their own crusades against clerical authority.[57] It's likely that Collins's belligerent, take-no-prisoners style at least partly encouraged the hard-edged and disputatious habit of "abrupt Contradiction" Franklin adopted for a while as a youth.[58]

Franklin's broad reading in the exhilarating New Learning, his angry resentment at religious and paternal authority, and his rebellious adolescent quest for identity all began to crystallize somewhere around his fifteenth year, spawning a scornful repudiation of supernaturalism and a zealous embrace of rational religion. He became a "thorough Deist." Deism in general is an austerely cerebral religion. But the version Franklin created for himself sometime around 1718, and which he endorsed for the better part of the following decade, was especially so. As we shall see in the next chapter, it was really more of a metaphysics than a faith. On the surface, it seemed light years away from the orthodox religion of his father. It professed an aloof, uninvolved deity who operated through secondary causes, and it asserted that humans were innately good and incapable of performing evil. Moreover, it endorsed a deterministic mechanism that consistently denied freedom of the will to humans. But scratch its surface, and traces of the New England theology Franklin absorbed as a youth and rebelled against as an adolescent are plainly discernible beneath the Newtonian veneer. During his deistic decade, Franklin spoke the language of Locke and Collins and Shaftesbury. But his Calvinist accent, try as he might, still broke through.[59]

It is impossible to appreciate fully this first stage of Franklin's ambiguous religious journey, the transition from cradle Calvinism to deism, quite simply because of the relative dearth of available biographical information. Franklin tells us next to nothing in the *Autobiography* about his childhood. True to the Enlightenment ethos in which he lived and reminisced, he reckoned there was little if anything of interest to be said about an individual's life prior to the first glimmerings of reason. (Rousseau, of course, is a notable exception to this general eighteenth-century tendency to treat childhood as if it didn't exist.) Consequently, all but a few facts about Franklin's early religious life, until around his twelfth year, are wrapped in shadow.

But it is still possible to reconstruct in broad terms the general lay of the land he trod in moving toward the deism of his adolescence and early manhood. After all, we do know something of the religious ethos in which he grew up; there is a scattering of intriguing autobiographical details; and the psychologist James Fowler, following the work of Jean Piaget, Erik Erikson, and Lawrence Kohlberg, has elaborated a model of religious development that can be enlisted as a conceptual grid to help fill in the remaining gaps.[60] Like all developmental schemata, Fowler's should be approached with some wariness. The rich complexity and occasional sheer unpredictability of persons and their behavior obviously stretch far beyond the boundaries of theoretical attempts to categorize them, and any attempt to shove individuals willy-nilly into stylized classifications is foolishly Procrustean. But when read as a heuristic rather than a recipe, Fowler's model does clear up some of the murkiness in the early stages of Franklin's religious journey.

Fowler argues that just as a careful observation of human behavior reveals several discernible stages of cognitive or normative development, so it likewise suggests that an individual's religious sensibility, or faith, also grows developmentally. For Fowler, "faith" is a person's way of "finding coherence in and giving meaning to the multiple forces and relations" that comprise his or her life. It focuses, as Paul Tillich argued, on "ultimate concerns," those "god values" that are the real foci of devotion and commitment. A faith journey is a search for an explanation or worldview or set of beliefs that will bestow transcendent meaning and purpose on human existence and call forth from us appropriate responses of love, gratitude, and devotion. Since human beings are dynamic creatures, it stands to reason that their faith journeys should expand, contract, or change directions over time.[61] But since humans are also psychobiological creatures, their religious development is neither chaotic nor completely unpredictable. A general pattern, expressed in a series of faith-stages, can be discerned.

Fowler also argues that following an initial (prelanguage) infancy stage in which patterns of trust and loyalty to one's immediate (familial) environment are either established or not, most individuals go through five and sometimes six subsequent moments in their faith development. The first three he calls the "intuitive-projective," the "mythic-literal," and the "synthetic-conventional" stages. Typically the first stage occurs between the ages of three and seven, the second when the child is "school-age," and the third in adolescence. A consideration of these first three stages is particularly helpful in filling in the gaps of Franklin's transition from Calvinism to deism.

At the intuitive-projective level of faith development, the child is bombarded with a continuous stream of novel perceptions "for which no stable operations of knowing have been [as yet] formed." "Uninhibited by logical operations," the imaginative processes are at full tilt, absorbing and recreating the episodic panorama of images and sensations. This imaginative play is the child's prelogical way of intuitively grasping the world in which she dwells. It engenders in her "feelings towards the ultimate conditions of existence" that may be either positive or negative but are certainly long lasting. At a later point in her life, she will have to reflect on and possibly exorcise these chthonic memories, but even then their residual effects are likely to remain.[62]

Entry into the second, "mythic-literal" faith stage is typically prompted by what might be described as the developing child's tendency toward "realism": he wants to distinguish between what is actual and what is only "pretend," and he wants to discern a pattern in the former. So he graduates from satisfaction with episodic images to the construction of stories—"myths"—that bestow coherency upon those images. But because he still operates from a one-dimensional perspective, he takes his myths literally. For him, they are not symbolic representations of the world. Instead, they are literal descriptions and thus serve in his mind to separate truth from falsehood. This literalness most often gives rise to anthropomorphic images of God as a bearded old man, or heaven as an actual city in the sky. It also encourages a rigid fidelity to the exact letter of moral rules and principles. In his own way, the child in this second stage of religious development is a fundamentalist, advocating a strictly inerrant reading of religious and normative stories. Words have only one meaning, and that is the most concretely obvious one.[63]

The first two stages of faith development are normally cultivated in the relatively closed environment of the family. Consequently, there is a nonthreatening homogeneity to first the episodic images and feelings and then the stories and values that constitute the raw material of a child's religiosity. But as she matures into adolescence she inevitably encounters a wider community that is heterogeneous in its religious beliefs, values, and attitudes. Her deepest religious and normative convictions are challenged simply by the sudden awareness that contrary ones exist, and she finds herself forced to cope with the emergent pluralism by taking a stand. Typically this stand means conforming to the "expectations and judgments of significant others" because she "as yet does not have a sure enough grasp on [her] own identity and autonomous judgment to construct and maintain an independent perspective." Not surprisingly, the significant others upon whose beliefs she models her own are often not her parents, whom she is likely now to see as stodgy or old fashioned. Also not surprisingly, the beliefs to which the adolescent person of faith conforms have not been, as Fowler says, "dwelt" in. They may satisfy the emotional need to rebel against parental example, and they may even exhibit a high degree of intellectual sophistication. But they typically are not owned or lived by the individual. They are simply appropriated, either unreflectively or, if reflectively, in an abstract, detached manner.[64]

Given what we do know about Franklin's early environment, and following Fowler's schema, it is not difficult to paint in broad strokes the first stages of Franklin's religious odyssey. He is born into a piously dissenting family that sets aside regular time for family devotions. His parents are loyal church members, and they undoubtedly begin taking young Benjamin to service long before he's capable of understanding the sense of the sermons. But he can and does pick up on the impassioned tones from the pulpit, the groans arising from the congregation, the stern, humorless faces as well as the occasional panic-stricken ones, the hard benches, the damp and coldness of the church in wintertime. These and hundreds of other powerful albeit episodic images that flash back and forth, and which he comes to associate with religion, are endlessly fascinating but also sometimes frightening. Moreover, during these early years Franklin's mother and father surely entertain him with colorful stories from the Bible, probably ones with the most obvious moral lessons, and these in turn likewise leave their mark on his imagination and memory. Tales of God's angry judgment of Adam and Eve, of Saul's destruction and David's chastisement, or of the unhappy fate of Sodom and Gomorrah—not to mention Lot's wife—leave him puzzled about the causal mechanism at work in these cosmic acts of retribution, but the accounts deeply impress him with disturbing images of violence and destruction, which later translate into the idea of a stern and punishing God-Father. The psychic tension so characteristic of New England Calvinism is thus sown, and births the danger, as Fowler puts it, of "the possible 'possession' of the child's imagination by unrestrained images of terror and destructiveness."[65]

The religious images and sensations of early childhood eventually begin to fall into more coherent patterns, and Benjamin now thinks in stories, ones heavily tinted with affective associations formed in earlier days. Whereas once he focused on fleeting impressions, now he searches for an underlying meaning to tie the images together. He listens carefully each Sunday to the sermons, and even though he still doesn't comprehend the theology, he seizes eagerly on the biblical stories and moral pronouncements. The God-Father in all the stories he hears takes on the image of an old man with flowing locks and heavy eyebrows, perhaps looking something like old Samuel Sewall, redoubtable father of South Church's minister. He begins to arrange everything he hears into two categories: true and false. The stories of the Bible and the moral teachings of his parents are true. Those stories that deviate from either in even the slightest way are false. Of course, Benjamin only hears about this second kind of story indirectly, as when some authority figure in his life invokes one as an example of error to be shunned. But he nonetheless knows that many persons mistakenly believe such stories to be true, because he has been assured that there are many wicked and godless people in the world, and particularly in Boston. It's not surprising that one of his favorite childhood books is Bunyan's *Pilgrim's Progress.*[66] Its allegorical account of redemption is a story that sketches the world in black and white, the forces of godliness engaged in a relentless battle against the Evil One's minions.

Ambivalence has already bubbled up in Benjamin's developing religious perspective. On the one hand, he implicitly trusts the moral and scriptural stories that are the raw material of his faith. He has heard them from both his minister and his father. The former he has been taught to venerate, and he loves and respects the latter. They would not deceive him. But faintly riding on all their stories, an ambience more than a palpable presence, are the residual feelings of uneasiness and anxiety associated with church and God imprinted on his memory in the days of early childhood. So long as Benjamin remains in the homogeneous and stable environment of his family, the ambivalence is quiescent. But his adolescent entry into a wider world awakens it, and the consequence is an explosion.

The wider world for Benjamin is initially encountered in books more than people, although it is certainly the case that some of his brother James's liberal companions also open his eyes. He forsakes Bunyan for secular history, then progresses to authors such as Addison, Shaftesbury, Locke, and Collins. The urbane, tidy, and sunlit worldview they defend captivates the boy. When he compares it to the Calvinist scheme of salvation in which he has been raised, the latter comes across as wintry, needlessly authoritarian, and hopelessly out of touch. He now smiles at the stories he once took literally, and the old unsettling images of the God-Father as autocratic and merciless reemerge to stand as accusers of his cradle religion.

Coupled with his recently adopted intellectual allegiance to the New Learning is his growing resentment against the old order. Perhaps it is first consciously felt when his father decides to make him a tradesman rather than a scholar; there is such an intimate connection in Benjamin's mind between Josiah and the family religion that anger at one inevitably bleeds over into anger at the other. Josiah, the wise and strong *paterfamilias,* has up to this point been perfect in young Benjamin's eyes. When the fall comes, it takes down not only the boy's devotion to his father but also his faith in the unquestionability of his father's religion.

Angry, nursing a resentful sense of betrayal, contemptuous as only an adolescent can be of what he perceives as the intellectual and moral inadequacies of his family's religious convictions, young Franklin is still too young and untested to strike out on his own in the rough waters of religious exploration. But no matter: he has discovered in his reading an alternative to Calvinism to which he can give his wholehearted allegiance. He throws his hat in with the deists and does so with single-minded zeal. His earlier scriptural standard of truth is now replaced by a Newtonian one. He has established for himself an identity, asserting his independence from both his father and Old South Church.

Or so he thinks. But in fact the deism he now embraces, and will continue to champion for the next few years, is never assimilated into his everyday existence in the same way his boyhood Calvinism was. Benjamin "converts" to rational religion because he is intellectually intrigued by its pristine orderliness, and because it represents a slap in the face of Boston orthodoxy. But deism never really sinks deep roots in his psyche. He becomes increasingly unsure of both its metaphysical presuppositions and its ethical implications, until he finally rejects it as one of his great "errata." This rejection, as we will see in succeeding chapters, signals his movement into the next of Fowler's religious stages.

Until his sixteenth year, Benjamin's rebellion was largely private, centered on the forging of a new identity on deism's anvil. But in 1722 Franklin took his revolt to the streets with the anonymous publication of the first "Silence Dogood" letter in his brother's *New-England Courant.*[67] Fourteen Dogood letters in all appeared, the first on 2 April and the last on 8 October 1722. They were the newly converted deist's first public salvo against the religion and institutions of his fathers.

The letters, heavily influenced in both style and substance by Addison's essays, purported to be from one Mistress Silence Dogood, the widow of a New England clergyman.[68] It is likely that Franklin intended her name as a punning reference to a sermon of Cotton Mather's entitled "Silentiarius: The Silent Sufferer," which had been delivered in late September 1721 and published shortly afterward.[69] In the very choice of a name for his mouthpiece, then, the young rebel thumbed his nose at the Boston establishment.

And not just with her name. Mistress Dogood has acquired the benign reputation in the years since her appearance as a rather simpleminded, sharp-tongued busybody who in her breathlessly gossipy way occasionally hits on some telling social and religious truths. While it's true that Franklin intended her to be humorous, it's also the case that she is much more than merely a Shakespearean clown. Her very being is an affront to convention. In the first place, she is a member of the "gentler" sex. That a woman should set herself up as a social critic, and moreover one who has things to say actually well worth listening to, was in itself a disturbing novelty, as Silence herself acknowledges in the third letter.[70] Second, the details of her biography go against the social grain by calling conventional class and gender categories into question. An impoverished servant, she crosses social boundaries to marry a clergyman, a member of the New England elite.[71] Although a wife and mother, she refuses to limit herself to womanly tasks and educates herself through reading.[72] A member of the sex to whom the doors of Harvard College are closed, she presumes to criticize both the curriculum and the graduates of that august institution.[73] In short, Mistress Dogood is herself a cause for scandal in the eyes of proper Bostonians, and that's exactly what Franklin intended. What he may not have intended, but certainly wound up doing, was revealing as much of himself as he did in the fictional Dogood. The humble son of a tallower who aspires to something greater in life and considers himself the equal of Boston's elite, an apprentice who nonetheless cultivates his mind and refuses to accept his lowly station, a poor youth for whom Harvard is an impossibility and who both scorns and envies its scholars: the young Franklin took himself as a model for Mistress Dogood.

Franklin used the Dogood letters to express his disgust with the moral and religious hypocrisy of Calvinist Boston. Like John Dunton a generation earlier, Silence sees the city on a hill shot through with religious and moral hypocrisy. The same citizens who sanctimoniously thump their Bibles and insist on strict attendance at church vainly adorn themselves in the latest fashions, indulge in the most philistine literary tastes, tolerate infringements on free speech, fail to provide for indigent widows and orphans, and legitimate relations between the sexes that promote hideous coquetry and shameless carousing.[74] Young Franklin quite early had read and been impressed by Mather's *Bonifacius* and Defoe's *An Essay upon Projects* and was afire with enthusiasm for the moral improvement of society. He had also absorbed Shaftesbury's insistence that the mark of true religion was its success in cultivating virtue. Since Calvinism countenanced and even encouraged egregious breaches of individual rectitude and social propriety, it must, he insinuated through Mistress Dogood, be false.

But the Dogood letters did not rest content with mere innuendo when they addressed religion; the coyness of a Shaftesbury wasn't for young Franklin.

Three of the letters overtly attacked. One argued that open infidelity was much less harmful to the social weal than private hypocrisy.[75] Another took aim at religious enthusiasm, complaining that "too many blind Zealots [are] among every Denomination of Christians."[76] And in the third, one of the finest in the series, Franklin vented his fury at social privilege as well as his scorn for the arcane metaphysics of Calvinist theology. Taking Harvard as his explicit target, he has Silence tell about a dream she has had of a great Temple of Learning. At its gate stand two sturdy porters named Riches and Poverty, "and the latter obstinately refused to give Entrance to any who had not first gain'd the Favour of the former." Unfortunately, almost the only students who manage to get past the porters are "Dunces and Blockheads." Those who opt to study theology once inside the temple emerge "as great Blockheads as ever, only more proud and self-conceited." This is little wonder, since their education in divinity for the most part consists in aping the ideas of others while claiming them as their own.[77] Franklin would return to his criticism of social privilege a few months later when he published a short essay in which he railed against distinctions based on inherited rank or wealth instead of merit.[78]

The word on the street soon had it that Franklin was the author of the Dogood letters. Coupled with his contentious love of argument—and, undoubtedly, his adolescent delight in shocking pious Bostonians with a carefully cultivated air of infidelity—he soon acquired the unsavory reputation he seemed to be aiming for. As he says in the *Autobiography,* "my indiscrete Disputations about Religion began to make me pointed at with Horror by good People, as an Infidel or Atheist."[79]

Franklin might have been content at this point in his life to remain in Boston as a gadfly to the religious and social establishment. But relations with his older brother James had gone from bad to worse. Although "not an ill-natur'd Man," James was prone to fits of rage that inevitably resulted in harsh words and blows. Probably, too, the younger brother's journalistic successes chafed James's pride and inflated Benjamin's, leading to even more tension between the two. To make matters even worse, their father, when called on to arbitrate, usually sided with James (another betrayal in Benjamin's eyes). The upshot was that in either September or October of 1723, when he was seventeen, Franklin ran away. He intended on settling in New York. Once there, however, he discovered little prospect of employment, so he went on to Philadelphia.[80] It was a propitious choice for a young freethinker. Philadelphia had a reputation for religious pluralism—so much so that twenty years after Franklin's arrival there, a shocked orthodox visitor observed that "there are no lack of Atheists, Deists, Materialists and Free Masons. In short, there is no sect in the world that is not cherished here."[81]

After his arrival in Philadelphia, the events of Franklin's life took on the dizzying pace of a Horatio Alger story. He found work with the eccentric Samuel Keimer (whom we will encounter again in chapter 3), met his future wife, exulted in the town's religious heterogeneity, and met some of its men of letters, whom he impressed with his knowledge of books and his self-assured air. Before long he came to the attention of William Keith, governor of the province, and the two concocted a farfetched scheme whereby young Franklin would set up his own print shop and Keith would feed him the province's business. (It's noteworthy that the erstwhile moral gadfly of Boston appears to have had no qualms about disloyally conspiring to run his employer Keimer out of business.) Franklin traveled back to Boston, complete with a letter from Keith, to enlist his father's financial assistance in purchasing a press and type. Josiah, wisely concluding that the governor "must be of small Discretion, to think of setting a Boy up in Business who wanted yet 3 Years of being at Man's Estate," declined to invest in the harebrained affair (yet another betrayal).[82]

On hearing that Franklin's journey to Boston had met with no success, the impulsive Keith announced that he would underwrite the financial costs himself, and he urged the young man to sail to England as soon as possible to purchase the necessary printing equipment. On 5 November 1724, Franklin stepped aboard the *London Hope.* He thought he was making only a brief trip to London. But in fact he was taking the next significant step in his lifelong religious journey.

2 A False Start

THE MATURE FRANKLIN, the spinner of salutary maxims and programs for moral improvement, was inclined to suspect that virtue and vice, regardless of how (or whether) they might be dealt with in the next world, frequently met their just deserts in this one. Industry, sobriety, honesty, and all the other virtues touted by Poor Richard were stepping stones to success and esteem, while vices such as arrogance, pride, and selfishness led to downfall in the long run. This was part of the just and natural symmetry of things taught by both deists and Calvinists.

The unhappy denouement of Franklin's high-hoped dealings with Governor Keith couldn't have illustrated the point better. Anyone given to moralizing might have drawn the reasonable conclusion that young Benjamin had risen too quickly and at the expense of too many persons. He had worried his parents, turned his back on his religion, betrayed his brother, thumbed his nose at respectable Bostonians with the Silence Dogood letters, connived to undermine Samuel Keimer, was admittedly disputatious and conceited, and at the tender age of eighteen self-importantly fancied himself ready, with Keith's financial backing, to become Philadelphia's leading printer. It was an inauspicious beginning for a young man who claimed to endorse the enlightened view that virtue is the highest form of worship, and who as a boy had been so taken with Cotton Mather's *Bonifacius*. Given the proportionality of natural justice, Benjamin was ripe for the sobering fall of discovering that Keith's assurances of patronage, while probably given in good faith, were so much smoke.

The governor promised that letters of credit for the purchase of London press, type, and paper had been deposited with the captain of the *London Hope*. But Franklin was dismayed to discover on arriving in England that none of the letters left by Keith in the captain's care so much as mentioned him. Worse, he soon learned that Keith's credit was no good in London anyway; the governor had an unhappy financial history of promising more than he could deliver. So the eighteen-year-old Franklin found himself tricked and abandoned an ocean away from home, with no companion but James Ralph, an irrepressible and roguish friend from Boston who had made the journey with Franklin and would drain his meager financial resources before finally breaking with him (and then using the rupture as a pretext for repudiating his debts).[1]

One of Franklin's fellow-travelers aboard the *London Hope* was a Quaker merchant named Thomas Denham. He took a liking to the young printer and, already having a low regard of Keith's character, willingly gave Franklin a shoulder to cry on and then a few good words of advice. Offer your services to a London printer, he told the youth. You will thereby not only earn money needed for immediate needs and eventual passage back to Pennsylvania. More important, you will increase your knowledge of the art and business of printing.

In spite of his adolescent arrogance, Franklin rarely passed up an opportunity for self-improvement. Besides, in this case, he really had no choice. He needed a job and he knew no trade save printing. So he heeded Denham's counsel and quickly hired on at Samuel Palmer's printing house in Bartholomew Close, Little Britain.

Franklin gained more than wages and experience at Palmer's. Within his first six months there (or so we think: the precise chronology is vague) he also wrote and printed a metaphysical treatise, *A Dissertation on Liberty and Necessity, Pleasure and Pain*, which attempted to summarize his religious beliefs up to that point. He would within just a few months move away from and even repudiate the *Dissertation*'s conclusions, going so far as to condemn the pamphlet as one of life's "great errata" that he would blue-pencil were he offered the opportunity of a second edition. As a statement of his enduring attitude toward religion, then, it was a false start. But it is an especially interesting and important false start.[2] There are at least three reasons for this.

The first is that the *Dissertation* is Franklin's attempt to take to their logical conclusions the New Learning's implications for religious belief. Problematic in places as the treatise's arguments may be, it can scarcely be denied that Franklin succeeded in this enterprise. In fact, the *Dissertation*'s religious conclusions are much more consistent with the Enlightenment's mechanistic worldview than were many other contemporaneous deistic accounts.

The second reason why the *Dissertation* is worth taking a serious look at is that it nicely illustrates Franklin's enduring ambivalence in religious matters. The treatise is the most unequivocal of his religious musings. It is written in a no-nonsense, sober style—quite unusual at the time for the sardonic, joke-cracking Franklin—that on a casual reading allows for no suspicion that the author might not be single-mindedly confident of his thesis. But in spite of its tone of certainty, the *Dissertation* is actually permeated with themes that have sneaked in from Franklin's Calvinist background. Franklin's uneasy position between the two opposing worldviews comes through even in this, his most overtly Enlightenment piece of religious writing.

Finally, the *Dissertation* is important because in spite of Franklin's later repudiation, it reflects one of the major themes of his more mature religious position: the notion of God as the distant, unapproachable First Cause. Franklin will later attempt to ameliorate, in a unique way, the inaccessibility of this divine First Principle, but he never forsakes the basic concept.

The immediate occasion for the *Dissertation*'s composition was Franklin's desire to respond to William Wollaston's (1659–1724) *The Religion of Nature Delineated.* In the early months of 1725 Franklin was given the task at Palmer's of setting type for the third edition (his *Autobiography* incorrectly says the second) of Wollaston's book.[3] Reading as he composed the type, Franklin tells us he became convinced that some of the book's arguments were less than "well-founded."[4] This is a classic Franklinian understatement. Given Franklin's love of disputation as well as the vehemence of his revolt against the orthodox Christianity of his childhood, all of Wollaston's conclusions must have fired him with a sense of outraged contempt. Franklin tried to mask the heat behind his treatise by adopting a geometrical style of axiom, proposition, and corollary similar to that employed by the cooler Wollaston. But the stiff mode of presentation is entirely unable to disguise a rather breathless urgency. One can imagine the manuscript dashed off at white heat in a single sitting. Franklin already wrote fluidly, partly because of his wide reading, partly as a consequence of the training in composition he had set himself as a youth.[5] But the ease and swiftness with which the *Dissertation* flowed from his pen must have surprised even him. This is not simply conjecture on my part. As I will argue later, this interpretation helps to make sense of why Franklin came to repudiate the document.

The Religion of Nature Delineated, first published in 1722, excited a large readership for at least a generation after its appearance.[6] It is a learned book, full of quotations from classical as well as biblical sources, and the style of argumentation, although somewhat tedious, is clear enough. But for the most part there is little in it that is original. Even Wollaston's most characteristic thesis, that goodness consists in acting according to the truth (a doctrine that subsequently drew the jeers of Thomas Jefferson, among others) is used to support a claim (that moral virtue is the essence of true religion) defended by most liberal religionists.[7] The book, then, is just one of dozens of more-or-less similar treatises on religion scribbled by liberal-minded British divines in the eighteenth century, and it repeats arguments and conclusions one expects from the genre.[8] Moreover, it is unfinished. Wollaston announces in his prefatory dedication that he will examine three questions: Is there a natural religion? What is its nature? and On what basis can humans decide between competing religious traditions? He deals with the first two, but the third is never really tackled and Wollaston died before he could rectify the omission in later editions.

Why does Franklin challenge this particular book when there were plenty of other defenses of natural religion just as well—or better—argued? Obviously, sheer accident was one factor. Franklin was given Wollaston's book, not someone else's, to typeset. But there is also a much more significant explanation. In spite of its unoriginality, Wollaston's book was a cause célèbre at the time Franklin composed its third edition. It was the talk of learned as well as polite society, and its merits and weaknesses were loudly and often debated in the London coffee houses young Franklin had begun to frequent. It was just the sort of Goliath that a freethinking eighteenth-century David would want to take on. In sending it crashing to the dust, Franklin by implication was also demolishing the enterprise of natural religion in general. His adolescent rebellion against the orthodoxy of his fathers had already eroded his fidelity to revealed religion, and he dismissed as "unintelligible" or "doubtful" typically Calvinist "dogmas of persuasion" such as election and reprobation.[9] But the option of a liberal Christianity, supposedly liberated from the more egregious superstitions of orthodoxy and instead founded on the dictates of reason and conscience, was for many enlightened minds a respectable alternative. It was this sacred cow that young Franklin now proposed to challenge in his *Dissertation,* and he did it by attacking the currently most popular defense of liberal Christianity. It was a bold move, and one that eventually proved so destructive that even Franklin was frightened by what he had done.

In assailing *The Religion of Nature Delineated,* then, Franklin was doing much more than merely responding to a rather mediocre defense of watered-down Christianity cum natural religion. He was up to nothing less than calling into question the Enlightenment confidence that such a religious model is an acceptable alternative to the Christian supernaturalist scheme. Both, he wanted to demonstrate, were contrary to reason. Before moving to an examination of the way he defends this conclusion, it will be helpful to take a brief glance at the main lines of Wollaston's argument.[10]

Unlike many of his fellow defenders of natural religion, Wollaston does not build his case primarily on a consideration of the *physical* evidence for God's existence. He certainly is not out of sympathy with such approaches, but he chooses to focus more closely on a different one.[11] Wollaston's strategy is to show that morality can be deduced from purely rational first principles, independent of revelation or sectarian belief. Then, after he has established the reality of good and evil on a purely natural basis, he infers from that conclusion the existence of a supernatural benevolent God who rewards righteousness and punishes wickedness in an afterlife. For Wollaston, "the foundation of religion lies in the difference between the acts of men, which distinguishes them into good, evil, indifferent. For if there is such a difference, there must be religion."[12]

It is possible for reason to distinguish good from evil, argues Wollaston, because both are natural qualities and accordingly open to rational investigation. They are natural qualities because they emerge from a consideration of true and false propositions, which in turn are identified by an appraisal of actual states of affairs in the world. Goodness is the action of conforming oneself to what is true, and evil arises when an action deliberately flies in the face of what is true. Thus stealing is an evil act because it violates the truth that the property taken belongs to someone else. Likewise, to treat another person as an object is also evil, because such a course of behavior denies—that is, rejects the truth about—what it means to be a human: a creature who is conscious, sentient, free, and so on.

Wollaston is satisfied that this connection between truth and the good on the one hand and falsehood and evil on the other establishes a criterion of human well-being or happiness. It provides us with a "great law of Nature," derived from reason rather than revelation, which states that "every intelligent, active, and free being should so behave himself, as by no act to contradict truth; or that he should treat every thing as being what it is."[13] Felicity is dependent on loyalty to this principle because conformity to it leads to actions that accord with the moral laws of nature, and such conformity is a necessary condition for happiness.

Two corollaries follow from this argument. The first is obvious: the reality of good and evil entails that humans are free agents. Unless humans are capable of distinguishing, choosing, and behaving in conformity with truth/goodness, no action is properly normative. Humans, then, possess free will.

The other corollary does not so obviously follow from Wollaston's central argument, but it is absolutely crucial to support his claim that the distinction between good and evil is the foundation of religion. According to the "great law of Nature" Wollaston derives from his analysis of good and evil, acting in accordance with the truth is conducive to well-being and happiness. Yet it is clear that many good persons in fact do not experience the well-being that ought to follow on their actions. Even more awkward, history is replete with instances of the success and apparent happiness of scoundrels, rogues, and even moral monsters intent on the pursuit of pleasure and power who, in their rejection of the truth, inflict much misery on good people. As Wollaston laments, "the history of mankind is little else but the history of uncomfortable dreadful passages, and a greater part of it, however things are palliated and gilded over, is scarcely to be read by a good-natured man without amazement, horror, and tears."[14]

But this gap between happiness and virtue, Wollaston assures us, is not as strong an objection to his position as it might seem at first. The great law of Nature cannot be doubted; the uniformity of creation is too obvious a first principle to be jettisoned because of an apparent exception. The only other option, then, is to explain away the asymmetry, and this Wollaston proceeds to do by concluding that unjustly miserable people will in some "future state" enjoy a situation "where the proper amends may be made."[15] Otherwise, there is no way to compensate the "multitudes whose griefs and pangs have far outweighed all their enjoyments; and yet who have not been able, either by their innocence, their prudence, or any power in them, to escape that bitter draught which they have drunk."[16] But such a conclusion depends on the immortality of the soul, and this in turn necessarily (at least in Wollaston's mind) points to the existence of a just and rational God. "So that the argument," he concludes, "is brought to this undeniable issue: if the soul of man is not immortal, either there is no God, upon whom we depend; or he is an unreasonable Being; or there never has been any man, whose sufferings in this world have exceeded his enjoyments, without his being the cause of it himself. But surely no one of these three things can be said."[17] Religion, then, is established, and on a liberal, rational basis. The characteristic tenets of Christian theism—free will, absolute good and evil, the benevolence of God, the immortality of the soul, heaven and hell—are all retained, albeit in a characteristically "enlightened" way.[18]

There is almost nothing in Wollaston's (or by implication anyone else's) liberal theology that the young Franklin endorsed. In his *Dissertation* he set himself the task of denying the existence of evil as well as human free will. He also refused to concede that most human lives are characterized by a disproportionality of either happiness or misery. Instead, he somewhat perversely contended that the two perfectly balance each other out in this life. Hence there is no unjust asymmetry to be redressed in a future state, and the immortality that Wollaston saw as normatively necessary is rendered irrelevant. Most important, Franklin showed that liberal religion's espousal of all these doctrines is inconsistent with its own fidelity to Enlightenment.

In spite of its grand purposes, *A Dissertation on Liberty and Necessity, Pleasure and Pain* is highly abbreviated. In scarcely five thousand words, Franklin presents us with the basics of an argument stripped to its barest essentials. As the title suggests, the work is divided into two parts. The first half argues that both free will and evil are illusory; the second, that pleasure and pain balance one another out, thus eliminating both the logical and the moral need for a heavenly compensation. I will examine each of the sections in turn.[19]

Franklin begins the *Dissertation*'s first half by introducing two propositions that all liberal religionists would accept: God exists, and possesses the absolute attributes of omnipotence, omniscience, and omnibenevolence. No attempt is made to argue for these claims although, given the fact that Franklin refers to God as the "First Mover," he undoubtedly has in mind at least one of the standard cosmological arguments for the existence of God. Instead, as was quite common in the eighteenth century, Franklin assumes that his two propositions are "allow'd and asserted by people of almost every Sect and Opinion."[20]

Several consequences immediately follow from this omni-attributed description of God. If the deity is omniscient and omnibenevolent, then "whatsoever he doth" must be all-wise and all-good. Moreover, given the deity's third characteristic, omnipotence, it follows that "there can be nothing existing or acting in the Universe against or without his Consent." In saying that God is omnipotent, Franklin means his claim to be understood in the strictest sense. Traditionally, he tells us, philosophers who discussed divine omnipotence distinguished between what the deity actually does and what he merely allows or permits to happen. But Franklin will have none of this, dismissing it as a sophism that undermines the sovereignty of God. If God merely *permits* a human action, the implication is that he lacks either the power or the will to prevent it or bring it about Himself. But either imputation does damage to the earlier stipulation that God is all-powerful and all-good. Consequently, Franklin concludes, God must be directly responsible for everything that is.

Franklin is now ready to present the first major argument of his *Dissertation:*

> (i) If God is all-wise and all-powerful, then nothing exists contrary to his will.
>
> (ii) If God is all-good, then his will is good.
>
> Therefore, everything that exists is good—or, as Franklin tersely says, "evil doth not exist."[21]

This stark conclusion is unsettling, and for good reason. All theogonic arguments such as this one elaborate denials of evil that are logically satisfying, because they eloquently follow from first principles, but morally distressing, because they appear to deny what is so palpably obvious to most: the widespread presence of undeserved pain and suffering in the world. Franklin is clearly aware that his conclusion is counterintuitive, for he quickly points out that he doesn't claim that pain and suffering do not exist, but only that they "are not in reality Evils, Ills, or Defects in the order of the Universe." How could they be, when their direct source, God, is all-good and hence incapable of giving rise to evil?

Franklin's next argument forcefully applies the same denial of evil to human agency:

> (i) Everything created by God is good.
>
> (ii) Humans are created by God.
>
> Therefore, humans are good, and "can do nothing but what is good."[22]

In denying that humans are capable of performing evil actions, Franklin not only consistently follows the direction of his original omni-attributed description of God. He also anticipates objections to his theogony that would concede that natural phenomena that cause suffering are not properly evil, but that actions perpetrated by persons with the malicious intent to harm others are. Franklin refuses to back down. If humans are indeed the products of an all-good God, then they, like all creation, necessarily must be good. Moreover, as we've already seen, Franklin refuses to accept the traditional theological distinction between doing and permitting when it comes to divine power. Orthodox Christians as well as natural religionists regularly tried to ameliorate the scandal of human evil by arguing that God permits it to exist as a means to some better end. But as Franklin says, "this Objection destroys itself; for whatever an infinitely good God hath wise Ends in suffering to be, must be good, is thereby made good, and cannot be otherwise."[23] Franklin's point is not to deny that humans commit acts that are conventionally *named* evil, but only that such actions are *in fact* evil.

The third argument in the *Dissertation*'s first half is the denouement toward which all of Franklin's efforts thus far have aimed:

(i) Human beings can do nothing but what is good.

(ii) But this means that human actions are bound by divine will.

Therefore, humans lack free will, or the "power to do or refrain an action."[24]

In defending this conclusion, Franklin is careful to point out that his insistence that human beings are bound by divine necessity is not inconsistent with the notion of human liberty. But this compatibility is possible only because Franklin takes a narrowly mechanical view of liberty as "absence of opposition." Human actions, therefore, can possess liberty, "but it is a Liberty of the same Nature with the Fall of a heavy Body to the Ground." The heavy body plummets earthward because there is no intervening event or obstacle to hamper it, but its fall, for all that, is still causally determined by antecedent events. Similarly with human actions. Even if they encounter no external opposition and hence are at "liberty," in Franklin's sense of the word, they are not thereby the products of free will, because they are the final outcome of a long sequence, beginning with God's will, of causal factors.[25]

A priori reasoning from the axiomatic descriptions of God's omni-attributed nature demonstrates that human beings lack free will. But Franklin also offers an empirical argument that he thinks points to the same conclusion. Let us suppose, he says, that humans in fact do possess free will. A myriad of choices faces each person on a regular basis, and each of those choices in turn can be evaluated on a sliding scale from "best" to "worst." Now, experience teaches us that no human is capable of taking a broad enough view to predict all the "intricate Consequences of every Action"; such consequences "are innumerable and incomprehensible by any Thing but Omniscience." It follows that everyone has "but as one Chance to ten thousand" of selecting the best course of action available to him or her, and this means that by rights "we should then be perpetually blundering about in the Dark, and putting the Scheme in Disorder." But this is not, asserts Franklin, an accurate description of the way things are. Disaster does not follow disaster in the human realm any more than chaos is characteristic of the natural one. The only explanation for this, concludes Franklin, is that human actions are "rul'd and govern'd"—that is, causally determined—by a mind powerful enough to fathom the whole of reality and benevolent enough to will the good of the whole.[26]

In his arguments against free will, Franklin shows more loyalty to the mechanistic tendencies of the Enlightenment than did most of his contemporaries. Eighteenth-century liberal Christians and deists alike were quick to endorse the view that the physical universe is best understood as an immense machine necessarily bound by intractable natural law. But they typically refused to follow this interpretation to its logical conclusion of rigorous determinism when it came to human behavior, even though humans are clearly constituents of the physical universe and hence presumably bound by its laws. Instead, liberal Christians and deists chose to defend a rather dissonant view of human nature that stressed freedom, virtue, and self-creation through education. These ideals accounted for the Enlightenment's intense humanism, but they are hardly consistent, as Kant would point out by century's end, with its physical mechanism.

Franklin, however, realized that defenders of a mechanistic universe couldn't have it both ways. Either reality is uniformly bound and defined by causal necessity or it is not. If the latter, then the bottom drops out of the Enlightenment worldview as well as its vision of a unifying science that explains nature's powers and bends them to the service of humankind. If the former, humans do not enjoy a privileged position in the great cosmic machine. That Franklin endorsed a thoroughgoing mechanism at this stage in his religious development, and hence was willing to throw over the possibility of free will, is further indicated by the strong language he uses in describing how incongruous the "Self-Motion" of humans would be in an otherwise mechanically predictable universe:

> It is as if an ingenious Artificer, having fram'd a curious Machine or Clock, and put its many intricate Wheels and Powers in such a Dependence on one another, that the whole might move in the most exact Order and Regularity, had nevertheless plac'd in it several other Wheels endu'd with an independent Self-Motion, but ignorant of the general Interests of the Clock; and these would every now and then be moving wrong, disordering the true Movement, and making continual Work for the Mender; which might better be prevented, by depriving them of that Power of Self-Motion, and placing them in a Dependence on the regular Part of the Clock.[27]

In denying free will, Franklin goes a long way toward deflating the Enlightenment's overblown humanism. But he ends the *Dissertation*'s first half on a note guaranteed to push the point home. He concludes that his previous arguments persuasively demonstrate that all aspects of creation "must be equally esteem'd by the Creator." Everything that exists must possess equal worth because created by an all-good God incapable of bringing about anything not similarly good. Although Franklin's immediate purpose here is to highlight his claim that human actions are identically good (and therefore "equally esteem'd"), his argument obviously applies to all other distinctions as well. Murder and sacrifice, usury and charity, are all without either merit or demerit and so equally esteemed by the Creator. But ants and geniuses, mud and Mona Lisas, cancer cells and concerts are also at qualitative par with one another. Franklin's *Dissertation,* then, is more than a rejection of the claims of liberal religion. When read against the backdrop of the Enlightenment's understanding of what it means to be a person, it is also an uncompromisingly antihumanistic manifesto. Franklin's youthful disputatious nature, as well as his disdain for religious conventionality of any sort, have taken him far indeed.

More immediately, however, Franklin has rejected the fundamental principles upon which Wollaston based his defense of religion. In asserting the absolute sovereignty of an all-good God, Franklin dissolves the distinction between good and evil that Wollaston posited as the foundation of all religion. Similarly, the rigorous necessitarianism defended by Franklin renders all talk of morality irrelevant. Cogs in a perfect cosmic machine, as Franklin himself notes, are neither praiseworthy nor reproachable. They simply do what they must. Consequently, Wollaston's effort to reduce morality to truth-abiding is perhaps interesting in an abstract way but actually quite beside the point. Humans, as Franklin made clear in his earlier-quoted reflection on the incongruity of free will with the divine plan, are *incapable* of acting against the truth. They are bound by the Ultimate Truth—divine will—and consequently are always in harmony with the universe.

In the second part of his *Dissertation,* Franklin continues the assault against Wollaston. Moreover, he amplifies the antihumanist tone he introduced in the first half. The cold-blooded way in which he now proceeds to reduce humans to the status of sentient automata manipulated solely by the desire to avoid pain is disconcerting even today. It is little wonder that Franklin later destroyed all copies of the *Dissertation* he could lay his hands on.[28]

But even though there is an obvious continuity in tone as well as target in the first and second halves of Franklin's treatise, there is also a decided break in the rigor of argumentation. When defending necessitarianism, Franklin's arguments are crisply syllogistic. If one faults them, it can only be because their premises are dubious, not because their conclusions do not logically follow. But Franklin's style of argumentation in the second part of the *Dissertation* is much looser. Instead of presenting the reader with a closely connected network of arguments, he here builds his case on a succession of five propositions that are less precisely defended. This is not to say that the conclusions he arrives at are fatally flawed, but only that for one reason or another he chose to change methods between the *Dissertation*'s parts. Such a modification could be accounted for by supposing that he wrote the two halves at different times, with a significant interval between them. But I doubt this. The second half is just as breathless in tempo, just as feverishly urgent, as the first, suggesting that the whole treatise was dashed out quickly as a whole. A more likely explanation for the difference in tone is that Franklin is less sure of his conclusions in the second half—as well as, quite possibly, less comfortable with them.

In this second part of his *Dissertation,* Franklin takes on Wollaston's orthodox claim that there is such unfairness in the distribution of pain and pleasure in this world that justice requires compensation in the next. In attacking Wollaston, Franklin defends a consistent reductionism that accounts for human behavior exclusively in terms of pain avoidance, argues that pleasure and pain in fact are equally distributed in life (and therefore that an otherworldly distribution is unnecessary), and all but denies that the soul is immortal. In short, Franklin demolishes the central core of Christian theism. Even a young man as angry at Calvinism as he must surely have felt some uneasiness at the enormity of such destruction.

Franklin launches his assault by positing what he takes to be a self-evident claim:

> (i) Humans are capable of experiencing pain or uneasiness.[29]

Such uneasiness, the causes of which originate "Somewhat without and distinct from the Mind itself" in the external physical realm, is a necessary condition for human consciousness. Obviously drawing from his reading of Locke, Franklin asserts that the mind is not "rous'd and put into Action" until acted on. But once its passive equilibrium is ruptured by stimuli, "it discovers its Powers and Faculties, and exerts them to expel the Uneasiness." In describing this process, Franklin revealingly invokes mechanistic metaphors: "Thus is the machine set on work; this is Life. We are first mov'd by Pain, and the whole succeeding Course of our Lives is but one continu'd series of Action with a View to be freed from it. As fast as we have excluded one Uneasiness another appears, otherwise the Motion would cease. If a continual Weight is not apply'd, the Clock will stop."[30]

Franklin's use of such language is not accidental. In his *Dissertation,* he quite deliberately likens humans to clocks and compares human activity to the mechanical movements of counterweights. Humans are merely physical objects, even if they do differ, in degree rather than kind, from inanimate ones. As such, they must conform to the same system of natural laws that defines the rest of reality. Newton argued that material things lack a principle of self-animation, and consequently that the movement of an object ultimately must originate from an external impetus. In insisting that the mind's activity is triggered by stimuli rather than by some sort of internal self-determination, Franklin is simply showing loyalty to his Newtonian convictions.[31]

Since humans are nothing more than relatively sophisticated clockworks, and since all machines are characterized by a measurable harmony in the interworking of their parts, Franklin thinks it stands to reason that

> (ii) Uneasiness produces an exactly proportionate desire to be freed from it.[32]

The clockweight of uneasiness begins to ascend, and its counterbalancing weight of desire compensates by exerting an equal force. Such proportionality is necessary in order to animate the human machine properly. Otherwise the risk of external stimuli destroying the actor before he or she (or it) reacts would be too great. This much is obvious. But what is more contentious is Franklin's subsequent claim that

> (iii) The desire to be freed from uneasiness is *always* satisfied.[33]

Thus far in the *Dissertation*'s second half, Franklin's arguments for his propositions have been sparse. At a stretch, the first two may be said to rest on an endorsement of Newtonian natural philosophy as well as on a rather naive psychology inspired by Locke. Even if there is little explicit argumentation in support of them, then, Franklin's points at least can be situated against a wider background. But in presenting his third proposition, he offers no evidence or argument whatsoever. Instead, he rests content with elaborating the point. He tells us that while the *end* of a desire is always predictable, the *manner* in which the end is brought about is not. An individual trapped in a house she believes to be in imminent danger of collapse, for example, experiences as a consequence a violent uneasiness or terror. This terror can be alleviated in any number of ways, but three immediately suggest themselves. The individual can flee the house, she can be persuaded that her fear is unfounded, or she can be crushed to death by the actual collapse of the house. The means differ, but the end is the same.

The problem, of course, is that Franklin's point about means and ends, interesting as it is, possesses importance only if the wider claim to which it is attached carries weight. But there is no good reason for supposing it in fact does. Even the most cursory data gleaned from introspection point to the unhappy fact that our desires to be free from one uneasiness or another are not always satisfied. To claim otherwise, as Franklin does, ignores the fact that psychological distress and uneasiness are usually so complex that it's not at all easy to know what will ameliorate them. Franklin's simplistic assertion takes on a special irony in light of the complex ambivalence of his own religious uneasiness.

Equally problematic is Franklin's next proposition:

> (iv) The satisfaction of a desire produces pleasure exactly proportionate in intensity to the uneasiness it replaces.[34]

As with the immediately preceding proposition, there is no real argument in support of this claim. In all honesty, it is difficult to see how Franklin could have provided a convincing one. The satisfaction of a desire, or the alleviation of a pain, in no obvious way entails that the ensuing psychological state is one of pleasure. This only follows if "pleasure" is rather unimaginatively defined as the mere absence of pain, and this move in turn runs the risk of conflating a positive sensation with the absence of sensation. The problem is one that had been recognized by philosophers for centuries but apparently escaped Franklin.

Or perhaps it didn't. For the assertion, doubtful as it is, that pleasure is exactly proportionate to the pain it replaces is a necessary condition for the ultimate step in Franklin's longer argument—so necessary that he may have turned a blind eye to its weakness. Franklin's final proposition affirms the following:

> (v) The sensation of pleasure and pain are equal, or "in exact proportion" to one another, in this life.[35]

The truth of this proposition, says Franklin, is syllogistically obvious: "As the Desire of being freed from Uneasiness is equal to that Uneasiness, and the Pleasure of satisfying that Desire equal to the Desire, the pleasure thereby produc'd must necessarily be equal to the Uneasiness or Pain which produces it: Of three Lines, A, B, and C, if A is equal to B, and B to C, C must be equal to A." Stated less elaborately, Franklin's point is that pain precedes pleasure, and pleasure always replaces pain. His counterweight metaphor is appropriate here: as the intensity of pain descends, the intensity of pleasure proportionally ascends, and "one cannot rise or fall without the Fall or Rise of the other." Pleasure and pain, then, continuously balance one another out. It is true, admits Franklin, that humans are often convinced that pains outweigh pleasures in their lives, but this is usually because "the former leave more lasting impressions on the Memory."[36]

Still, Franklin acknowledges, it is often the case that some individuals pass the greater part of their lives in pain, sorrow, and distress. Doesn't this falsify his claim that there is no inequality of pleasure and pain in human existence? Only, Franklin responds, if one erroneously insists (as Wollaston did) on measuring pain and pleasure in terms of *duration.* Instead, the two by rights ought to be measured in terms of *intensity.* This done, it is obvious that "the Pain, tho' exquisite, is not so to the last Moments of Life, the Senses are soon benumb'd, and render'd incapable of transmitting it so sharply to the Soul as at first: She perceives it cannot hold long, and 'tis an exquisite Pleasure to behold the immediate approaches of rest." In other words, a lifetime of continuous pain, measured in intensity rather than duration, can be counterweighted by the intense pleasure that the relief of imminent death brings: "One single Moment of Pleasure may outweigh and compensate an Age of Pain."[37]

The target at which Franklin has directed his five propositions is now in sight. It will be recalled that Wollaston, along with other eighteenth-century liberal apologists, argued that the existence of a just God and the immortality of the soul are both necessary if undeserved pain (or pleasure) ultimately is to be compensated. Wollaston went so far as to claim that the intuition that justice demands such compensation is the foundation of religion. But Franklin skewers this entire approach by denying that life's pleasures and pains are in fact unequally distributed. The obvious outcome is that "there is not, on that Account, any Occasion for a future Adjustment."[38]

With this conclusion, the sly, innuendo-loving Franklin of the Silence Dogood letters resurfaces. He does not come right out and insist that religion—or at least Christian theism, as well as any of its liberal redactions that insist on an otherworldly compensation—is a sham. But in denying the necessity for compensation beyond this life, he rejects Wollaston's foundation for religious belief and hence, by implication, religion itself.

Just to make sure that his indirect rejection of religion isn't missed, Franklin ends the second part of his *Dissertation* with a rather out-of-place paragraph that argues that even if the soul is immortal, there is no good reason to suppose that it retains either consciousness or a sense of personal identity after death. Ideas, says Franklin the good empiricist, depend on physical experience: they are "first admitted by the Senses and imprinted on the Brain." The soul, in turn, is nothing more than the faculty of "contemplating on and comparing" ideas. It follows that when the body dies, the ideas "contain'd in the Brain" are destroyed, as is the possibility of acquiring or retaining new ideas. The soul, therefore, "tho' incapable of Destruction itself, must then necessarily cease to think or act." It is as if we enter into an unthinking "sound Sleep" or "Swoon" for all eternity. And, as Franklin discomfitingly reminds us, "to cease to think is but little different from ceasing to be."[39]

Franklin's *Dissertation* renounces, in a disturbingly relentless way, the two major intellectual and normative traditions of his time: supernaturalism and Enlightenment humanism. In rejecting the claims that evil exists, that humans are free agents, and that virtue is rewarded and wickedness punished in an afterlife, Franklin closes the book on both Christianity and those enlightened attempts to retain theism stripped of its more objectionably orthodox tenets. In rejecting any moral or metaphysical privilege for humans, Franklin likewise breaks with the inconsistent humanism defended by the eighteenth-century savant. All that remains from the *Dissertation*'s iconoclasm is the former's bare assertion of a Supreme Creator and the latter's postulation of a mechanistic universe.

Franklin himself admits that his reduction of humans to causally determined cogs in a rigid clock-universe is a bitter pill for many to swallow. He recognizes that "Mankind naturally and generally love to be flatter'd" and that it "sooths our Pride" to be elevated "above the rest of the Creation." Such an exaltation, of course, is endorsed by liberal religionists and deists alike. But Franklin cautions that "our *Geese* are but *Geese,* tho' we may think 'em *Swans;* and Truth will be Truth tho' it sometimes prove mortifying and distasteful."[40]

But what exactly *is* the truth here? What are we to make of Franklin's *Dissertation*? Should we take it at its word, reading it as a sincere condemnation of both natural religion and humanism? Or should we instead approach the text as yet another example of the youthful Franklin's love of satire, reading it as a clever parody of the learned windbags of his day? If we conclude that Franklin's denunciation of natural religion is sincere, what are we to make of his implicit condemnation of enlightened humanism? Is it intentional, or did he inadvertently crush humanism in steamrolling over religion? And what of the treatise's insistence that whatever is, is right—a particularly surprising assertion from a young man who recently had been bamboozled and stranded on foreign soil by a likable but unreliable Governor Keith? Is the *Dissertation* really a defense of what Basil Willey so memorably dubbed "cosmic Toryism"?[41] Or is it rather a reductio ad absurdum, a sly effort on young Franklin's part to highlight the absurdity of all overintellectualized attempts to deny moral responsibility by pushing the doctrine of theogony to its logical and perverse conclusion? The fact that the thesis defended by Franklin in his *Dissertation* is so out of kilter with his opinions both prior to and after the treatise's publication only underscores the pertinence of these questions.

William James once argued that the manner in which we philosophize and the directions in which our thoughts are likely to flow ultimately are triggered by sentiment.[42] Our most "abstract" and "objective" judgments, in other words, are motivated and colored by our passions. If there is anything to James's claim, two implications for authorship immediately arise. The first is that it is often (if not always) the case that an author is not completely clear in his own mind about precisely what he's up to. He articulates to himself one agenda, but there may be several more at work under the surface that he is only dimly aware of. Second, the author frequently is propelled by the passion guiding his thought in directions and toward conclusions he neither anticipated nor intended. He means to defend one thing, but the force of his argument pushes him toward another to such an extent that, after the heat of creativity is cooled and he steps back to examine what is written, he is sometimes startled by the result.

The invisible hand of sentiment or passion is at work in all intellectual writing, but especially so, I suspect, in Franklin's composition of the *Dissertation.* He was a young man of burning convictions and equally strong aversions. One of his strongest convictions at this point in his life was that the God defended by traditional Christianity is intellectually unacceptable. Accordingly, one of his strongest aversions in these years was to the orthodox Calvinism in which his father had struggled to rear him. Part of the reason for his strong dislike obviously came from his wide reading in the empiricist New Learning. But as we saw in the previous chapter, his rejection of the New England scheme of salvation was also to some extent a revolt against a resented father. As is often the case with adolescents in Fowler's third stage of religious development, Franklin rebelled against his family's religiosity by eagerly embracing one as antithetical to it as he could find.

We also know that Franklin was a youngster afire with ambition, and this again is compatible with another characteristic of Fowler's third stage: the adolescent's need to assert his own identity. He wished to make a mark on the world of letters and wanted to do so quickly. His early adventures in print, the Dogood letters he published in his brother's Boston newspaper, brought him just enough acclaim to whet his appetite. He possessed the brimming self-confidence and earnestness of the self-educated, and consequently he was more than ready to champion provocative, unconventional positions that older (and perhaps wiser) people would have avoided. He needed to be spotlighted, particularly during the first months of his unintended stay in London, where he was just another journeyman in just another printing house in a city that dwarfed Boston and Philadelphia. Finally, as Franklin himself later admitted, he was of a disputatious bent in his youth, loving to argue endlessly about religion, ethics, and literature with his companions. He found intellectual duels exhilarating and sought them out with an avidity he eventually condemned.[43]

It seems reasonable, then, to presume that Franklin genuinely wished to debunk Christian belief in the pages of his *Dissertation.* His passionate dislike of his father's religion made him ripe for "infidelity," and his ambition and love of disputation goaded him to court the public eye by defending an unpopular position. But for all his eagerness, he wasn't foolhardy. He knew it was much safer to take on liberal religion than Christian orthodoxy. Anyway, destruction of the former, at least in Franklin's judgment, would pull down the latter as well.

But in addition to his strong aversion to religion, Franklin also possessed an abiding conviction in the truth of the humanism defended by enlightened liberals such as Addison and Steele, Shaftesbury and Collins, each of whose writings he had devoured. It was, after all, an essential part of the deistic perspective to which he tied his identity. The dignity of humanity was one of the keynotes running through their works. It was precisely the clarity and promise of such a conclusion that so appealed to a young Franklin repulsed by Calvinism's gloomy assessment of human potential.

Moreover, one of Franklin's strongest allegiances both before and after the *Dissertation* was to "good works." As we saw in the previous chapter, Franklin early in his life converted to the spirit of individual and civic responsibility preached in Mather's *Bonifacius* and Defoe's *An Essay upon Projects.* The Dogood letters reflected this high estimation of "doing good." In fact, Franklin's emphasis on self-improvement, the constant theme throughout his life from his early efforts to teach himself composition, was based on the assumption that human behavior is legitimately judged in terms of good and evil (not merely, as we will see in chapter 4, in terms of prudence).

It would amount to an inexplicable *volte-face,* then, had Franklin intentionally set out in his *Dissertation* to demolish the humanism he had learned from British poets and deists and the high moral tone he had imbibed from Mather and Defoe. We can only conclude that his agenda of demolishing liberal religion, based as it was upon an uncritical acceptance of reductive mechanism, took him in directions he neither intended to go nor approved of when he stepped back to scrutinize his work. After the dust settled, Franklin discovered among the rubble remnants of structures he had not meant to knock down.

What happened, then? There are two likely answers. The first is that the young Franklin, scribbling the *Dissertation* at a furious pace, became so caught up in the logical flow of his thought that he allowed it to drive him to a conclusion his heart really couldn't endorse. Franklin himself appears to agree with this diagnosis. As he tells us in the *Autobiography,* his treatise at second glance "appear'd now not so clever a Performance as I once thought it; and I doubted whether some Error had not insinuated itself unperceiv'd into my Argument, so as to infect all that follow'd, as is common in metaphysical Reasonings."[44] By "metaphysical Reasonings," Franklin meant the a priori style of argumentation he employed in the *Dissertation,* particularly its first half. The more mature Franklin resolutely turned his back on such abstract speculation, insisting that all sound reasoning proceeds from hypotheses based on experimentation. Probably one of his reasons was the unhappy memory of the corner he had painted himself into by his youthful foray into a priori reasoning. Bacon, after all, had cautioned against such ventures on the grounds that the result might be a perfectly logical argument that utterly failed to say anything significant or true about the real world. Franklin probably never read much Bacon, but he certainly learned from hard experience the Baconian lesson.[45]

Actually, it is likely that Franklin began to have reservations about the direction his logic was taking him even before he finished the *Dissertation.* I suspect this is the explanation for the less authoritative, somewhat hesitating tone of the *Dissertation*'s second half. The propositions he presents there are for the most part undefended, or at best defended less rigorously than the ones in the first part, and although the pace is still breathless, the logical flow is less precise. Even the *Dissertation*'s final rhetorical salvo, where Franklin tells us that truth is truth even though we might wish otherwise, has a rather hollow ring of bravado to it, as if Franklin is trying to convince himself as much as his readers.

But there is another explanation for why the *Dissertation* went further in its destruction than Franklin consciously intended. One need not agree with James's claim that passion underlies even our most objective judgments to recognize that religious convictions are not entirely, nor even primarily, the products of dispassionate analysis. There is obviously an intellectual component to any religious worldview, namely, the attempt to justify one's convictions in a rational, orderly way. This is what theology is all about. But prior to such second-order operations are those visceral responses to both inner and outer environments that serve as the raw material of religious sensibility. These felt, scarcely articulated needs, fears, hopes, rages, resentments, and loves that develop from infancy onward influence our subsequent attitudes to existence and our yearnings for meaning in foundational, inescapable ways. (Recall Fowler's analysis of the lasting affective impressions left by the imaginative absorption of episodic images in stage 1 faith.) Jonathan Edwards and Friedrich Schleiermacher after him were correct in this regard: genuine religion is affective, composed of heartfelt emotional urges that are only subsequently veneered with layers of theology.[46] Very often the zealot's rage for divine vengeance on a corrupt society and the saint's drive to self-sacrifice are fueled by sublimated emotions originally directed at quite different objects.[47]

So, besides the fact that Franklin's white-hot rush of composition outstripped his thoughts, my guess is that the *Dissertation* took the direction it did because he unintentionally threw into it all the anger and frustration and disgust—spiced with youthful bravado and arrogance—that had slowly built up in him over the previous five or six years. Things came to a head for him, as it were. Meaning to write a learned reply to Wollaston, he wound up venting anger. *Calvinism's notion of an angry God was foolish and hurtful, as is its insistence on human depravity.* Fine. But as the pot boiled it overflowed. *When you think about it, all notions of God except that of a distant metaphysical principle are foolish. And so are class or economic distinctions, such as those that permeated Boston society: all humans are equally valuable. But when it comes right down to it, what's so special about being a human anyway? Humans are just sophisticated, windup toys, not wingless angels or lowly worms. . . .* And so on. One can almost feel Franklin's urge to destruction mushrooming as the *Dissertation* unfolds. It is as if the floodgates have crashed opened and he cannot stop the flow of spleen cascading through them.

It is also important to keep in mind that at this point in his religious development, Franklin probably didn't live or "own" the mechanistic deism he intellectually endorsed. Stage 3 religious conversions are marked more by the adolescent's need to establish an identity by belonging to a religious "group" than by a genuine change of heart and mind. As pointed out in chapter 2, this is why adolescent religion tends to be either unreflective or too abstract. In a youngster as precocious as Franklin, the move from Calvinism to deism, while certainly addressing a lived, emotional need on one level, was primarily bookish and expedient. He needed an escape route from Calvinism, and deism had the advantage of offering one that stimulated his mind. That the deistic roots sank no deeper than his intellect is suggested by the fact that the *Dissertation*'s logic damaged his newfound religion as much as it did Christian theism. In short, for all the *Dissertation*'s cockiness, its author was a young man still religiously adrift.

The upshot is that what Franklin intended to do in the *Dissertation* and what he finally did are two different things. He intended to express his scorn for both liberal and (by implication) orthodox Christianity. But because he based his arguments against them on first principles derived from a rigid determinism, and because his anger got the better of him, he wound up rejecting free will, human dignity, and morality as well. When his ardor cooled, he realized he had gone too far. Although he likely enjoyed the notoriety his pamphlet brought him among the coffee house set,[48] and although its publication certainly led to his being "more consider'd by [his employer] as a young Man of some Ingenuity,"[49] his conscience soon got the better of his ambition and he repudiated the *Dissertation.*

But it mustn't be supposed that his eventual rejection of the *Dissertation*'s uncompromising mechanism meant that he wholeheartedly embraced the more palatable Enlightenment ideal of human dignity. It is because Franklin ultimately was unable to stomach the very necessitarianism he had defended in the *Dissertation* that he steered clear of the period's encomiums to human goodness. He came to accept that humans are capable of making free choices, and that this means some will deliberately choose self-aggrandizement at the expense of their fellows (exactly, by the way, what Wollaston had argued). The youthful Franklin already had too much unhappy life-experience with his abusive brother James, the roguish Governor Keith, and the irresponsible James Ralph to buy into the notion that there is an inherent splendor to being human. Still, again because he rejected the necessitarianism of the *Dissertation,* Franklin came to deny that humans were pawns either of the cosmos or their own pasts. They could improve themselves with education and effort, and this conviction, if not the uncritical humanism of the Enlightenment, was at least cause for guarded optimism.

Nor did Franklin's repudiation of the *Dissertation*'s denial of good and evil throw him back into an endorsement of Christianity's supernaturalist explanation of value. His rejection of Christianity was too vehement, and his absorption of the Enlightenment ethos too deep, for him to believe that value is based on the arbitrary will of an all-powerful deity. "Revelation," he tells us, "had indeed no weight with me as such; but I entertain'd an Opinion, that tho' certain Actions might not be bad *because* they were forbidden by it, or good *because* it commanded them; yet probably those Actions might be forbidden *because* they were bad for us, or commanded *because* they were beneficial."[50] Having been burnt once by abstract reasoning that had no connection to the real world, Franklin insisted for the rest of his life that the basis of good and evil had to be sought in close scrutiny of observable behavior. His later (unrealized) plan to write a book-length program for moral improvement was based on the conviction that adherents of any or no religious sect could agree on what was right or wrong simply by exercising their reason and their hearts.[51]

But all this was in the future. In 1725, the young Franklin had to face one of the great ironies of his life: that his first major publication defended a thesis he himself increasingly found unacceptable. Moreover, to compound the irony, he had no articulated alternative to the necessitarianism and moral and religious nihilism he had lately advocated.

And the irony did not end there. While it is certainly true that the *Dissertation*'s denial of free agency and moral accountability overtly departs from Franklin's Christian background, it is not the case, as two recent commentators claim, that the treatise "marks a drastic break with his Puritan past."[52] Elements within it are reminiscent of the very Calvinism Franklin thought he had left behind. Most obvious is the similarity between Calvinism's doctrine of predestination and the *Dissertation*'s mechanistic determinism. A less obvious but not unreasonable connection can be drawn between Franklin's claim that humans are incapable of rising above the laws of sensation that define and control behavior, and the traditional Calvinist ascription of utter depravity to humans, which prevents them from overcoming the limitations imposed by original sin. Finally, there is a much more obvious similarity between the *Dissertation*'s insistence that God is supremely powerful, willing each and every event in the physical realm, and the typically monarchical concept of God preached by the Calvinist divines of Franklin's youth. The point is not that Franklin deliberately attempted to write a natural philosophy that would accommodate itself to Calvinist doctrine. He clearly retained no *conscious* allegiance to the Presbyterianism of his boyhood by the time he penned his response to Wollaston. Instead, the claim is that an excavation of the *Dissertation* exposes two intertwined threads of influence: the predominant one of Enlightenment mechanism and the less recognizable but more ancient one of Calvinist Christianity. Franklin's essential religious ambivalence reveals itself, then, even in the one document in which he appears to be the most confident of his religious opinions.[53]

So the *Dissertation* was a false start. Since only a hundred copies of it had been printed, it was relatively easy for Franklin to collect and destroy most of them. He did so not only because he thought the philosophical points in the document flawed. He also wished to keep it out of the hands of impressionable readers who might take its religious nihilism to heart. Franklin feared that his earlier defenses of deism had already "perverted" some of his companions.[54] But those defenses were small beer compared to the heady brew of the *Dissertation.*

Painful as the false start was, it taught Franklin three lessons that stayed with him for the rest of his life. First, as indicated earlier, the unexpected paths down which the *Dissertation*'s abstract reasoning took him cured him of any future interest in "metaphysics." He became convinced that a priori first principles could be invoked to justify any number of absurd and even contradictory positions, and swore henceforth to let experience be his guide. As he wrote in middle life to Thomas Hopkinson, "The great Uncertainty I have found in that Science [metaphysics], the wide Contradictions and endless Disputes it affords; and the horrible Errors I led my self into when a young Man, by drawing a Chain of plain Consequences as I thought them, from true principles, have given me a Disgust to what I was once extremely fond of."[55] Moreover, such reasoning not only explained little; it had no concrete value whatsoever. It led neither to invention nor the redress of present ills: "Are there twenty Men in Europe at this Day, the happier, or even the easier, for any Knowledge they have pick'd out of Aristotle? What Comfort can the Vortices of Descartes give to a Man who has Whirlwinds in his Bowels? The Knowledge of Newton's mutual *Attraction* of the Particles of matter, can it afford Ease to him Who is rack'd by their mutual *Repulsion,* and the cruel Distensions it occasions?"[56] Never again would Franklin allow himself to be seduced by logic for its own sake.[57]

Second, Franklin learned from his brush with nihilism that one denies the distinction between good and evil at great peril. The logic of mechanism told him there was no qualitative difference between charity and homicide, saint and sinner, and that pain was always exactly recompensed by pleasure. But experience of the world and his instincts cried otherwise. The boy had learned his Mather and Defoe too well to forsake them for a pristinely argued but ultimately vapid defense of moral nihilism. The consequences of ignoring the lessons those mentors had taught him were fraught with danger to himself as well as others. Henceforth, Franklin tells us, he "grew convinc'd that *Truth, Sincerity and Integrity* in Dealings between Man and Man, were of the utmost Importance to the Felicity of Life."[58]

Finally, and perhaps most important, the *Dissertation* episode sparked in Franklin a valuable insight into the nature of religious convictions. In his treatise he defended a purely intellectual notion of the deity. The *Dissertation*'s god was described in formal, abstract language that perfectly fit its own aloof and impersonal divine character. This god truly was the distant First Cause, unapproachable by humans and, for all apparent purposes, indifferent to their fate.

Even if a Spinoza can glean personal satisfaction from an intellectual love of such a deity, most people cannot. Franklin was no exception in this regard. Although he had rejected orthodox Calvinism, he was not prepared (nor would he ever be) to reject outright the notion of a god who is involved in the lives and destinies of humans. The cold-blooded intellectuality of the religious position defended in the *Dissertation,* Franklin came to see, was incapable of providing either the emotional comfort or existential security necessary for getting through life's trials. In short, the *Dissertation*'s abortive attempt to reduce religion to a handful of abstract metaphysical principles taught Franklin that true religious sensibility was more of the heart than the head. Metaphysics may serve as an amusing diversion to be explored in one's spare time, but it cannot lend a sense of purpose or meaning to an individual's existence. Only a religion that speaks to the heart can do that.

It was precisely such a religion that the youthful Franklin set out to discover.

3 The Great Insight

"I NOW TOOK LEAVE of Printing, as I thought, for ever." With this dismal conviction, Franklin departed England after a year and a half and returned to America.[1] He was little better off than when he had first sailed into London. True, he had picked up valuable experience at Palmer's printing house, published a metaphysical treatise, and enjoyed the acquaintance of a handful of British men of letters. But he had saved almost no money (thanks largely to James Ralph, but also to Franklin's own careless habits) and had no prospects. Moreover, he suffered from an uneasy conscience and great mental confusion. The *Dissertation*'s hatchet job on free will and ethics was responsible for the former,[2] and Franklin's growing disaffection with its thoroughgoing mechanism accounted for the latter. He was a young man adrift, as uncertain about what he believed as how to earn a livelihood.

Fortunately for him, an old acquaintance reappeared and offered him a second chance. Thomas Denham, the Quaker merchant who had helped Franklin pick himself up in the wake of the Governor Keith debacle, had now concluded his business in England and was ready to sail home to Philadelphia.[3] Denham obviously took a liking to the young man (he was probably unaware of the scandalous *Dissertation*) and offered Franklin a position as bookkeeper and general factotum in his mercantile business. The *Dissertation*'s author considered himself first and foremost a printer and man of letters, but he had wearied of London and wanted to return home. Denham was willing to advance him funds for his passage. So in the final days of July 1726 Franklin embarked from Gravesend, bound for America and a new beginning.

Arriving in Philadelphia in the middle of October, Denham set up shop and Franklin, as he tells us, "attended the Business diligently, studied Accounts, and grew in a little Time expert at selling."[4] This was experience he would put to good use later when he became a Philadelphia merchant in his own right, but he gained something even more valuable from Denham. The two men lodged and boarded together and so were in each other's company continuously. Denham offered the young Franklin a friendship quite unlike the ones he had previously known. They had been based on a love of disputation, vanity, and pleasure, and had dissipated without doing the parties involved any good. But the relationship with Denham was one based on mutual respect and affection. Denham provided Franklin with the steadying influence he needed at the time. He "counsell'd me as a Father," Franklin tells us, and his description of Denham's rectitude, patience, and sound sense are remarkably like his autobiographical recollections of Josiah Franklin's character.

Denham's counsel probably extended far beyond the pragmatics of business. The two could well have discussed the religious doubts that continued to plague Franklin. Franklin may even have shared the distasteful conclusions of the *Dissertation* with his mentor. At any rate, an almost familial bond, unusual for employee and employer, grew between them. As Franklin says about Denham, "I respected and lov'd him."[5] It may be that Franklin's lifelong affection and respect for Quakers was sparked, or at least certainly underscored, by his timely encounter with Thomas Denham.

Franklin's iconoclastic *Dissertation* represents the high point of his allegiance to a minimalist religion of nature. Deists such as Shaftesbury and Collins had provided him with what he needed at the time he first read them: an alternative to his father's faith, a substitute religion he could use as a reference point in his rebellious struggle for an identity. The irony is that his adolescent battle to attain some degree of independence amounted to the rejection of one religious tradition for whole-cloth conformity to another. In his zeal to leave behind a Calvinism he found repugnant, he too uncritically embraced its opposite (or at least what looked like its opposite). Consequently, young Franklin's "conversion" to deism was not a genuine emancipation so much as an act of voluntary bondage to another religious master. Being something of an infidel initially exhilarated Franklin, prompting him to push the limits of his newfound natural religion, taking its precepts and first principles as far as reason would allow. But an adventurous spirit coupled with an overblown esteem for logic are, after all, flimsy foundations for an enduring fidelity to a religious perspective. Predictably, Franklin soon found himself straining against his new harness.

Fowler maintains that the unreflective certainty of adolescent religiosity (stage 3) begins to break down for a number of reasons, thereby preparing the way for the advent of the fourth, "individuative-reflective," stage. The two primary causes of the transition are "serious clashes or contradictions between valued authority sources" and an "encounter with experiences or perspectives that lead to critical reflection on how one's beliefs and values have formed and changed." The frequently painful experience of "leaving home," either literally or emotionally, can precipitate the affective turmoil that shakes the foundations of the adolescent's faith and self-image.[6]

It is not difficult to discern this pattern of conflict, confusion, and conscience in the young Franklin. Since his fifteenth year he had endorsed a religious perspective that discounted, at least in his own mind, the moral strictures of Calvinism. True, deism argued that virtue was the highest form of worship, but because Franklin's allegiance to natural religion was abstractly intellectual it was easy for him to give a cerebral nod to this principle and go his merry way. Deism proved a convenient religion indeed for an adolescent lad desperate to escape Jehovah's censuring eye.

After his arrival in England, with the entire Atlantic separating him from both his parents' and their God's disapproval, Franklin sowed his wild oats. Prompted by the ever ready James Ralph, he threw himself into the entertainments London offered. As he discretely puts it in the *Autobiography*, the two regularly frequented "Plays and other Places of Amusement"—so much so that Franklin's wages were spent as fast as they were earned, and he and Ralph "just rubb'd on from hand to mouth." Of course, no funds were laid aside for Franklin's passage back to Philadelphia.[7]

There were also intrigues with women. Ralph had left a wife and child behind in Philadelphia but once in London blithely forgot them and set up household with a milliner, one "Mrs. T." Encouraged by his companion's example, Franklin visited a few prostitutes and even went so far as to attempt "Familiarities" with Mrs. T. in Ralph's absence (which, he writes, "she repuls'd with a proper Resentment").[8]

In addition, Franklin fell in readily with the urbane and cynical London intellectuals who frequented taverns and coffee houses and talked incessantly about ideas and books (mainly, of course, their own). Franklin the rough-edged colonial must have been captivated by the razor sharp wit of a raconteur like de Mandeville (Franklin describes him as "a most facetious entertaining Companion") and impressed by the nonchalance with which the men of letters savaged all the social and moral institutions he had been raised to venerate. Although there is no clear record, it's not unreasonable to speculate that at least some of the *Dissertation*'s radical claims were inspired by the iconoclastic discussions Franklin heard in the coffee houses.[9]

Finally, there was the *Dissertation* itself. As we have seen, the treatise demolishes both religious faith and moral principle, leaving the reader with a nihilistic perversion of Dryden's dictum that "whatever is, is right." The world is reduced to an elaborate deterministic machine, and human actions are rather insignificant but necessary movements within the machine's interior. Have you squandered your resources in licentious revelry? You were determined to do so. Have you abandoned wife and child for an adulterous affair with a milliner? Whatever God creates is good, because God is good by definition. Have you defended ideas that shatter the foundations of rectitude and purposefulness? Our Geese are but Geese, even if we call them Swans. The arrogance and the destructiveness of Franklin's *Dissertation,* even today, are breathtaking.

The young man who had been raised by piously dissenting parents, who as a child had devoured volumes of sermons along with Bunyan's complete works, who had faithfully attended Sunday meetings and dwelt in a home where daily prayers were a family ritual, could not but have felt conflicted by the life he led in London. Bred to the virtues of frugality and chastity, young Franklin squandered money and eagerly pursued sexual adventures. An ardent admirer of Mather's and Defoe's books on doing good, and a rather self-righteous, even priggish, commentator on morals in the Dogood letters, he violated his own best instincts on a daily—or nightly—basis. The contradictions between his childhood values and his London behavior are, at least in hindsight, striking. Even at the time, he tells us, they gave him "great Trouble."[10]

Even had Benjamin been able to turn a blind eye to the conflicts in his own life, he could scarcely deny what he observed in others. He had converted Ralph to deism—in fact had dedicated the *Dissertation* to him—and Ralph was a person for whom the words "honesty" and "loyalty" meant absolutely nothing. Governor Keith had deceived and abandoned Franklin, and he too was "another Freethinker."[11] In addition, Franklin must have observed that many of the London men of letters he associated with were as loose in their virtue as in their religion.

But besides these sorry examples of the wages of freethinking, Franklin also encountered during this period happier illustrations of the fruits of piety and rectitude. Denham was one, and perhaps the most significant in Franklin's life. But two other persons Franklin met in London seem to have made a profound impression on him as well. One was a widow with whom he lodged in Duke Street opposite the "Romish Chapel." Although she was not well off financially and lame with gout, Franklin found her the best of companions, cheerful, amusing in conversation without indulging in the cruel wit of his pothouse associates, and generous with both her advice and meager resources.

The other person whose life impressed Franklin at this time was a "Maiden Lady of 70" who lived "in the most retired Manner" in the garret of his lodging house. She, like his landlady, was Roman Catholic. In her youth she had aspired to be a nun, but living in a Protestant England unadorned with convents, "she had vow'd to lead the Life of a Nun as near as might be done in those Circumstances." She gave away her estate to charity and limited her own income to a pound a month, a good deal of which she likewise gave away. Her sole food was gruel, which she boiled herself, and she permitted herself a fire only when cooking. Her room was as stark as any nun's cell, furnished with but a mattress, a stool, a crucifix and Bible, and "a Picture over the Chimney of St. Veronica, displaying her Handkerchief with the miraculous Figure of Christ's bleeding Face on it." She lived quite alone, receiving almost no visitors except a priest who came to give her the sacraments each day. Franklin was allowed to visit her once.[12]

It is significant that the memory of these two elderly women should have remained in Franklin's memory so long, and that he would have thought his time with them important enough to record in his memoirs. Doubtless part of the attraction was their eccentricity. Except for her religion and location, his landlady could have been Silence Dogood. And the saint in her garret cell must have struck both his Calvinist soul and his enlightened mind as a fascinating illustration of supernaturalism's excesses.

But it would be an error, I think, to suppose that Franklin was drawn to these two women solely on account of their quaintness. The impression they made on him went deeper than that. Franklin's landlady reminded him of the innocent pleasures, solid goodness, and unfailing faith found in simple, homey people. When he contrasted her with his more worldly friends, he cannot have failed to be shaken by the difference. In addition, the pure, selfless faith of the old woman in the attic, though excessive in the eyes of the world, testified by deeds rather than mere verbal assurances that not all piety reduced to hypocrisy and cant. When Franklin compared the devil-may-care behavior of himself and his freethinking companions to these two aged saints' cheerful and charitable holiness, his allegiance to the amoral deism lately defended in the *Dissertation* further eroded.[13]

It will be recalled that two of the primary causes for the breakdown of stage 3 religiosity are the escalating clash between valued authorities, and encounters with experiences and persons that call into question religious beliefs and values. Franklin's own account of his London years clearly suggests that both factors were at work in his retreat from deism. But there was also a third factor that brought his growing dissatisfaction with the *Dissertation*'s minimalist religion to a head, and that was what Fowler describes as the sense of "leaving home."

By the time he was ready to return to America, Franklin had left home several times. One leave-taking was the waning of his regard for his father and his subsequent rejection of his father's religion; another was his fleeing from Boston to Philadelphia; a third was his voyage to England. In the final months of his London sojourn, Franklin took the first steps toward yet another departure, one probably more painful and frightening than any of the others. He began to take leave of the deism on which he had grounded his self-image for the better part of a decade. Once again he found himself caught between two worlds, floating in a limbo of religious indecision and nagging self-doubts. Unable to return to the simple faith of his boyhood, unwilling to remain with a religious alternative he had begun to see as perverse, he felt truly abandoned.

Fowler sees the anticlimax of religious indecision, confusion, and forlornness that succeeds adolescent dogmatism as the transition from stage 3 to stage 4 faith, what he calls the "individuative-reflective" stage. This stage, which occurs in late adolescence or early adulthood, is marked by a new mood of critical examination in which the individual, no longer self-defined by allegiance to one external group or another, begins the arduous task of genuine scrutiny and worldview formation. This is the true beginning of autonomy as well as selfhood, but it can frequently be a rather bleak interlude in an individual's religious development, arising as it does from the ruins of earlier beliefs.[14]

By the time Franklin set sail for America with Denham, he had begun this process of self-exploration. His earlier attraction to virtue and genuine piety had been reawakened, but as yet he did not know where to go with it. He had not and never would renounce his fidelity to the New Learning's Newtonian cosmology or its high regard for reason, but he knew that the extremes to which he had taken both were unacceptable. For the next two years he would bide his time, searching for a way out of his impasse, inviting the gods, as D. H. Lawrence would have put it, to come forth.

Franklin's relationship with Thomas Denham was the one point of stability during this period of religious and moral confusion. Unfortunately for him, it did not endure. Scarcely five months after their return from England, both Franklin and Denham took ill. Franklin's "Distemper" was pleurisy, and he very nearly died from it. Denham contracted a wasting fever that lingered some time before finally carrying him off.

In his *Autobiography,* Franklin's description of these events is especially terse. He matter-of-factly summarizes Denham's final illness in one abrupt sentence, and of his own brush with death he says merely: "I suffered a good deal, gave up the Point in my own mind, and was rather disappointed when I found my Self recovering; regretting in some degree that I must now some time or other have all that disagreable Work to go over again."[15] But the rather glib, detached way he writes about these events is revealing. Franklin is reticent, even for an eighteenth-century memoirist, when it comes to recounting events in his *Autobiography* that affected him deeply. And these two, his near and Denham's actual death, must have devastated him. He lost a man who had become a second father to him, and he was forced by illness to confront his own mortality. If there were any remaining scraps of allegiance to the cold-blooded mechanism defended in his *Dissertation,* they were certainly scattered. The hard school of experience—the only one Franklin ever really respected—taught him by brutal example that pain is much more than the mere absence of pleasure. It also added urgency to his growing realization that the *deus absconditus* of deism is of little use to humans desperately in need of spiritual succor and hope.

It was Denham's passing that returned Franklin to the printing he thought he had forsaken once and for all. After Denham's death, his business was taken over by executors who saw no need for retaining Franklin's services. So Franklin decided to return to his first and best-loved profession and soon found himself once again working for Samuel Keimer.

The eccentric Samuel Keimer (1688–1742?) could have walked straight out of a Henry Fielding novel.[16] A rapscallion, maker and loser of modest fortunes, printer, author, versifier (although, according to Franklin, an "indifferent" one), and newspaper publisher, Keimer had immigrated to Philadelphia from London in 1722, leaving behind him both a wife and a load of debt. While still in London, he had thrown in his lot with a group of religious enthusiasts who called themselves the "French Prophets." Although he later abandoned and published a polemic against the sect, Keimer never lost his taste for unconventional religion. He seems to have been obsessed with discovering that core of belief which served as the essence of all true religion, but which he felt had been obfuscated by sectarian and historical rigamarole.[17]

When Franklin had worked for him the first time around, for example, Keimer had been busy working out details for the elaboration of a new religion that would avoid its rivals' confusions. Perceiving that his young employee was quick on his feet in disputation, Keimer tried to enlist him as one of the budding sect's prophets: Keimer would write and preach doctrine, and Franklin would engage opponents in debate. Franklin is not specific in telling us the proposed sect's creed. All we know from him is that "Keimer wore his Beard at full Length, because somewhere in the Mosaic Law it is said, *thou shalt not mar the Corners of thy Beard.* He likewise kept the seventh day Sabbath; and these two Points were Essentials with him," and presumably with his new religion.[18]

Franklin seems not to have shared Keimer's zeal. Probably the older man was too much of an amusing oddity to take seriously, particularly when it came to his hobby horse. But the example of a man who, dissatisfied with conventional religion, was presumptuous enough to invent his own gave Franklin pause. His own religious confusion stemmed in large part from his belief that in religious matters one had only two equally undesirable alternatives from which to choose: mechanism with its absentee First Cause, and Calvinism with its angry and capricious Jehovah. Keimer, crackpot though he was, taught Franklin that there were other options.

The painful realization that the impersonal clockmaker god of his *Dissertation* was spiritually as well as ethically bankrupt; his close brush with death, and the death of his fatherly counselor Thomas Denham; the recollection of the good-heartedness of his London landlady and the piety of the holy recluse who lived in her attic; and the example of Samuel Keimer's carving out a personal religion for himself: each of these events impressed themselves on Franklin. By the time he was twenty-six years old, the lessons from these and other experiences had penetrated deeply. For almost three years, Franklin had searched for a new religious home as well as a new identity. By the early winter of 1728, things began to fall into place for him. On 20 November, he took a sheet of foolscap and wrote "Articles of Belief and Acts of Religion" across its top. He had had his great insight. He had discovered the key to religion Keimer had pursued. In Fowler's terminology, he had moved beyond the soul-searching of the fourth stage into the creative resolution that characterizes the fifth.

Fowler labels the fifth stage "conjunctive" because in it occurs the integration or conjunction of the self with a consciously adopted religious outlook. This outlook Fowler describes as "porous and permeable." The individual in search of a religious perspective has experienced the dangers of dogmatic conformity as well as the alienation from self that follows its breakup. Both now serve as cautionaries against the dangers of black-and-white religious thinking, making him more tolerant of ambiguity in both his own and others' religious beliefs. As Fowler puts it, he is "alive to paradox and the truth in apparent contradictions." He is also more receptive to "the voices of [his] 'deeper self'" and willing to allow himself to be vulnerable "to the strange truths of those who are 'other.'"[19]

The individual who has reached this faith stage is more appreciative of the affective dimension of religious belief than he might have been earlier, and he tends to take seriously the meaning-ladenness of symbols. Following Paul Ricoeur, Fowler refers to this willingness on the part of the believing individual to allow himself to be instructed and guided by symbols as a "second" or "willed" naivete. He now accepts as "axiomatic that truth is more multidimensional and organically interdependent than most theories or accounts of truth can grasp." This understanding convinces him that all sectarian beliefs are relative to a deep, underlying religious reality that they seek, in their separate ways, to express. This doesn't mean that he has no real commitment to the specific tradition he himself endorses, but rather that he appreciates the wide range of traditions that may evoke commitment. Fowler calls this "ironic imagination": "a capacity to see and be in one's or one's group's most powerful meanings, while simultaneously recognizing that they are relative, partial and inevitably distorting apprehensions of transcendent reality."[20]

Conjunctive faith is obviously a stage in which the demands of the ego have been forsworn, at least to some extent, so that the believing individual can cultivate a receptivity to deep meaning. In traditional Christian idiom, it is a dying to self in order to make room for God, a humbling of one's pride in order to acknowledge the radical limitations of one's capacity for knowing the supreme reality. In stretching toward this point of willed naivete with his "Articles of Belief and Acts of Religion," Franklin left behind the self-assured and combative dogmatism of his *Dissertation.* He would never again experience the religious certitude that more or less characterized his decade of deism. But what he lost in intellectual surety he gained in spiritual richness.

Unlike the *Dissertation,* the "Articles of Belief and Acts of Religion" was not written for publication. It is a private memorandum, intended by Franklin for his own eyes only. The second half of the document is missing, but the section of the "Articles" that has come down to us, divided into two separate parts, is clearly a credo and a liturgy. The credo, which comprises the first part, is made up of seventeen short paragraphs. The liturgy, found in the second, is complete with readings and prayers of adoration, petition, and thanksgiving. The "Articles," then, obviously served as a guide for Franklin's personal devotions. But in all likelihood it also was an opportunity, especially in the credal section, for him to sort out his newly discovered religious beliefs by getting them down on paper.

The initial section of the "Articles," entitled "First Principles," is by far the more important. In it, Franklin clearly is trying to describe the lay of his own religious landscape in order to distinguish it from deism on the one hand and orthodox Christianity on the other. The statement is eloquent in its simplicity, as all credos are (or ought to be). It has none of the scholastic-like argumentation Franklin utilized in the *Dissertation.* Instead, it is a lyrical but bare-boned encapsulation of religious belief. As we shall shortly see, the abbreviated style of the "Articles" gives it an ambiguity that has encouraged a number of conflicting interpretations.

For all his ambivalence, there is one religious belief Franklin never forsook. It appeared in his *Dissertation* and it plays a major role in the "Articles." This belief is that "there is one Supreme most perfect Being,"[21] impassable and aloof. In the *Dissertation* this First Cause was little more than a logical postulation, and Franklin's description of it was impersonal and dispassionate. But in the "Articles" the distance between the individual and God is described in a melancholy, awed tone:

> [W]hen I stretch my Imagination thro' and beyond our System of Planets, beyond the visible fix'd Stars themselves, into that Space that is every Way infinite, and conceive it fill'd with Suns like ours, each with a Chorus of Worlds for ever moving round him, then this little Ball on which we move, seems, even in my narrow Imagination, to be almost Nothing, and my self less than nothing, and of no sort of Consequence.
>
> When I think thus, I imagine it great Vanity in me to suppose, that the *Supremely Perfect,* does in the least regard such an inconsiderable Nothing as Man. More especially, since it is impossible for me to have any positive clear Idea of that which is infinite and incomprehensible, I cannot conceive otherwise, than that He, *the Infinite Father,* expects or requires no Worship or Praise from us, but that he is even INFINITELY ABOVE IT.[22]

There is no difference between the God of this passage and the God of the *Dissertation.* Both are immeasurably distant from human comprehension or accessibility. But the description of divine inaccessibility here is poignant, whereas that of the *Dissertation* is lifeless. Here, the aloofness of the deity isn't simply asserted. Instead, the reader is made to feel the distance in Franklin's description of the vastness of space as well as the relative insignificance of the world and the puny creatures, reduced to "less than Nothing, and of no sort of Consequence," who inhabit it. Why should the "Supremely Perfect," the Creator of all that is, pay the slightest attention to less than nothing, either requiring anything of it or caring for its welfare? There is a despair in these words reminiscent of Pascal, a despair that comes from the young Franklin's post-*Dissertation* floundering. The urge to make a name for himself as an iconoclast among the London literati had prompted his metaphysical treatise. But the "Articles" arises from a sense of profound alienation from God. It is, at least in part, a moving cry of pain.

The otherness of God is particularly painful because, says Franklin, there is in each of us "something like a natural Principle which inclines [us] to DEVOTION or the Worship of some unseen Power."[23] Although this is expressed more prosaically than Augustine's famous claim that our hearts are restless until we return to God, the sentiment—and the passion—is the same. The point both Franklin and Augustine are making is that persons cannot live in a godless world. The fragility of being human requires divine support, just as the ache of human love ultimately demands a divine object. How much more tragic, then, that the "Supremely Perfect" is sublimely indifferent.

But Franklin was the product of an age where deist and Christian alike saw the universe as a great Chain of Being in which there is a sufficient reason for everything that is.[24] Consequently, he reasoned, if there is a longing for God within the human heart, it cannot be gratuitous. It must be part of the fixed and planned order of things, and therefore plays a role in the divine economy. It is our duty to explore this longing and discover means to assuage it. But how, given the remoteness of the First Cause?

Franklin's answer to this question is both fascinating and perplexing. He says that the "Supremely Perfect" is not merely the Creator of heaven and earth, but also the "Author and Father of the *Gods* themselves" (my emphasis).[25] It is these subordinate "Gods" to whom we properly direct our natural inclinations to devotion and worship. They serve as intermediaries between us and the unapproachable Supreme Architect. As Franklin says, "I CONCEIVE then, that the INFINITE has created many Beings or Gods, vastly superior to man, who can better conceive his Perfections than we, and return him a more rational and glorious Praise. As among Men, the Praise of the Ignorant or of Children, is not regarded by the ingenious Painter or Architect, who is rather honour'd and pleas'd with the Approbation of Wise men and Artists."[26]

Franklin goes on to say that these "created Gods" may be immortal or "it may be that after many Ages, they are changed, and Others supply their Places."[27] But whichever is the case, they are "exceeding wise, and good, and very powerful," and worthy of our praise, love, and adoration. They share an element of the passion as well as the reason implanted within us. This means that there is an ontological link between the gods and humans that allows for more of an interpersonal bond than is possible between humans and the First Cause. Moreover, says Franklin, the gods are good, and hence are "pleased and delight[ed] in the Happiness" of humans. Since virtue is the only true path to felicity, the gods also delight in virtuous behavior among persons. Thus, exults Franklin in speaking of the "particular wise and good God" who is the "Owner" of *this* planet and *this* age,

> I *love* him therefore for his Goodness and I *adore* him for his Wisdom.
>
> Let me than not fail to praise my God continually, for it is his Due, and it is all I can return for his many Favours and great Goodness to me; and let me resolve to be virtuous, that I may be happy, that I may please Him, who is delighted to see me happy. Amen.[28]

There is a striking contrast between these words of hope and affirmation and the earlier passages of the "Articles" that reflect the alienation of a soul infinitely distant from God. Clearly, Franklin has made a breakthrough here that he found personally liberating and fulfilling, and its secret lies in his mysterious talk about "gods." But what exactly is he getting at?

As I stated in the introduction to this book, the standard interpretation of the meaning of the "Articles" is Alfred Owen Aldridge's reading that Franklin intends to defend a literal polytheism. In his credo, Franklin writes that intermediate gods are in charge of particular planets and solar systems, and Aldridge argues that this points to Franklin's acceptance of a plurality of lesser deities.[29] Aldridge suggests that such an idea was in the air in the early eighteenth century. Isaac Newton tossed around the possibility of "intelligent beings superior to us who superintended [the] revolutions of the heavenly bodies" in 1725, and John Ray and other physico-theologians of the seventeenth century had speculated in a similar fashion.[30] Although Franklin never had the opportunity to meet Newton during his eighteen months in London, he did make the acquaintance of several British natural philosophers, and it is possible that he heard such a theory from them.[31]

Aldridge claims that Franklin never abandoned the polytheism expressed in his "Articles," and he backs up the point by appealing to a handful of texts from Franklin's later years. For example, Aldridge believes Franklin alludes to polytheism in a 1757 letter when he writes that "the Gods will doubtless take Care of those they love" and closes his remarks with "a Dieux" instead of the singular "a Dieu." In 1768, Franklin speaks of "superior beings in better worlds." In 1782, Franklin again refers to "superior Beings," and that same year, in a letter to a French abbé, remarks that "superior beings smile at our theories, and at our presumption in making them." Shortly thereafter, in a letter to the president of the Royal Society, Franklin once more writes about "Beings of a . . . nature far superior to ours," saying that they have made and launched the sun and heavenly planets.[32] Aldridge takes these scattered remarks as compelling evidence that Franklin literally accepted a plurality of gods until the end of his days.

A competing interpretation is Elizabeth Dunn's more recent contention that the "Articles" is a sly joke written by a smiling Franklin who tries to walk "a thin line [between] serious imitation [and] cleverly disguised irreverence."[33] She concludes that the document is best looked at as a Swiftian satire in which Franklin pokes good-natured fun at the religious sensibilities, deist as well as Christian, of his day. It naturally follows that she dismisses the "Articles" as a reliable source of Franklin's religious convictions.[34]

Both of these interpretations, I believe, are erroneous. Aldridge errs in reading Franklin too literally, and Dunn errs in not reading him literally enough. The "Articles" was neither a bizarre defense of literal polytheism nor an elaborate joke.

There are three main problems with Aldridge's interpretation. In the first place, Aldridge fails to establish a line of influence. He suggests that the idea of polytheism was in the air in the early eighteenth century, but he gives no indication of how or when Franklin might have picked up on it. Newton's espousal of the idea was voiced only in private correspondence to which Franklin had no access.

Second, and more important, the advocacy of a literal polytheism, in which each heavenly body has its own protecting spirit that serves as a messenger between humans and the First Cause, seems highly out of character for Franklin. Polytheism, at least in modern times, is after all a bizarre position to hold. Newton may have tossed the idea around, but Newton's religious musings were notoriously eccentric.[35] Franklin wasn't the hardheaded scientist that some commentators make him out to be, but neither was he a mystic or a man likely to embrace arcane religious positions that smacked of Platonic metaphysics. Both before and after his unfortunate *Dissertation,* Franklin was an experimentalist who insisted that beliefs are legitimated by utility *and* empirical evidence.[36] Even if one grants that there is a certain psychological utility to the belief in a pantheon of lesser gods (that is, that the belief ameliorates our cosmic alienation), there is no conceivable empirical evidence for the claim. It is simply incredible that Franklin, who had renounced Calvinism because he had been unable to swallow its more extreme doctrines, would so quickly turn around to embrace a religious position that is at least as implausible. Moreover, such a move is out of keeping with the rest of his beliefs about reality.

Finally, there simply isn't the textual evidence Aldridge claims to support his polytheistic interpretation. Scrutiny of the particular passages he cites from

Franklin's letters reveals that Aldridge has consistently misread either their context or their purpose. The 1757 letter cited by Aldridge, which contains the expression "the Gods will doubtless take Care of those they love. A Dieux then, Dear Sir," is taken from a letter to a British colonel that is jocular in tone throughout. In the paragraph immediately preceding the passage Aldridge quotes, Franklin recommends the colonel to an "ingenious Physician of my Acquaintance who knows the Rule of making cool, weak, refreshing Punch, not inferior to the Nectar of the Gods."[37] This reference to "Gods" is obviously playful, and conforms to the tone of the entire letter. It is not unreasonable to suppose that the passage Aldridge quotes can be interpreted in the same way.

In the 1768 reference to "superior Beings in better Worlds" cited by Aldridge, Franklin is praising Pierre Samuel du Pont de Nemours's political treatise *Physiocratie.* As was the custom of the day, Franklin heaps encomiums on the book and its author. Franklin moves from expressing a "high Opinion of the Doctrines" espoused by du Pont de Nemours to praising the "goodness mixt with the Wisdom" of his philosophical principles, and effusively winds up by saying that "it is from your Philosophy only that . . . [desirable] Maxims . . . and more happy Conduct are to be drawn, which I therefore sincerely wish may grow and increase till it becomes the governing Philosophy of the human Species, as it must be that of superior Beings in better Worlds."[38] The latter reference is simply a flowery convention. To read it as anything else is to mistake both its context and intent.

In a similar vein, Aldridge misreads the reference to "superior beings" in Franklin's 1782 letter to Joseph Priestley. Serious discussion of theology is the furthest thing from Franklin's mind in this letter, although he *is* making an earnestly held ethical point. After deploring the violent nature of human beings, Franklin spins a parable to illustrate his point. The parable comments on human nature by pretending to tell us "in what light we are viewed by superior Beings." A young angel is sent to earth on unspecified business, and an "old courier-spirit" is assigned to show him the sights. After gazing for a few minutes on a furious sea battle, the angel turns on his guide, angrily blustering that "you undertook to conduct me to the Earth, and you have brought me into Hell!" The courier predictably replies that "Devils never treat one another in this cruel manner; they have more Sense, and more of what Men (vainly) call *Humanity.*" At the end of this humorous but telling parable, Franklin, turning to other matters, immediately says, "But to be serious, my dear old Friend," thereby clearly indicating, if there was ever any doubt, that he had been speaking tongue-in-cheek up to that point.[39]

In the other reference to "superior beings" of that same year, Franklin is expounding his theories about the formation of the earth to the Abbé Soulavie. After going on for two quite lengthy paragraphs, Franklin pulls back with a display of false modesty that is just as conventional as his purple praise of du Pont de Nemours in the 1768 letter. He says, "I will not trouble you at present with my fancies concerning the manner of forming the rest of our [planet]. Superior beings smile at our theories, and at our presumption in making them." This is surely a self-deprecating stylism, not a serious theological observation.[40]

Aldridge thinks that the most important passage in support of his polytheistic thesis is found in Franklin's 1783 letter to Joseph Banks, president of the Royal Society, about the recent launching of a hot air balloon in France. The entire passage runs as follows: "Beings of a frank and [*sic*] nature far superior to ours have not disdained to amuse themselves by making and launching balloons, otherwise we should not have enjoyed the light of those glorious objects that rule our day and night, nor have had the pleasure of riding round the sun ourselves upon the balloon we now inhabit." Taken in itself, this sentence raises visions of gods juggling interstellar objects such as suns and planets. But when one reads it in context, it is clear that Franklin's intended meaning is quite different. Just before this passage, Franklin chides Sir Joseph and the stiff British in general for not experimenting with hot air balloons themselves. He good-naturedly says that the British, unlike the French and Americans, are so afraid of being laughed at that they refuse to undertake investigations that might appear foolish. But, he continues, this "does not seem to me a good reason to decline prosecuting a new experiment which apparently increases the power of a man over matter. . . . We should not suffer pride to prevent our progress in science." It is at this point that Franklin makes his remarks about the gods launching celestial balloons. His point, in light of the friendly dressing down he has just given Sir Joseph, is clear: where would we be if the Supreme Architect had refrained from the experiment of creation for fear of botching the job? If God doesn't mind taking a risk, neither should we. Once again, as in the Priestley letter, Franklin uses a parable (this time an extremely abbreviated one) to get across his meaning.[41]

There is actually another occasion where Franklin refers to "supreme beings" that Aldridge might have cited but does not. In a 1749 encomium to Newton, Poor Richard asks "what is all our boasted knowledge, compar'd with that of the angels? If they see our actions, and are acquainted with our affairs, our whole body of science must appear to them as little better than ignorance." But, Poor Richard continues, now and then a human is born who perhaps may, "by his most refined speculations," approximate their wisdom. Newton is such a man; as Pope said of him,

Superior beings, when of late they saw
A mortal man unfold all nature's law,
Admir'd such wisdom in a human shape,
And shew'd a Newton, as we shew an ape.[42]

Clearly Franklin is neither defending nor even suggesting polytheism here. Instead, he is dramatically comparing the genius of Newton to the legendary genius of divine creatures in order to express his intense admiration for the mathematician. Many of the stylisms in Franklin's later letters that Aldridge takes as evidence of a belief in polytheism are likewise found here: the paltriness of human affairs when viewed *sub specie aeternitatis,* the presumptuousness of human learning. But they are poeticisms, pure and simply.

Elizabeth Dunn's contention that the "Articles" is better read as a joke than a sincere expression of belief can be dismissed more quickly. It is clear that she reads the "Articles" as a joke because she cannot bring herself to believe that Franklin takes seriously the polytheism Aldridge ascribes to him. But as I've argued, Aldridge fails to provide us with a convincing argument for his polytheistic reading. Consequently, one of Dunn's reasons for interpreting the document as a spoof vanishes. Moreover, there is no evidence that suggests Franklin ever considered publishing the "Articles." Yet this is the same man who never lost an opportunity to wisecrack in print. What is the point of a joke that's never told to anyone? Why would Franklin go to the trouble of writing a rather elaborate religious satire only to hold it back from an audience? Just as tellingly, the language in which the "Articles" is written is innocent of the lighthearted tone Franklin almost always took when indulging in written gags. As we have seen, the opening lines of the credo express a disturbingly profound sense of alienation. Finally, we know that Franklin returned periodically to his "Articles" as a substitute for more conventional worship opportunities in Philadelphia (more of this in chapter 6). This is hardly the behavior one would expect if Dunn's evaluation of the "Articles" is correct.

Dunn is quite mistaken, then, when she fails to see Franklin's "Articles" as the single most important religious writing of his life. Aldridge correctly appraises the importance of the "Articles" but misinterprets it as a defense of polytheism. So the question remains: what is Franklin up to?

Franklin provides a clue in the epigraph to the "Articles." It is taken from the tragedy *Cato,* written by Joseph Addison, always one of Franklin's favorite authors:

> Here will I hold—If there is a Pow'r above us
> (And that there is, all Nature cries aloud,
> Thro' all her Works), He must delight in Virtue
> And that which he delights in must be Happy.[43]

Most immediately, the sentiment expressed in this passage suggests that Franklin had come full circle from the *Dissertation*'s earlier dismissal of any distinction between good and evil. There he denied the possibility of virtue on necessitarian grounds and concluded that whatever is, is right. Here, however, he approvingly quotes a passage that asserts that virtue (and, by implication, evil) is very real indeed, and that God's response to human actions is not uniformly positive but instead proportionate to the degree of virtue manifested by them. This is a transparent hint that what follows in the "Articles" represents a reversal of Franklin's earlier position.

Less obvious is the epigraph's clue about the psychological motive behind the "Articles." The Addison quotation is taken from the fifth act of his play. In it Cato, in despair and contemplating suicide, ponders the question of human immortality. The question has obvious religious significance, and Cato is in the midst of a crisis that is in large part religious. He cannot doubt that God exists, but he is unsure of anything else and weary of his uncertainty. He knows what he ought to do (follow the Roman code of honor and commit suicide), but his fearful questions paralyze him with indecision. Finally, after uttering the words Franklin selects as the epigraph for the "Articles," Cato shakes off his torpor and declares, "I'm weary of conjectures—This [grasping his sword] must end 'em."[44]

The scene could not have failed to strike Franklin forcefully, because it echoes the religious ambivalence and confusion he had lived with for years, which had only temporarily abated during the deistic decade and had grown especially painful after his repudiation of the *Dissertation.* Cato, in dealing with his confusion, wrests himself from spiritual and moral paralysis by a sheer act of will. He admits he can never know with certainty the answers to his moral and metaphysical questions. But instead of continuing to agonize, he once and for all chooses one of the options available to him. This is precisely what Franklin finally has done. The specifics of the decisions are different, but the resolve is identical. Cato cries out that he is weary with fruitless conjecture, and will put an end to it by suicide. Franklin, in appealing to this scene from *Cato,* gives notice that he is similarly weary and will put an end to his own religious paralysis with the religious choice of the "Articles." It is the sword he uses to slay the doubts and indecision that had pulled him back and forth for the previous three years.

From the very outset, then, we know that the "Articles" is something quite different from the *Dissertation.* The latter was a closely reasoned but impersonal philosophical treatise. The former is an intensely personal, even passionate statement in which the author (contrary to Dunn) has invested himself heavily. It is just as much a proclamation of Franklin's liberation as it is an attempt to express his new religious point of view.

Franklin's emancipatory vision rests on several points. The first is his steadfast belief in the existence of a God more like a metaphysical first principle than a personal, loving deity whom persons can adore and supplicate. Franklin thinks this clockmaker God's existence is indisputably suggested by observable design in creation, but of a very select kind of design. Most proponents of traditional design arguments point to two features of the natural order from which the existence of a Creator can be inferred: its rationality (orderliness) and its suitability to human flourishing (providence). Franklin bases his implicit acceptance of the design argument exclusively on the claim that the physical universe, ordered as it is by uniform natural law, could not have originated by chance. Because he cannot bring himself to believe that the First Cause is anything more than a distant principle with no knowledge of or concern for humans, he cannot argue for its existence on the grounds that the natural order displays signs of divine benevolence. As we will see in the next chapter, however, the essential ambivalence of Franklin's religiosity, even after the great insight, occasionally caused him to overlook this point.

Second, Franklin was struck by the psychological and ethical inadequacy of this concept of the divine. He had already begun to doubt its value even as he finished the *Dissertation.* Subsequent experiences and reflection served only to articulate and strengthen those doubts. An unapproachable God, Franklin suggests in his *Autobiography,* has little more regulative utility than no God at all. Certainly the more freethinking of his friends had, in Franklin's estimation, gone bad. Looking back on his London days, he was also uncomfortable with the memory of his own moral transgressions—so much so that he actually deleted the record of some of them from the final draft of his memoirs.[45] All this convinced Franklin that the average person needs an incentive to pursue the path of virtue and that the aloof deity of the philosophers is incapable of such inspiration. The First Cause may give rise to intellectual awe, but its divine indifference does not encourage humans to follow courses of action pleasing to God.

Judging again from the experiences of his boon companions in the early days, but even more from his own, Franklin also concluded that the distant God of the philosophers is incapable of helping humans arrive at a sense of meaning or purpose in their lives. As a boy, Franklin may have felt suffocated by the ever-present Calvinist God. But later he also came to feel adrift, abandoned by the mechanistic alternative. A rudderless existence, Franklin saw, is an unhappy and, most likely, less than virtuous one. Other thinkers in another time may have found a way to guide themselves through life's journey without God, but such an option was unthinkable for a person like Franklin. He was too steeped in religion since boyhood to find any satisfaction or fulfillment in a godless universe.

Finally, Franklin was struck by the wide diversity of religious belief. He recognized, of course, that other major religious traditions besides Christianity commanded the hearts and allegiances of worshippers. But he was also intrigued by the diversity of sects within the Christian tradition. Anglicans, Presbyterians, Quakers, the Moravians: these and many more denominations, each with its own sectarian inflection, were encountered every day in Philadelphia. Some of these sects, particularly those heavily influenced by Calvinist doctrine, at times infuriated and disgusted him. Others, such as the Quakers and Anglicans, were more agreeable to him. But what began to impress Franklin about this religious pluralism was the core of common belief shared by all the denominations and, indeed, by all the world's religious traditions, a thread of continuity that bound them together, regardless of their disagreements about specific creeds and doctrine. All accepted the concept of a God who is both creator of the universe and sustainer of life. All believed that virtue was pleasing to this God. All cultivated a sense of purposefulness in their believers.[46]

Now, Franklin the philosopher found himself unable to subscribe rationally to any other concept of God than the First Cause one. This entailed that the only intellectually sound religious position was one of theistic agnosticism, in which God's existence is affirmed but the possibility of any detailed knowledge about God's nature denied. But Franklin was also too perceptive a psychologist to ignore the fact that religious strivings are as much a matter of the heart as the head, that the average person needs a God who can serve as moral inspiration, source of meaning, and comforter in troubled times—that, in short, a thoroughgoing agnosticism about God's nature and ways is destructive. Moreover, he was also of a strong experimental bent, and more than willing to judge beliefs and theories on the basis of their practical, regulative consequences. So as he pondered the moral and psychological insufficiency of the First Cause, and with Cato-like indecision asked himself what he should believe, it slowly dawned on him that he and everyone else should and in fact did believe what they needed to in order to sustain themselves spiritually and ethically. In religious matters, in other words, necessity is the mother of invention. This was Franklin's great insight, one that served as the nucleus of his religious musings for the rest of his life. The "Articles" is an attempt to give devotional expression to it.

This insight—this theistic perspectivism—can be simply stated. Religious traditions, sectarian doctrine, and private beliefs are cultural symbol systems, influenced by historical place and time as well as individual temperament. These systems orient humans by providing them with images of the divine to which they can relate on a personally meaningful basis. Worshippers are not, of course, explicitly aware of the contrived nature of their religious beliefs. They generally consider them to have objective reference, although every religious tradition acknowledges that the essential ineluctability of God entails that human concepts always miss the mark to one degree or another.

In short, Franklin's great insight is that all religious expressions, except the stark postulation of a First Cause, are stories or symbols—poetic, metaphorical attempts to talk about God and reality in terms that are less forbidding than the coldly impersonal vocabulary of metaphysics.[47] These stories, or "perspectives," describe deities that are all-knowing, all-loving, and all-powerful, and different traditions and denominations within traditions add their own individual accents. They put faces on an anonymous universe, enabling humans to think the unthinkable and grasp the unattainable.

These perspectival deities, I submit, are the "gods" in Franklin's "Articles." They are reckoned by their worshippers to be "vastly superior to Man," to be "exceeding wise, and good, and very powerful." Some people call their god Allah, others Jesus, others Shiva, still others Jahweh. Each of these gods provides its devotees with a personal point of reference in an otherwise vast and indifferent universe. They serve as benevolent "Powers" to whom we can direct our prayers, our hopes, our thanksgiving, and our fears. Because they result from human attempts to express the divine symbolically, they are more accessible to the mind and comforting to the heart than the aloofly abstract Supreme Architect. In this sense they truly are intermediaries between humans and the distant First Cause. But for all that, they are "created Gods," products of place and time, who "after many Ages . . . are changed, and Others supply their Places."

It must not be supposed that Franklin is saying that the gods humans worship are merely anthropomorphic projections, and that religious belief, as a result, is illusory and detrimental. Hobbes and Hume appear to have defended such a position, and Feuerbach and Freud clearly did.[48] But Franklin was no village atheist. He never ceased to believe in the reality of the First Cause, even though he saw its mere existence as little if any comfort to suffering humankind. Nor would he have admitted that religious perspectives are illusory. Because these symbolic representations are founded in and motivated by an intuition of the First Cause's reality, they are not simple fabrications. Like all symbolic constructions, they stand for and shed light on something other than themselves. They are not accurate descriptions, but neither are they total illusions. Put another way, the gods may not be factual, but this does not make them untrue or meaningless.

Franklin's gods, and the religious doctrines and dogmas that attend them, are better described as "useful fictions" than as illusions.[49] They are instruments that aid humans in orienting themselves in the world, but they are not copies of the world, even if their users generally think otherwise. They can be said to possess a functional truth-value. Since their purposes are to maximize orientation, to facilitate a sense of normative purposefulness, and to provide opportunities for worship and succor, theistic perspectives are "true" in proportion to how well they fulfill these functions. Religious beliefs and, indeed, religious traditions, sometimes disappear from history because, for one reason or another, they lose their capacity to speak to people in meaningful ways.[50] Moreover, certain tenets and doctrines espoused from existing religious perspectives can diminish in importance and eventually disappear because of their failure to orient or succor. In short, religious beliefs are testable in an experimental crucible. Perspectives on the divine that are too anemic—or too harsh—to nourish the human spirit tend to disappear or mutate over time.

As already pointed out, there is a factual basis (in Franklin's judgment) to religious perspectives even if they themselves are not factual. This is the reality of the First Cause, whose existence all religious traditions grasp and toward which they grope by means of the particular useful fictions they adopt. Consequently, religious belief does, ultimately, have an objective reference. It is simply that so little can be known about that referent, and so little can be gained from it spiritually, that humans ameliorate its inaccessibility through historically conditioned perspectives.

Franklin, then, is not at all in the same camp with freethinkers such as Hobbes, Hume, Feuerbach, or Freud. All these men agree that religious beliefs are human inventions, but they also maintain that the sooner the race disabuses itself of such illusions, the better off it will be. Franklin, on the other hand, thinks the illusions are necessary and beneficial. They encourage the practice of virtue, they sustain a certain general level of happiness, and they ameliorate the loneliness into which humans are born. They satisfy the hunger created by our natural inclination to devotion.

A corollary of Franklin's conviction that religious perspectives are a necessary way in which humans deal with religious alienation is that some perspectives may be better than others. That this is Franklin's position is clearly indicated by his approval of certain religious traditions and his strong disapproval of others (more of this in chapter 6).

Since religious perspectives are interpretations, their evaluation cannot be based on the same standards by which we appraise "factual" statements. Rather, there are two other criteria that are more properly invoked. The first of these is coherence: a good story is one that does not contradict itself. A self-contradiction is inherently implausible, and consequently the credibility of any religious perspective is determined in part by its degree of coherence. The other criterion is utility. As we have already seen, a religious perspective possesses a functional truth value. It follows from this that the greater the utility displayed by a religious belief—that is, the more meaning and purposefulness it bestows on human existence—the better the belief.[51] As we saw in chapter 1, one of the reasons why Franklin turned his back on the Calvinism of his childhood was because of its emphasis on guilt and fear. In the language of theistic perspectivism, Franklin denied the capacity of that tradition to enhance happiness, virtue, and meaning in his life.

Franklin's great insight of theistic perspectivism clearly displays the characteristics of Fowler's conjunctive stage of faith. It recognizes and indeed relishes the rich diversity of religious symbols and their psychological importance in grounding the believer. It accepts ambiguity as an inevitable characteristic of religion's efforts to express the divine, thereby recognizing the need for humility in regard to one's own beliefs and tolerance in regard to the beliefs of others. It takes seriously the affective dimension to religious faith and willingly listens to the deep-seated intuitions and needs—Lawrence's gods that come forth—that can be expressed and fulfilled only through image and symbol, not logic and theory. It is, to use Ricoeur's phrase, a "second naivete," in which Franklin chose to throw in his lot with the heart rather than the head.[52]

Or perhaps it's more accurate to say that Franklin embraced the heart *and* the head. His earlier allegiance to deism had been primarily an intellectual affair, even though he originally adopted it at least in part because of a violent emotional antipathy to religious and paternal authority. From his days with the *New-England Courant* up through the publication of the *Dissertation,* he found a religious sensibility centered around *logos* more than adequate. After all, his New Learning mentors had assured him that reason was supreme, the highest faculty in humans, the only necessary tool for exploring an equally rational universe. Since the universe was rational, its creator must be likewise. Consequently, religion was reduced to reason, spirituality to science: logic brought one to God just as easily as to laws of nature. The reign of logos would be supreme when humans succeeded in exorcising their own irrationalities to such a degree that they become as antiseptically logical as the universe and its God.

A tidy religion, with all the corners neatly tucked in. But experience and conscience began to chip away at it, gradually demonstrating to Franklin that neither human yearning for the divine nor the divine itself is as manageable as his adolescent logos religion supposed. Logic could write philosophical treatises that contained impeccable arguments, but it was utterly hopeless in helping mortals sustain a sense of purposefulness, much less in succoring souls in pain or distress. Logic could satisfy the mind but did nothing to feed the hunger deep within for God.

As a consequence, Franklin came more and more to appreciate the psychological and normative importance of *mythos* in religious belief. It is the symbol, not the syllogism, that grounds and expresses ordinary human faith. Attempts to map the universal logos are really second-order operations undertaken by theologians or philosophers who have already hearkened, perhaps without fully realizing it, to the mythos of their specific traditions. These cerebral exercises are important. They help us to articulate and reflect on the emotion-laden symbols that emerge from us and speak to us. They give us the "gods" we worship, and they express the doctrines we subscribe to. But for all that, logos is not the original response to the human longing for connection with a loving, caring deity. Logos abstracts, classifies, defines. Mythos is lived. Mythos is primary. Mythos is foundational. It is the raw material from which our theistic perspectives are drawn.

But if this is what Franklin had in mind when he wrote his "Articles," why didn't he simply say so? This is a reasonable question. There are at least two reasonable responses to it.

First, the "Articles" is not a philosophical treatise. It was written as a private liturgy and credo, and as such it was intended to be evocative and devotional rather than analytical. There are no arguments in it, none of the precise syllogistic reasoning found in the *Dissertation.* Instead, the style is aphoristic, poetical. Since we know that Franklin was capable of thinking and writing in a rigorously logical manner, we can only conclude that he deliberately chose not to do so in the "Articles." His decision is not surprising. The document is clearly a testament of faith, hope, and thanksgiving, not an exercise in metaphysical logic-chopping.

The second reason why Franklin may not have spelled out in explicit terms the details of his great insight is that he might not have completely articulated them to himself at the time he wrote the "Articles." Although what I have here called theistic perspectivism is strongly suggested by Franklin's temperament as well as his texts, this is not necessarily to suggest that Franklin was as aware as subsequent readers of the direction in which he was going. His native religious ambivalence, coupled with uncertainty over the implications of his claim that particular religious doctrines and images of God are perspectival in nature, could have coalesced to render him much more comfortable in expressing his thoughts metaphorically in liturgy than discursively in a philosophical tract. Although this is only speculation, I would suggest that Franklin may well have intended the missing second part of his "Articles of Belief and Acts of Religion" to be a more formal discussion of theistic perspectivism but for one reason or another found himself unable to complete it.

Franklin's lack of complete clarity ought not to surprise us. We know, from personal experience if nowhere else, that religious beliefs regularly run ahead of their logical justifications. It is often difficult just to express cogently, much less defend, our deepest religious intuitions, and as a consequence all of us find ourselves appealing to poetry, metaphors, and symbols as ways of indirect communication. If my reading of Franklin is correct, this is precisely what he did when he first hit on the idea that all religions, although having the same goal, speak in different languages and hence follow different paths.

Theistic perspectivism is the insight that liberated Franklin from the religious confusions of his boyhood and youth. As will become clear in subsequent chapters, its influence is reflected in his later writings on providence, morality, and tolerance—indeed, it is only through the prism of his great insight that his views on these subjects can be fully appreciated. This does not mean that ambivalence was cleared from his religious thought. It remained, particularly, as we will see in the next chapter, when it came to his views on providence. But for the rest of his life, Franklin had an explanation of and justification for religious belief that he appealed to time and again.

The influence of theistic perspectivism on Franklin's later thought will be traced in chapters to come. But it is instructive to note here an instance in later life in which Franklin drew on the doctrine. This example is interesting for two reasons. First, it illustrates even more explicitly than the "Articles" Franklin's conviction that gods and religious beliefs are cultural artifacts. Second, the incident in question is invoked by Aldridge as a powerful illustration of his claim that Franklin's "Articles" is really an apology for polytheism.[53] An examination of it shows just how forced such an interpretation is.

In January 1774, some forty-five years after the drafting of the "Articles," Franklin, then residing in London as a lobbyist for Pennsylvania and Massachusetts, was humiliated in the Privy Council over the unfortunate Hutchinson Letters affair.[54] He was dismissed from his post of deputy postmaster-general, and there were rumors that his arrest was imminent. Although he eventually wound up staying in London for another eighteen months, Franklin was sufficiently frightened at the time to make plans for immediate departure. While his private papers were being collected and prepared for shipping, Franklin "took refuge from [the] political storm" in the Chelsea home of David Williams, who later wrote about the visit in an unpublished memoir.[55]

Williams (1738–1816) was a Welsh dissenting minister who eventually forsook the pulpit for the teacher's lectern and the literary world. The author of several works attacking religious cant and defending his philosophy of education (which minimized book-learning and maximized experimental training), Williams is best known as the founder, in 1790, of the Royal Literary Fund, which took as its special charge the financial relief of "distressed talents."

Williams belonged to a small Chelsea club that called itself "The Thirteen," a reference to both its numerical limit on membership and its scorn of superstition. The Thirteen included luminaries such as Josiah Wedgwood and James "Athenian" Stuart, and Franklin was welcomed as an honorary member during his stay at Williams's home. At one of the club's convivial meetings, Williams tells us, the discussion turned to religion and the observation that none of the members, though all good men, ever attended church regularly. Although some of the members undoubtedly let it be known that they felt no need for religious devotion, Franklin demurred. According to Williams, "Franklin, with some emotion, declared he never passed a Church, during Public Service, without regretting that he could not join in it honestly and cordially."[56] Franklin then went on to express an ardent desire for a public liturgy that suited persons of philosophical temperament. He probably refrained from mentioning the private liturgy he had written almost half a century earlier; at any rate, Williams makes no mention of it. But Franklin's comment prompted The Thirteen to form a committee to draft such a liturgy and accompanying credo. Franklin, naturally, was one of its elected members. The liturgy went through no fewer than six drafts before it satisfied the club's general membership, and a version of it was eventually published by Williams as *A Liturgy on the Universal Principles of Religion and Morality* (1776).

In his memoirs, Williams summarizes the main points of the credo. His recollections are worth quoting at some length.

> The God of Newton was probably the regulating Principle or Good of the Solar System. The God of a Nation or of a Sect is always the Spirit of that Nation or Sect, whatever be its nature. These are local Gods.
>
> What Principles may govern or preserve other Systems we know not, and therefore know not their Gods. It is probable that all the Systems of Nature are

> governed and preserved by a relative Principle or Law, and that governing Principle is the Universal God.
>
> It is to local Gods, those of various Nations, Sects and Parties that Theologists have generally ascribed the dominion of the Universe, and the ministers of these Gods have imputed to them their own Properties, to sanctify their own Views, and that they have justified the imputation by the Sophism "that causes and effects are similar."[57]

One can hardly fail to be struck by the similarity between this summary of the credo drafted by Franklin in 1774 and the one included in his 1728 "Articles." Aldridge reads the later document as a "direct link" to Franklin's youthful "polytheism," but the polytheistic interpretation is even more difficult to justify here than in the "Articles." There are several reasons for this.

Williams's summary makes clear that the only actual God that exists is the "God of Newton"—the distant First Cause that governs all "Systems of Nature" and is the "Regulating Principle" of the universe. But in addition to this First Cause divinity, there are lesser gods that serve as the foci of our adoration and worship. These are referred to as "local" gods, the "Spirits" of nations and sects. By "spirits" in this context, Williams and Franklin clearly do not mean disembodied entities so much as expressions of a nation's or sect's essential qualities, values, and beliefs (as, for instance, in the phrase "the *spirit* of 1776"). It is to these gods, who come and go along with the nations and sects that adore them, that sectarian worshippers and theologians direct their attentions, not realizing that they are symbolic perspectives and, indeed, frequently anthropomorphic projections.

This is a much clearer statement of the fundamental intuition behind theistic perspectivism than found in the 1728 "Articles." Nor is it surprising that it should be. By 1774 Franklin had had almost fifty years to think through his youthful insight and was able to articulate more clearly what he wanted to say. The only thing missing from Williams's account of the later document is Franklin's contention that the local (or "lesser") gods serve a necessary and beneficial regulatory function. Indeed, there is a hint that the perspectives are far from desirable, reflecting as they do the self-centered delusions of "Theologists." But this negative appraisal is less disturbing if one keeps in mind that it comes from the pen of David Williams, a man who, unlike Franklin, had no use for sectarian belief of any kind and insisted that the only honest credo was "I believe in one God." There is no cause to think that Franklin shared Williams's disparaging view of human attempts to symbolize the unknowable Regulator. In fact, given the obvious parallel between the credo of The Thirteen and the credo of the "Articles," there is every reason to suppose a continuity in Franklin's positive valuation of religious perspectives as well.

Close to a half century after he wrote his "Articles of Belief and Acts of Religion," then, Franklin still subscribed to the great insight he had recorded therein. It was the central religious belief of his life, and it had nothing to do with polytheism.

There is a certain resemblance to Franklin's theistic perspectivism and William James's later will-to-believe doctrine. James argued that we have the right to choose to believe in God if there is an absence of compelling evidence one way or another, and if not believing so empties our lives of meaning and happiness that they become unbearable.[58] Of course, most people who believe do so without being quite aware of why they believe. They haven't taken the time to reflect seriously on the nature of their religious beliefs or to study the pertinent theological or philosophical literature. Most commonly, they are born into one religious tradition or another, and at a certain point in late adolescence they acquiesce to (or "choose") the tradition, symbolized by appropriate rites of passage such as bar mitzvah or confirmation. But in spite of the rather passive, unarticulated nature of their choice, many of these same people would find their existences seriously impoverished were they to lose their faith. It serves as a valuable regulator in their lives, providing them with a normative as well as spiritual reference.

But Franklin (and presumably James) does not belong to this category. He instead is a member of the much smaller class of people who have *deliberately* chosen to believe certain religious propositions—that God is personal, loving, benevolent, and so on—while at the same time intellectually accepting that the only thing about God that can be rationally demonstrated is its existence as First Cause. This immediately raises the question of whether Franklin's great insight was simply a sort of defense mechanism against an indifferent universe.

Defense mechanism it certainly was, but not *simply* so. All religious beliefs are partially grounded, immediately or remotely, in fear and insecurity. This is a commonplace psychological observation that does nothing to undermine the value of religious belief; instead, it merely states an obvious factor in its emergence.[59] This factor clearly was present in Franklin's theistic perspectivism. Buffeted by religious doubts from boyhood, and shaken by Denham's death and his own near-fatal illness, Franklin reached a point where he simply could not endure the alienatingly abstract deity he had intellectually accepted since his conversion to deism at the age of fifteen. Like Addison's Cato, he drew a line in the sand and determined to rescue himself from indecision and fear by positing his "lesser gods" as proper objects of worship, supplication, and reverence. In part, Franklin's resolve was prompted by fear and weariness. But there was more to it than that. It was also, as he said, a way of appeasing his natural inclination to devotion, a hunger left untouched by the rarefied atmosphere of theistic agnosticism. It was a way of providing himself with a sense of meaning and direction far more important than the transient worldly success he also desired. This is why the "Articles," where Franklin expressed his newfound credo, was the most important religious document he ever wrote.

The Great Awakening preacher George Whitefield, anxious for Franklin's conversion, many years later would "humbly recommend" that he study and pursue "the mystery of the new-birth." Whitefield had no way of knowing that Franklin had already undergone a new birth some twenty-five years earlier.[60]

Even if it is granted that Franklin's theistic perspectivism is not dismissible as a "mere" defense mechanism, isn't there a large element of playacting or pretending to it? Franklin acts *as if* there really is a personal and loving God, all the time knowing that this and all religious beliefs are nothing more than perspectives, historically fashioned contrivances that come into being and pass away as cultural artifacts. Useful fictions such beliefs may be, but they are, for all that, still fictions.

This is a real problem for the believer who has reached the fifth stage of religious belief. Recall that Fowler says this level is characterized by "ironic imagination." The believer recognizes that all religious perspectives are relative, imaginative or symbolic constructs that ought not to be taken literally. But how, then, can one *commit* to a specific faith perspective in any but a provisional, ironical way? Logos cannot feed heart hunger. But, surely, neither can a mythos that is acknowledged as nothing more than a contrived human artifact, historically conditioned, destined to wear away with time.[61]

Fowler responds to this problem by reminding us that the symbolic perspectives we acknowledge as relative are all *relative to* an unconditioned, absolute Reality. This clearly is also Franklin's position. Religious beliefs may be fictions, but in Franklin's estimation they are not thereby untrue. This is because, as Fowler says, they ultimately point to an independently existing deity that is rationally unknowable. In fact, there is some cause to think that the symbolic ways in which humans attempt to approach this distant God are closer to the truth than reason can fathom. Keep in mind the claim of the "Articles" that humans have a natural inclination to devotion. Franklin is enough of a child of his century to deny that anything as ubiquitous as the human hunger for God is gratuitous. Given the lawlike nature of reality, there must be a reason for the inclination, as well as a way to appease it. Even if we cannot intellectually come to an awareness of God's nature, it stands to reason that there must be something within it that essentially addresses this natural inclination, something toward which our hunger is directed. Even if we are incapable of rationally directing the hunger, we can do so by means of poëtry, metaphor, music, and stories. We can symbolize what we cannot cognize, using our natural inclinations as guides in the symbol-making process.

This means that the symbols we construct—what Franklin refers to in the "Articles" as "lesser gods"—are the real intermediaries between us and God. This is the bottom line of his theistic perspectivism. God exists: of that Franklin was convinced. Humans have an innate need to worship God: he was equally convinced of this. The distant First Cause is incapable of filling this need. Therefore it only makes sense that symbols, which can fulfill the need and at the same time point beyond themselves to reveal something of divine nature, should be allowed to substitute. As Franklin revealingly has one of the characters in his 1755 "A Parable against Persecution" say, "I do not worship thy God, neither do I call upon his Name; for *I have made to myself a God,* which abideth alway [*sic*] in mine House, and provideth me with all Things" (my emphasis).[62]

In his own private meditations and worship, Franklin was satisfied with this. Of course, he differed from most people in that he was perfectly aware that the "gods" he worshipped were symbolic, cultural perspectives. But because he took the symbols to be revelatory, even if only dimly, they appeased his natural inclination.

Moreover, they clearly gave him a sense of emancipation. He no longer felt constrained by any one religious tradition or any one set of religious idioms. That this is the case is evidenced by his embrace of any number of religious tenets throughout his life, some of which in fact were so incompatible that they violated the criterion of coherence. The supreme irony of Franklin's great insight is that although he felt it to be a Cato-like resolution of his own religious indecision, it in fact legitimized and hence reinforced his tendency to veer from one side of the religious spectrum to the other, leaning sometimes toward deism, sometimes toward supernaturalism, and occasionally trying—unhappily—to marry beliefs taken from both.[63]

4 A Comfortable Belief

A YEAR BEFORE HE wrote his "Articles of Belief and Acts of Religion," Franklin brought together a group of like-minded young men in Philadelphia who thirsted for knowledge, wished to succeed in life, and were possessed of a hearty civic-mindedness. Organized into "a Club for mutual Improvement," they called themselves the Junto, or Leather Apron Club.[1] The club, which met each Friday evening, offered its members the opportunity to discuss the latest theories in mechanics and natural philosophy; peruse recently published books (the Junto began building a library, which eventually spun off into the Philadelphia Library Company, the "Mother of all the N[orth] American Subscription Libraries"[2]); debate different projects designed to enhance the public weal; and collaborate in the interests of one another's careers. The spirit of the Junto was utilitarian through and through. Its members were not interested in knowledge for knowledge's sake but rather for what inventions and social or civic improvements it gave rise to. The members, nothing if not earnest, pledged themselves to be "serviceable to *mankind,* to their country, to their friends, [and] to themselves."[3]

Given Franklin's background and interests, it is hardly surprising that he founded a society like the Junto. As mentioned in chapter 1, two of Franklin's favorite boyhood books were Cotton Mather's *Bonifacius* and Daniel Defoe's *An Essay upon Projects.* Both of these books strongly advocate the establishment of clubs (Mather calls them "Associated Families" and Defoe, "Friendly Societies") in which members agree to help one another and improve the general educational and economic level of the society in which they live.[4] Moreover, while in England Franklin had observed and been struck by similar goals promoted by British Masonic lodges.[5] He was also appreciative of the utilitarian bent of the Royal Society and could have been inspired by its example.[6]

Franklin himself drew up the bylaws and rules of the club. They mandated that every member "once in three Months produce and read an Essay of his own Writing on any Subject he pleased." The essays were then debated and discussed, but Franklin obviously wished to avoid the "disputations" he had engaged in as a youth, and which he felt most often resulted in little more than hot tempers and angry words. He therefore stipulated that the Junto debates were "to be conducted in the sincere Spirit of Enquiry after Truth, without Fondness for Dispute, or Desire of Victory," and even provided for financial penalties for offending members.[7]

A scan of a few of the "queries to be ask'd the Junto" provides us with some idea of just how practical its concerns were: "Whence comes the Dew that stands on the Outside of a Tankard that has cold Water in it in the Summer Time? Does the Importation of Servants increase or advance the Wealth of our Country? Would not an Office of Insurance for Servants be of Service, and what Methods are proper for the erecting of such an Office? Does it not require as much Pains, Study and Application to become truly Wise and strictly Good and Virtuous as to become rich?"[8] Quite obviously, these are questions concerned with curiosities from natural philosophy or matters affecting one's pocketbook. It is a bit unusual, then, that Franklin delivered an address to the Junto membership sometime between 1730 and 1732 dealing with a strictly theological topic. It was entitled "On the Providence of God in the Government of the World."[9]

The essay was unusual in another regard as well. In it, the same Franklin who had rejected the basic tenets of his parents' orthodox Calvinism defended a very orthodox doctrine of Calvinism indeed. On the surface, this seems like yet another one of his strange religious flipflops: first, the "piously dissenting ways" of his parents, then the necessitarianism of the *Dissertation,* then on to the theistic perspectivism of his "Articles," and now a return to Calvinism. And, to be sure, there is a certain amount of waffling here that reflects

Franklin's deep-seated ambivalence in religious affairs. But the unexpectedness of his 1732 views on divine providence, as well as the seeming impropriety of his airing them before a society dedicated to practical knowledge, is ameliorated if interpreted as the latest twists in his fundamental conviction that all doctrinal beliefs are useful fictions.

A belief in divine providence is common to Judaism, Christianity, and Islam, but those Christians who pledge their loyalty to the theology of John Calvin have especially emphasized it. The doctrine of providence has it that God is not merely the Creator of the universe, but also, as Calvin put it, the "Disposer Supreme" who oversees and regulates the world in such a way as to provide for the well-being of its inhabitants. Divine agency "disposes" in three ways: it sustains the very existence of the created order, it influences the daily activity of living beings, and it guides all created things to their proper, appointed end. "Herein," declares Calvin, "lies the unfathomable greatness of God: not only did he once create heaven and earth but He also guides the whole process according to His will."[10] The traditional doctrine of providence has no patience with the enlightened notion of God as a *deus absconditus* who sets the universe in motion and then retreats into celestial silence: "he who confesses God as Creator while supposing that He remains tranquilly in heaven without caring for the world, outrageously deprives God of all effective power."[11]

Calvin argued in his *Institutes* that the theological doctrine of providence had scriptural foundation. In Genesis 22:8, the first explicit reference is made to it when Abraham tells his son that "God will provide" (*Deus providebit*).[12] Calvin interprets this passage not only as an assertion of divine foreknowledge of future needs, but also as an invitation for the believer to place himself in the hands of a deity who actively provides what is necessary. Moreover, scores of other scriptural passages testify to this. God raises a wind in the desert, for example, to carry to the wandering tribe of Israel a flock of birds (Exodus 16:13), or sends forth a wind to raise a tempest so that Jonah will be tossed overboard (Jonah 1:4). All the scriptural examples of divine providence have one thing in common: each consists in action, demonstrating that God plays an active role in the affairs of the world. It is, therefore, ignorant trifling to interpret divine providence as mere prescience.[13] Calvin clearly intended this argument to deflect the obvious (and traditional) criticism that providence of this sort eliminates human free will as much as chance or luck. The torturous debates over liberty and divine knowledge that later raged between Calvinists of varying sects, as well as between Calvinists and their enlightened critics, suggest that these efforts to forestall controversy were unsuccessful.[14]

But it ought not be supposed that divine providence is limited to God's regulation of the natural order only, because it extends beyond that to the overseeing of individual actions. Not a sparrow falls to the ground but what God knows and intends it to happen. Disasters occur to awaken humans from sin and pride, and great rewards honor great virtue. The benevolence of God is such that he will not withhold his guidance from humanity, the pinnacle of his creation, when he exercises it throughout the rest of the universe. For although humans are made in God's image, they are particularly susceptible to physical hardships:

> [I]t is a puerile cavil to limit the [government of God] to the influence and course of nature. And they not only defraud God of his glory, but themselves of a very useful doctrine, who confine the Divine providence within such narrow bounds, as though he permitted all things to proceed in an uncontrolled course, according to a perpetual law of nature; for nothing would exceed the misery of man, if he were exposed to all the motions of the heaven, air, earth, and waters. Besides, this notion would shamefully diminish the singular goodness of God towards every individual.[15]

Calvin does not intend the knowledge of God's providential care of individuals to be solely a matter of rational inference. True, the human intellect is capable of discerning God's governance in the physical realm. The presence of immutable natural laws and the predictability of natural events persuade the mind that the workings of nature are designed and overseen by a Supreme Architect. But "faith ought to penetrate further" into the divine plan than reason can. Once the mind has perceived that God is the creator, governor, and preserver of the immutable system of natural laws, it stops. But faith enables the believer to see that providence protects (or punishes) the individual as well, until he or she can say with Paul that "we live, and move, and have our being" in God (Acts 17:28).[16]

Early Puritan immigrants to the American shore took the Calvinist notion of providence seriously. Providence as God's overarching regulation of the natural order was always assumed, but an increasing stress was laid on the notion of God's providential care for individuals—what became known as "particular" or "special" providences. Partly, perhaps, because of the frequently brutal living conditions they encountered in the new world, partly out of their acute sensitivity to the presence of sin and human dissimulation, the Puritans were quite taken with the notion that God could and would interfere in the natural workings of nature to rescue hapless saints. The darker side of this was the equally strong belief that divine anger likewise intervened to smite the ungodly.

Two of America's earliest Puritan documents, John Winthrop's *Journal* and William Bradford's *Of Plymouth Plantation,* provide ample illustrations of both kinds of special providences. Winthrop tells us, for example, that

> One Smith of Watertown had a son about five years old, who fell into the river near the mill gate, and was carried by the stream under the wheel, and taken up on the other side, without any harm. One of the boards of the wheel was fallen off, and it seems (by special providence) he was carried through under that gap, for otherwise if an eel pass through, it is cut asunder. The miller perceived his wheel to check on the sudden, which made him look out, and so he found the child sitting up to the waist in the shallow water beneath the mill.[17]

The Smith boy's good fortune, to the Puritan mind, was a clear manifestation of God's active intervention to protect the innocent from harm. But the other aspect of special providence was never forgotten: it also served as punishment for the wicked and warning for the righteous. In describing the voyage from England to Plymouth, William Bradford provides a chilling example.

> I may not omit here a special work of God's providence. There was a proud and very profane young man, one of the seamen, of a lusty, able body, which made him haughty; he would alway [*sic*] be contemning the poor people in their sickness and cursing them daily with grievous execrations; and did not let to tell them that he hoped to help to cast half of them overboard before they came to their journe's end, and to make merry with what they had; and if he were by any gently reproved, he would curse and swear most bitterly. But it pleased God before they came half seas over, to smite this young man with a grievous disease, of which he died in a desperate manner, and so was himself the first that was thrown overboard. Thus his curses light on his own head, and it was an astonishment to all his fellows for they noted it to be the just hand of God upon him.[18]

Both these stories point to a characteristic of the Puritan faithful: the habit of scrutinizing themselves and their environment for signs of divine favor or anger. Although always a fixture of the Puritan ethos, this preoccupation with special providences probably hit its high point in the closing years of the seventeenth century. Increase Mather's 1684 *An Essay for the Recording of Illustrious Providences,* which promised to provide guidelines for identifying authentic special providences (thereby to Mather's mind dramatically demonstrating "a design of this Nature, so as shall be indeed for Gods Glory"), was a bestseller by the day's standards. Even into the eighteenth century, thundering jeremiads proclaiming providential displays of divine wrath or pious sermons of thanksgiving for providential rescue were common. The threat of or deliverance from Indian massacres, blazing comets, monstrous births, yellow fever, earthquakes, thunderstorms, locusts, or droughts were occasions for lengthy and portentous sermons on either the restraining or smiting hand of God Almighty.[19]

As late seventeenth-century Calvinism danced with the Enlightenment, less theological emphasis came to be placed on special providences and more on God's overarching regulation of the natural order. Ultimately, among deistic-minded intellectuals as well as many liberal Christians, providence became synonymous with natural design and was discussed in exclusively philosophical, nonbiblical, terms. Special providences were rejected as irrational superstitions that more insulted than underscored divine wisdom. But in popular piety, a strong belief in special providences held on. It is more than likely that the household in which young Franklin was raised accepted them wholeheartedly. It is certain that John Bunyan's *Pilgrim's Progress,* which Franklin read and reread as a lad, regularly and fervently refers to them.

The doctrine of special providences was well known, then, to Franklin, partly because of his pious rearing, partly because he could have not have failed to absorb it from the atmosphere of early eighteenth-century Boston. As we saw in chapter 1, Cotton Mather, clearly the dominant theological voice in Boston during Franklin's boyhood, shared his father's belief in special providences and frequently preached and wrote about them.[20] But the conviction that God can and does interfere in the natural order to deliver or smite saints and sinners was rejected by the adolescent Franklin along with other Calvinist tenets that violated the dictates of reason. Certainly the *Dissertation*'s defense of an aloof deity uninterested in the activities or fates of humans suggests as much. Yet, curiously, Franklin's 1732 Junto address appears to be an endorsement of the traditional Calvinist doctrine.

"On the Providence of God in the Government of the World" is written in a relaxed, friendly style, exactly the tone one would expect from an address delivered, as Franklin tells us, to "intimate Pot Companions." He begins by loosening up his audience, jocularly worrying that none of his listeners "who have heard me say a 1000 silly Things in Conversation" are likely to take seriously any remarks he might make on such a weighty subject as providence. But he promises to do his best, forsaking both the "Glosses of Oratory" and an emotionally charged delivery that may be persuasive but in substance no more than "unmeaning Noise."[21]

Franklin, in typical early eighteenth-century fashion, offers in his address no overt argument for the existence of God. Instead, he assumes his audience is not so "ignorant of what all Mankind in all Ages have agreed in" as to need one. But in order to set the stage for his specific arguments about providence, he reminds his listeners that the very structure of the universe offers the best reason to believe in God. It operates in accordance with uniform laws of motion and is constructed in such a way as to be conducive to "Life to so many Creatures," each of which has been provided with "plentiful Sustenance." Whoever "attentively and thoroughly" examines the matter cannot fail to be "astonish'd and swallow'd up in Admiration" at the design that permeates nature. Consequently, it is reasonable to infer the existence of a Supreme Designer, and likewise to posit unlimited wisdom, power, and goodness as three of the divine attributes. For only an entity totally wise and powerful could blueprint and build such an orderly world, and only a completely good one would make sure it is conducive to the well-being of its inhabitants.[22]

Now, asks Franklin, if "the World was at first made by a Being of infinite Wisdom, Goodness and Power," what may we conclude about that Being's present relation to creation? There are only four possibilities:

> 1. Either he unchangeably decreed and appointed every Thing that comes to pass, and left nothing to the Course [of] Nature, nor allow'd any Creature free agency. or
>
> 2. Without decreeing any thing, he left all to general Nature and the Events of Free Agency in his Creatures, which he never alters or interrupts. or
>
> 3. He decreed some Things unchangeably, and left others to general Nature and the Events of Free agency, which also he never alters or interrupts; or
>
> 4. He sometimes interferes by his particular Providence and sets aside the Effects which would otherwise have been produced by any of the Above Causes.[23]

There is no doubt that the Franklin of the *Dissertation* would have opted for the first possibility. But several years and much reflection separated the youngster who dashed out his impetuous reply to Wollaston from the respectable printer who addressed the Junto. Now it was the fourth option that Franklin would defend.

The first possibility is dealt with easily enough. If it is the case that everything that is must be, then, says Franklin, several unacceptable consequences follow. In the first place, a thoroughgoing necessitarianism eliminates the very need for God. In determining the entire course of nature and events for all time, the deity "divest[s] himself of all further Power" since there is nothing left to be done. "[H]e has ty'd up his Hands, and has now no greater Power than an Idol of Wood or Stone." Second, belief in necessitarianism goes contrary to the traditional notion that God is benevolent, for experience all too clearly teaches us that frequently the wicked prosper and the good suffer. Yet the first possibility, which claims that the deity is responsible for everything that is, would have it that God is also responsible for such injustices. Finally, if God truly has appointed the nature of all that is, "Prayers to him both in private and publickly in great Assemblies" are absurd. The hopes and fears that humans have brought to God in prayer for centuries are thrown into an unhearing, indifferent universe. And yet, as Franklin wrote in his 1728 "Articles," we have a natural inclination for worship and reverence. This must mean in part that prayerful supplication and adoration are not in vain. As Franklin says, "Surely it is not more difficult to believe the World was made by a God of Wood or Stone, than that the God who made the World should be such a God as this."[24]

The second possibility, that God has "left all to general Nature and the Events of Free Agency in his Creatures," is an equally unacceptable extreme. Like the first possibility, it violates the notion that the deity is all-loving and benevolent. Of what value is a God, Franklin asks, who sits on the cosmic sidelines and passively observes suffering and injustice in the world without intervening, or who gazes at unselfish virtue without rewarding? This sort of spectator God creates merely to abandon, and that in itself is absurd: "there can be no Reason to imagine [God] would make so glorious a Universe meerly to abandon it." But far worse is God's moral indifference. Franklin's fear of this God, his terror at the thought of being abandoned by such an uncaring divine parent, comes through clearly:

> [I]magine the Deity looking on and beholding the Ways of his Creatures; some Hero's in Virtue he sees are incessantly indeavouring the Good of others, they labour thro vast difficulties, they suffer incredible Hardships and Miseries to accomplish this End, in hopes to please a Good God, and obtain his Favour, which they earnestly Pray for; what Answer can be made them within himself but this: *take the Reward Chance may give you, I do not intermeddle in these Affairs;* he sees others continually doing all manner of Evil, and bringing by their Actions Misery and Destruction among Mankind: What can he say here but this, *if Chance rewards you I shall not punish you, I am not to be concerned.* He sees the just, the innocent and the Beneficent in the Hands of the wicked and violent Oppressor; and when the good are at the Brink of Destruction they pray to him, *thou, O God, art mighty and powerful to save; help us we beseech thee:* He answers, *I cannot help you, 'tis none of my Business nor do I at all regard these things.*[25]

This description of God is as dispiriting as the lonely fear of the vast emptiness of space that comes across at the beginning of the "Articles." Franklin is not merely speculating in an abstract, impersonal fashion here. "On the Providence of God" is as much confession as it is theology. In its own way, it represents another Cato-like resolve of the will on Franklin's part to "put an end" to his religious melancholy by refusing to believe in anything less than a beneficent universe.

Franklin also rejects the third possible interpretation of providence, once more on the grounds that it too violates the notion of God as the Supreme Designer. If God has decreed some things but left others to unsupervised chance or free will, then he would be just as "unGod[ed]" as he is by the first possibility of rigorous necessitarianism. He refuses to interfere in order to bring about justice or prevent wickedness; he will not respond to petition; he refuses to reciprocate love. He has "nothing to do; he can cause us neither Good nor Harm; he is no more to be regarded than a lifeless Image, than Dagon, or Baall, or Bell and the Dragon." He is, in a word, an "Absurdity, which when considered or but barely seen, cannot be swallowed without doing the greatest Violence to common Reason, and all the Faculties of the Understanding."[26]

What Franklin has done in rejecting the first three accounts of divine providence is to employ a rather simple reductio ad absurdum. He entertains each of the possibilities just for the sake of argument, examines the consequences to which they give rise, and shows that those consequences are in conflict with the very definition of God. He concludes, naturally, that claims having such perverse implications must themselves be flawed and accordingly rejected. The reduction to absurdity of arguments with which one disagrees is an ancient logical strategy, and it is certainly one Franklin frequently invoked.[27] But as we shall see shortly, he had a special reason for emphasizing the disastrous consequences of denying, as the first three possibilities do, the traditional Puritan doctrine of providence.

Franklin doesn't offer a positive argument in defense of the account of providence he wishes to maintain. Since he has asserted there are only four possible interpretations, and since he has rejected three of them, it follows that he accepts as "most probably true" the remaining one: God "sometimes interferes by his particular Providence and sets aside the Effects which would otherwise have been produced" by the course of nature or human agency. Franklin asserts here that God can and sometimes does intervene in natural affairs by acting providentially—saving the Smith boy from drowning under the waterwheel, or smiting Bradford's impious sailor with a fatal illness. In affirming this, he turns away from deism's insistence that the doctrine of special providences insults the deity and destroys the immutability of the natural order, thereby endorsing the popular piety of his day.

Franklin rounds out his address with a quick nod toward those who might worry that the notion of a miraculously intervening deity does violence to human free will by stating (without defending) his conviction that nonetheless "Men are in some Degree free Agents, and accountable for their Actions."

Clearly, however, he doesn't wish to tackle this thorny problem in "On the Providence of God" and promises a "separate Discourse hereafter" on the topic "if I find Occasion."[28] As the next chapter will show, Franklin never did find occasion, but he was preoccupied with questions of freedom and moral responsibility for the rest of his life.

The bottom line of his 1732 reflections on divine providence, then, is that "'tis highly reasonable to believe a [special] Providence because tis highly absurd to believe otherwise." The opportunity cost of denying the reality of special providences is the burden of living with the alienating knowledge that God is utterly indifferent to the affairs and well-being of humans. Franklin found himself unable to face such a chilling conclusion even as he finished work on his *Dissertation,* and he subsequently reaffirmed his dislike of it in the "Articles." So far as he was now concerned, a belief in God's ability and willingness to intervene in history and nature is "the Foundation of all true Religion."[29]

"On the Providence of God" is an interesting example of how Franklin deals with religious matters because it illustrates the two essential features of his approach to things of the spirit. In the first place, it conveys a good sense of his divided loyalties to the Calvinism of his boyhood and the Enlightenment ethos he embraced as a youth, a split that is the root of the ambivalence that runs through most of his religious writing. On the one hand, Franklin is intellectually convinced, along with the deists, that the only thing we can really know about God is his role as First Cause; this would suggest that he ought to have little patience with the supernaturalisms of revealed religion. On the other hand, however, his heart leads him to an interpretation of God's governance of the world—special providences—that would have gladdened the seventeenth-century spirit of Increase Mather. On the one hand, Franklin is the founder and proud member of a society that devotes itself to the promotion of useful knowledge. On the other, he delivers an address to this same society that smacks more of otherworldly than secular concerns.

But in the second place, "On the Providence of God" is also a good example of how Franklin cashed out the theistic perspectivism of his "Articles" when it came to dealing with specific doctrines. The key to appreciating what Franklin is up to here is his great insight that religious beliefs function as useful fictions.

In "On the Providence of God" Franklin has underscored how unbearable the world would be if not for the fact that we believe God to be so benevolently concerned with our welfare that he occasionally intervenes in our affairs. As pointed out earlier, Franklin does not provide an argument for this claim but rests content with emphasizing the opportunity costs of believing otherwise. As he tells us, "'tis highly reasonable to believe a Providence because tis highly absurd to believe otherwise." "Absurd" in this context takes on a meaning similar to what the twentieth-century existentialists intended when they used the word. It is alienating, destructive, terrifying, to deny special providences: that is Franklin's real message here. Much better to believe the contrary, even if the belief is nothing more than a useful fiction, a culturally bound perspective that has no objective referent but gets us through the day. It is significant that Franklin ends his address by telling us that religion founded on this notion of providence (rather than, for instance, a cold and abstract religion that has as its only tenet the affirmation of a First Cause) is a "Powerful Regulater of our Actions, give[s] us Peace and Tranquility within our own Minds, and render[s] us Benevolent, Useful and Beneficial to others."[30] Although the enlightened intellect may balk at special providences, it and similar supernatural doctrines provide a sense of meaning and purposefulness that both regulates and edifies. They feed our natural hunger for God.

When Franklin began his address by claiming to "offer . . . nothing but plain Reasoning," he was not being disingenuous. It was not so much the abstractions of logical reasoning he had in mind (although they are clearly present in his employment of the reductios) as what might be called "instrumental" or perhaps, following Pascal, "heart" reasoning. If reasoning is seen as cogitation about that which is most useful or instrumental in promoting happiness, virtue, and purpose, then Franklin's advocacy in his address of a useful fiction is nothing but "plain Reasoning." It speaks to the heart as well as the head, with the implicit intention of defending our right to believe in a religious doctrine solely on the basis of its existential utility. Once more, logos makes way for mythos, this time a mythos replete with a sense of ultimate purposefulness. In a curious way, then, Franklin's choice to speak about Providence to the Junto is not as far out of place as it originally seemed. What could be more utility-laden than those beliefs about the nature of reality that meaningfully orient humans along life's way?

Still, the ambivalence was there, and it would continue throughout his life. Ironically, as indicated in the previous chapter, Franklin's doctrine of theistic perspectivism tended to exacerbate the very ambivalence it was intended to dispel. After his great insight of 1728, Franklin would always be conflicted in the religious realm between what he wished to believe and what he could assent to intellectually. The first category was much more inclusive than the second, which basically boiled down to the belief in a First Cause. Within the category of what he wished to believe were several more or less traditional Calvinist notions—providence being one of them—that Franklin came to see as necessary for a meaningful existence.

The problem is that Franklin appears at times to have conflated theistic perspectivism as an explanation of the origins of religious belief with theistic perspectivism as a justification of his own religious sentiments. The doctrine of useful fictions acts primarily as a way of understanding why different sects believe in different doctrines. It claims that those doctrines are in large part products of place and time, seized on because they serve to make life more bearable than it would be without them. But the doctrine as Franklin uses it in his "Articles of Belief" has another significance as well. This is what might be described as its "Jamesian edge," namely, that an individual has the right to accept as true those religious beliefs for which there is no clear evidence but which improve the quality of his or her existence.[31]

Franklin, much more of a social conservative than he is typically given credit for, believed that religion serves as a necessary regulator of human behavior.[32] As he asks in a 1786 letter (possibly to Tom Paine), "If Men are so wicked as we now see them *with Religion* what would they be if *without it?*"[33] Clearly, when Franklin the student of comparative religion perceives that humans believe in all sorts of regulatory religious doctrines that almost certainly do not accurately describe the true nature of things, he approves. Better for the crowd to accept fictions than for it to lose the checks on behavior that religion mandates as well as the psychological comfort it bestows.[34] But when Franklin the private, soul-hungry individual searches for his own religious beliefs, he is not under the same illusion of objective reference that the crowd is. He knows that the beliefs he settles on are not true in a literal sense but only in a functional and symbolic way. Thus his commitment to them, as Fowler suggests, is properly "ironic." Sometimes this is good enough for Franklin. But at other times the loneliness of an indifferent universe begins to close in and he longs for a less perspectival, less fictional, foundation for his beliefs. Thus his tendency to waffle on central religious tenets, sometimes expressing fervent belief in them, other times skeptically poking fun at them. I do not think this ambivalence points to confusion—much less hypocrisy—on Franklin's part so much as it is a predictable outcome of knowingly trying to steer one's life around the buoys of useful fictions. Even if we intellectually think that the only truth religious beliefs can have is a functional one, we still occasionally long for them to be fortified with a more Platonic solidity. Such, I believe, was the situation Franklin found himself in, not only about providence but about other traditional religious doctrines as well.

But of all the useful fictions he endorsed at one time or another in his religious journey, providence appears to have been the most personally significant one. In "On the Providence of God," he remarks that a belief in providence is the "Foundation of all true Religion." Fifty-two years later, in the 1786 letter, he just as strongly says that even more than "general Providence" a belief in "the Doctrines of a *particular* Providence" is "the Foundation of all Religion" (my emphasis).[35] Obviously, then, Franklin maintained a lifelong conviction that a belief in providence was important. In fact, as will be shown shortly, his appreciation of the doctrine seems to have grown as time passed. But still, there were occasions when his head overruled his heart.

In 1745, for example, he made fun of the notion of providence in a letter to his favorite brother, John (1690–1756). The letter was written in the midst of King George's War and it referred to the public announcement of a "fast and prayer day" during which inhabitants were enjoined to offer up prayers for victory. "I compute," writes Franklin, "five hundred thousand petitions were offered up to the same effect in New England, which added to the petitions of every family morning and evening [since January] makes forty-five millions of prayers." If no victory ensues, continues Franklin, "I fear I shall have but an indifferent opinion of Presbyterian prayers in such cases as long as I live." At any rate, he concludes, "I should have more dependence on *works,* than on *faith*" when it comes to attacking strong towns. Doubtless there is the intention here to entertain his older brother with a few sardonic words about a troublesome current event, but it is significant that Franklin chose the doctrine of providence as the butt of his joke.[36]

It is also revealing that it takes a catastrophe like war to shake Franklin's faith in the doctrine of special providence. Throughout his life, the experience of pain and suffering, either his own or (more usually) someone else's, prompted him to feel more deeply the indifference of the universe and, consequently, wounded his faith in providence. In a 1782 letter to James Hutton in which he describes a recent massacre of Indians by frontiersmen, Franklin laments that "the dispensations of Providence in this World puzzle my weak Reason. I cannot comprehend why cruel Men should have been permitted thus to destroy their Fellow Creatures. . . . I wonder at this."[37] The same melancholy over undeserved pain comes across in a letter written five years later to a French correspondent. After praising the Comte de Buffon's contributions to natural philosophy, Franklin goes on to deplore the fact that Buffon suffered terribly from stone, and wonders at the wisdom and goodness of a deity who allows it: "I do not understand these dispensations of Providence, though probably they are for the best. But it seems to me that if you or I had the disposition of good and evil in this world, so excellent a man would not have an hour's pain during his existence."[38] True, one man's propensity to stone is not of the same magnitude as the slaughter of innocent people, but Franklin is not indulging in a tasteless levity here. Suffering is suffering, regardless of its scale, and it is always hard to swallow when it befalls those who deserve better.

On at least one occasion, Franklin found himself forgetting that providence is a useful fiction. In 1769 he wrote a letter to his friend the revivalist George Whitefield that bespeaks a melancholy bordering on despair: "I *see* with you that our affairs are not well managed by our rulers here below; I wish I could *believe* with you, that they are well attended to by those above: I rather suspect, from certain circumstances, that though the general government of the universe is well administered, our particular little affairs are perhaps below notice, and left to take the chance of human prudence or imprudence, as either may happen to be uppermost."[39]

Two things are especially interesting about this gloomy letter. First, although it appears that Franklin rejects the notion of special divine intervention, thereby reverting to the third possible interpretation of providence he had discussed in his address before the Junto, he really is not. At the last moment he pulls up, as if he has only then realized the road his reflections are taking him down: "It is, however, an uncomfortable thought, and I leave it."[40] In this terse sentence, one is reminded of the young Franklin who, in imitation of Addison's Cato, put an end to his doubts and confusions by a sheer act of will. The head tells him one thing, but the heart cannot bear to hear it. The tussle continues. The human soul, as Lawrence said, is a vast and tangled forest.[41]

The second noteworthy thing about this letter is that it expresses what is a more or less constant conviction of Franklin's: a belief in *general* providence. Even when Franklin in his moments of gloom questions whether God's governance extends to individuals or groups of individuals, he almost never doubts, as he puts it to Whitefield, that the "general government of the universe is well administered."[42] Presumably this is because he was intellectually convinced that the apparent rationality of the physical order points to the presence of a supervisory Designer. As he wrote to his sister Jane Mecom, "I see so much Wisdom in what I understand of [the world's] Creator and Government, that I suspect equal Wisdom may be in what I do not understand."[43]

Part of Franklin's steadfast confidence in the reality of general providence can probably be traced back to his Calvinist roots. It will be recalled that Calvin in the seventeenth century had concluded that nature's orderliness impresses a sense of providence on the intellect. But I suspect that a much stronger reason for Franklin's conviction was his absorption of the Enlightenment worldview. Cold, indifferent, alienating, and psychologically damaging as that model might be, it at least provided rational guarantees that the universe was predictably governed by immutable natural laws that could be discovered and to a certain extent manipulated by reason. Franklin's scientific interests were founded on this belief, and it is one he never relinquished. But it was incompatible with the orthodox doctrine that God directly intervened in the clockwork universe.

Still, in spite of the times when he fell into gloom and doubt, and notwithstanding his intellectual loyalty to a Newtonian cosmology, Franklin tended to hang onto the belief that God personally intervenes in the affairs of humans. As we have seen, the cost of abandoning it was simply too great. Just as he tended to doubt in moments of catastrophe or crisis, so his belief tended to soar during times of triumph. Two examples in particular are worthy of attention. Both are drawn from political speeches, and consequently one needs to be wary of mere rhetorical appeals to higher powers and the guiding hand of God. But beneath the conventional flourishes, Franklin's sincere endorsement of special providence is clearly detectable.

The first example is from a 1788 letter to the *Federal Gazette,* in which Franklin castigates antifederalist opponents of a national constitution. He begins in a typically disingenuous way by saying that he would not want to be misunderstood to mean that the General Convention was divinely inspired when it drafted the federal constitution. Yet, he continues, "I must own that I have so much Faith in the general Governance of the World by *Providence,* that I can hardly conceive a Transaction of such momentous Importance to the Welfare of Millions now existing, and to exist in the Posterity of a great Nation, should be suffered to pass without being in some degree influenc'd, guided, and governed by that omnipotent, omnipresent, and beneficent Ruler, in whom all inferior Spirits live, and move, and have their Being."[44]

Although Franklin uses the language of general providence in this letter, his point is clear: a special intervening act of God swayed the minds of ambivalent delegates to approve of a national constitution. This conviction that specific political agendas that promise to improve the lot of human beings must be inspired and guided by a benevolent deity is likewise expressed in Franklin's earlier motion for prayers in the Constitutional Convention. The aged Franklin took a back seat at the convention, but in the early summer of 1787 he rose to plead that each session of the convention be opened with prayers of petition and thanksgiving. Oddly, the motion was simply ignored by the delegates. But it contained as eloquent a defense of special providence as Franklin ever wrote: "the longer I live, the more convincing proofs I see of this Truth, *that* GOD *governs in the Affairs of Men.* And if a Sparrow cannot fall to the Ground without his Notice, is it probable that an Empire can rise without his Aid? We have been assured . . . in the Sacred Writings, that 'except the Lord build the House, they labour in vain that build it.' I firmly believe this; and I also believe, that, without concurring Aid, we shall succeed in this political Building no better than the Builders of Babel."[45]

As he grew older and found himself famous, respected, and wealthy, Franklin tended to slide further away from his intellectual conviction that belief in special providences was nothing but one of those useful fictions that help humans get through the occasionally nasty business of living. The belief had become so important to him that he seems to have forgotten what his head told him about it. Instead, he followed his heart.

The importance of the belief is especially evident when Franklin speaks of the possibility of an afterlife. Franklin became progressively convinced that he would continue after physical death. His grounds for this conviction rested in part on an orthodox reading of providence. He tells George Whitefield in a 1764 letter, for instance, that "thro' almost threescore Years [God] has been continually showering his Favours upon me, whose very Chastisements have been Blessings to me[;] can I doubt that he loves me? And, if he loves me, can I doubt that he will go on to take care of me not only here but hereafter?"[46] The argument here appeals to special providence as its major premise: God has bestowed so many blessings on Franklin in the past that he must love him. Then, calculating that enough blessings have appeared to establish a pattern on which reasonable predictions about the future can be made, Franklin concludes that the blessings will continue after bodily dissolution. As he succinctly sums up his method, "Hope of the Future, built on Experience of the Past."[47] And his recollections of past experiences were refracted through the doctrinal prism of providence.

By the end of his life, Franklin was confident that the doctrine of special providences, as well as God's great frugality (that is, general providence), which makes the Creator loath to waste any part of His creation, guaranteed his continuation after death.[48] The wickedness he had encountered in the world had also left its mark, and he came to believe that a wise governance of the world necessitated that successful evil in this life be punished in the next. As he wrote in 1782, "the more I see the Impossibility, from the number and extent of his Crimes, of giving equivalent punishment to a wicked Man in this Life, the more I am convinc'd of a future State, in which all that here appears to be wrong shall be set right, all that is crooked made straight."[49]

Five weeks before his death, he reaffirmed his hope in the reality of providence. "Having experienced the Goodness of that Being in conducting me prosperously thro' a long life," he wrote, "I have no doubt of its Continuance in the next."[50] Franklin had come full circle from the early days in which he had criticized Wollaston so harshly for defending the very same doctrine.

Religious worldviews are never absolutely coherent. There are always breakdowns in consistency or murky areas of downright confusion that the believer resists (and probably rightly so) dragging out into the light. Religious beliefs deal with matters that by their very nature transcend the human ability to know. They are also beliefs in which subscribers have invested major emotional capital. They are not simply or even primarily intellectual theories about the nature of reality. Rather, they are boulders to which believers sometimes desperately cling in order to wait out the storms of life. It is no wonder that any given individual's religious worldview appears a bit patchworked or even tattered to an outside observer.

Franklin's religious views are no exception, and this is especially apparent in his attitude toward special providences. After 1728 he accepted the regulatory importance of traditional religious perspectives such as providence because he saw them as enriching an individual's sense of meaning and encouraging a certain degree of social stability (more of this in the next chapter). They were fictions, perhaps, but very useful ones. But as the years wore on, Franklin became so comfortable with (or perhaps reliant on) the fiction of providence that he tended at times to forget it *was* a perspective. What he had once defined as a cultural invention now became a reality—and yet, in his more soberly reflective moments, as in the 1745 letter to his brother John, Franklin acknowledged it as merely a useful fiction. On at least this issue, then, Franklin's religious thinking was at times uncomfortably dissonant. The head believed one thing, the heart another, and Franklin, caught in the middle, at times leaned toward one, at times toward the other. The doctrine of providence, in short, was one of those religious beliefs he simply could not give up, even though his intellect told him that it was not rationally justifiable. He himself had an at least vague awareness of the conundrum. "The Dispensations of Providence," he wrote in 1782, "puzzle my weak Reason. . . . *but I cannot therefore part with the comfortable Belief of a Divine Providence*" (my emphasis).[51] In the long run, the pull of Franklin's "piously dissenting" boyhood outweighed his later Enlightenment convictions on this issue.

5 Taming Wolves

WHEN FRANKLIN DEPARTED from England in 1726, the voyage back to Philadelphia took about two and a half months. To help while away the long weeks at sea, he began a journal. Most of its entries are taken up with observations on sea animals, the weather, and shipboard gossip. But as Franklin recollected in his *Autobiography,* there was something else in it as well, "perhaps the most important Part": a plan for the regulation of his "future Conduct of Life."[1]

The plan is a brief memorandum that sets out four "resolutions": to be frugal, truthful, industrious, and to "speak ill of no man whatever." In themselves, these pledges are unremarkable. They are no more than what one would expect from a precocious and ambitious youth intent on self-improvement. What's more interesting is the short paragraph that prefaces them. In it, Franklin notes that "those who write of the art of poetry teach us that if we would write what may be worth the reading, we ought always, before we begin, to form a regular plan and design of our piece; otherwise, we shall be in danger of incongruity." He goes on to reflect that the same may be said of life. His own brief existence, suffering from a want of "regular design," hitherto has merely been "a confused variety of different scenes." But now, with his four resolutions, he settles on a "scheme of action" he hopes will make his life worth the reading.[2]

These reflections, as opposed to Franklin's rather run-of-the-mill resolutions, are somewhat startling, coming as they do from a young man who up to that point appeared to have been unbothered by the lack of regular design in his life—indeed, seemed to have relished it. As we have seen, Franklin liked the fast-paced, cosmopolitan air of London. He sought out the company of quick-witted and sharp-tongued men of letters, frequented coffee houses, attempted (unsuccessfully) at least one seduction, consoled himself with "some foolish Intrigues with low Women," ran up debt, and in the process acquired a bit of a reputation as the freethinking author whose *Dissertation* at least implicitly condoned license by arguing that anything humans do is right.[3]

But exciting as this life was, Franklin in time began to feel he was adrift. Pangs of conscience about his own behavior, coupled with a gradual disgust with the unpredictable and unseemly behavior of many erstwhile companions such as James Ralph and Governor Keith, prompted a reaction—or, as Fowler would say, a transition to stage 5 religiosity. He felt the need for principles by which to regulate his own behavior, ones that would infuse an element of purpose and direction in his life. The Plan of Conduct articulated four such principles and, at least in Franklin's mind, they were effective. As he recalled years later, he "pretty faithfully adhered to [them] quite thro' to old Age."[4]

In drawing up his Plan of Conduct, Franklin was renewing the marked interest he had shown as a boy in moral issues and self-improvement. Raised as he was in a pious household, he could hardly have helped imbibing the Calvinist emphasis on soul-searching, discipline, and sacrifice. Moreover, as we saw in chapter 1, he devoured the works of John Bunyan as well as numerous "Books in polemic Divinity" that comprised the bulk of his father's library, all of which stressed the importance of good works in the life of a regenerated Christian. Two books in particular so impressed him that he went out of his way to mention them in the *Autobiography:* Daniel Defoe's *An Essay upon Projects* (1697) and Cotton Mather's *Bonifacius: An Essay upon the Good* (1710).[5]

Defoe's book is a celebration of progress, brimming with early Enlightenment optimism. In late seventeenth-century idiom, a "project" was a scheme of improvement, invention, or good work. Defoe primes his readers at the beginning of his treatise by asserting that "past ages have never come up to the degree of projecting and inventing . . . as we see this age arriv'd to," and he then proceeds to defend a number of projects he thinks are in society's best interest.[6] For example, he advocates the establishment of fire and insurance companies as well as old-age pensions; lobbies for a national academy for women, a national military academy, and a national academy for regulating the English language; and argues for reformation of the banking system and the bankruptcy laws (this last project must have been especially close to the heart of the perennially impecunious Defoe). Throughout the book, which was the first he published under his own name, Defoe was more interested in practical suggestions than theoretical analysis. His goal was reformation, not speculation about political economy, and he accordingly highlighted the nuts and bolts of social cooperation, which he saw as the key to success in the promotion of good works.

Mather's *Bonifacius* (or, as it is more commonly called, *Essays to Do Good*) is likewise more concerned with promoting good works than with theorizing about them. Mather calculates at the beginning of his book that upward of seven million people now inhabit the earth, and then, in an exuberant display of the zeal that punctuates all his writings, concludes that there is an "ample field among all these, to *do good* upon!"[7] Three goods in particular are especially needed: the good of Christianity, the good of correcting evils wrought by humans and the good of succoring those in misery. Mather, ever orthodox, does not wish to substitute good works for the Calvinist scheme of salvation by grace, but he does go so far as to concede that "to be *saved* without *good works,* were to be *saved* without *salvation.*"[8]

In order to achieve his three desiderata, Mather, like Defoe before him, recommends cooperation (or what Mather calls "Good Neighborhood") as the prime mover. He urges the creation of voluntary philanthropic societies devoted to local work in the family, the church, and the community. Moreover, Mather warns against the sin of pride masquerading as benevolence. The person who genuinely desires to do good does not wait in idleness for a grand opportunity. Instead, he or she perseveres in daily work, anonymously and selflessly, to improve the lot of immediate neighbors. "One great way to prove ourselves *really good,* is to be *relatively good.*"[9]

Two features of Mather's book especially reflected its author's Calvinist background. First, Mather insisted that any attempt to help one's fellows had to begin with an internal examination and evaluation of one's own weaknesses. This was in keeping with the traditional Calvinist emphasis on self-examination, but Mather's call for a scrutiny of "heart and life" extended beyond the strictly Puritan project of ascertaining whether or not one belonged to the elect. It also served, from a normative perspective, to put one's life in order so that one could do good for others.

Second, again in typical Calvinist fashion, Mather emphasized that depraved human nature would lead men and women to scorn the efforts of well-meaning reformers to do good. The pride and selfishness that contaminate even the best of persons, our inheritance from Adam, are likely to prompt derisive jeers whenever instances of genuine sacrifice and selflessness are encountered. As Mather rather acidly warns, "*Essays to do good* shall be derided, with all the *art* and *wit,* that [Satan] can inspire in his *Janizaries.* . . . Exquisite *profaneness* and *buffoonery* shall try their skill to laugh people out of them. The men who abound in them shall be exposed on the *stage; libels,* and *lampoons,* and *satires,* the most poignant that ever were invented, shall be darted at them; and *pamphlets* full of lying stories, be scattered, with a design to make them *ridiculous.* Hic se aperit Diabolus!"[10]

Franklin's reading of Defoe and Mather—the latter of whom, he tells us, "perhaps gave me a Turn of Thinking that had an Influence on some of the principal future Events of my Life"—colored his ruminations about the nature of morality.[11] He was so taken with what they had to say that, except for the brief lapse of the *Dissertation,* their ideas served as reference points for his own moralizing for the rest of his life. Both men, for example, taught him the value of cooperative societies. Similarly, both impressed upon him the realization that an orderly existence was a necessary condition for improving either oneself or others. Defoe's enthusiasm for the possibility of unlimited projects nicely dovetailed with the Enlightenment optimism Franklin picked up from his adolescent reading of the deists, while Mather reinforced his belief that self-inquiry is necessary if a person seeks to do good. But Mather also pushed home the Calvinist conviction that humans are inherently corrupt and consequently resistant to doing good. Even after they "*have done all,*" Mather warned, doers of good are still "*unprofitable servants*" who have "exceedingly falled short of [their] *duty.*"[12]

Once again, as will become clear in this chapter, Franklin was caught in a worldview clash that led to a good deal of ambivalence in his thought, this time about the nature of morality. As an Enlightenment figure, he spent a lifetime refining his Plan of Conduct, honing the habit of virtue down to what he optimistically considered a science, or calculus, of morality. Moreover, beginning with the Junto, he devoted over half a century to the careful nurturing of cooperative societies for the betterment of society. But as the son of a piously dissenting household, he never completely shed the Calvinist penchant for continuous self-examination, nor a pessimism about human nature bred from the deep-seated but usually unarticulated conviction that humans are essentially depraved. As with his more explicitly religious reflections, his head told him one thing, his heart another, and these mixed signals frequently resulted in a certain degree of dissonance.

In examining Franklin's writings on morality, then, we see a parallel to his straightforwardly religious reflections. Both are deeply ambivalent, trying as they do to marry disparate elements from two different traditions, and Franklin attempts to ameliorate the tension in each with his doctrine of theistic perspectivism. Doctrinal and theological fictions supply symbols that infuse life with meaning and purpose. Moral ones provide normative and social regulation by sanctioning the otherwise indefensible belief that humans are potentially perfectible, rather than inescapably corrupt, creatures. These two sets of useful fictions, religious and ethical, intersect in the doctrine that heaven is the ultimate reward of the righteous and hell the inevitable punishment of the wicked.

When one hears Franklin's name today, one tends to think, along with D. H. Lawrence, of the supreme optimist, the prophet of progress, prosperity, and human perfectibility. The *Autobiography,* Franklin's testament to the world, the way he wished to be remembered, certainly supports this popular perception. It is the prototypical rags-to-riches account of how an ambitious lad pulls himself from obscurity by sheer force of will and industry. Implicit in his recollections is the Enlightenment assurance that human beings are perfectible over time, learning from past mistakes and constantly endeavoring to improve themselves. What could be a more optimistic reading of human potential than this?[13]

It is true that at times Franklin endorses the eighteenth-century notion that humans are good (or at least normatively neutral) by nature, and that as science progresses and wealth increases, humans will become better and better. But there is a dark side to all this that too often has been ignored, a pessimistic vision of human nature and the possibility of doing good that dramatically conflicts with the Enlightenment optimism Franklin presented to the public.[14] Franklin had little doubt that progress in the sciences would continue at an amazing rate, and on at least one occasion he lamented that he could not live to see all its achievements.[15] But he was much more skeptical about a parallel advance in morality. As he wrote to Joseph Priestley in 1780, "it is impossible to imagine the height to which may be carried, in a thousand years, the Power of Man over Matter." But he more pessimistically added, "O that moral Science were in as fair a way of Improvement, that Men would cease to be Wolves to one another, and that human Beings would at length learn what they now improperly call Humanity!"[16]

Franklin frequently expressed his doubts about the moral fiber of humankind. His pessimism stemmed from two basic beliefs: the depravity of human nature and the depravity of reason. In the Calvinist scheme of salvation that Franklin was brought up on, both of these characteristics were attributed to original sin. Franklin came to reject the doctrinal explanation, even though the conclusions lodged themselves in his mind. Original sin, he tells us in one of his more angry essays, is a "Notion invented, a Bugbear set up by Priests . . . to fright and scare an unthinking Populace out of their Senses, and inspire them with Terror, to answer the little selfish Ends of the Inventors and Progagators." He goes on to argue that the very idea of original sin is "ridiculous," because "to suppose a Man liable to Punishment upon account of the Guilt of another, is unreasonable; and actually to punish him for it, is unjust and cruel."[17]

This is Franklin the deist speaking, founding his rejection of original sin on the grounds that it both violates reason and oppresses humankind. One expects him to conclude by declaring that the human spirit is not weighed down by any inherent corruption, as manipulative "Priests" would have us believe. But in fact he does not. Instead, he tersely remarks that "Moral Guilt is so personal a Thing" that it cannot be transferred from one generation to the next. "So *personal* a Thing": this is a chilling observation, implying that moral guilt is embedded deeply within each of us. There is something broken in humans that nudges them toward wickedness, but the explanation does not lie in the Bible or Calvin's *Institutes.* It is to be found in the types of creatures we are.

In order to account nontheologically for the fallen nature of humans, Franklin adopts a psychology reminiscent of the model Hobbes employed to describe human behavior in his hypothetical State of Nature. In fact, in a letter to James Logan, Franklin actually says that Hobbes is probably "nearer the Truth" in claiming that humans are naturally vicious than the contrary Lockean position, which views "the State of Nature [as] a State of Love."[18] Humans are intrinsically avaricious and driven by self-interest; there is a "Badness" in their material.[19] They are lazy and prone to a "life of ease" and "freedom from care and labour."[20] When they do muster the energy to act, they do so out of egoism: "Almost every Man has a strong natural Desire of being valu'd and esteem'd by the rest of his Species; but I am concern'd and griev'd to see how few fall into the Right and only infallible Method of becoming so."

Even men in public affairs act with a view to their own good, rather than to the good of their country; fewer still act "with a View to the Good of Mankind."[21] They have not learned that if they "were as industrious to become Good, as to make [themselves] Great, [they] should become really Great by being Good."[22] They are, Franklin says elsewhere, hypocrites, fools, dunces, and blockheads who prefer to remain precisely that.[23] Their avarice is "infinite," and "Half the Lives" a physician might save in fact "are not worth saving, as being useless; and almost the other Half ought not to be sav'd, as being mischievous."[24]

Moreover even those persons (if they can be found) who are neither worthless nor mischievous are crippled by passions that inevitably lead them astray.

The most pernicious of these passions—and the most difficult to subdue—is pride or self-love. "Disguise it, struggle with it, beat it down, stifle it, mortify it as much as one pleases, it is still alive, and will every now and then peep out and show itself."[25] Given this dismal take on what it means to be human, it is not surprising that Franklin viewed the race as more an object of disgust than one of admiration. As he wrote in 1782 to his old friend Priestley, nonconscious, physical phenomena are much worthier of the natural philosopher's attention:

> I should rejoice much, if I could once more recover the Leisure to search with you into the Works of Nature; I mean the *inanimate*, not the *animate* or moral part of them; the more I discover'd of the former, the more I admir'd them; the more I know of the latter, the more I am disgusted with them. Men I find to be a Sort of Beings very badly constructed, as they are generally more easily provok'd than reconcil'd, more disposed to do Mischief to each other than to make Reparation, much more easily deceiv'd than undeceiv'd, and having more Pride and even Pleasure in killing than in begetting one another.

Franklin concludes that the zeal with which humans kill one another would be lamentable "if the Species were really worth producing or preserving." But, he adds, "of this I doubt."[26]

It is not simply human nature that is corrupted. Reason likewise is fallen, at least when it is directed toward normative rather than scientific inquiry. In the latter arena, Franklin is as enthusiastic about the stretch of human reason as any other Enlightenment thinker. But when it comes to moral analysis, he fears that reason most often twists itself into self-serving rationalization.[27] Two well-known examples, both found in the *Autobiography,* illustrate this point.

When Franklin was around sixteen years old and still serving as apprentice to his brother James, he discovered a book by Thomas Tryon "recommending a Vegetable Diet." Franklin was immediately convinced (although one suspects his conversion was prompted as much by an adolescent desire to be different as by intellectual assent) and undertook to eliminate meat from his diet. He coaxed his brother into paying him half the money that otherwise would have been spent on his weekly board, and thereafter he prepared his own meals. Franklin boasts that this new arrangement not only provided him with more cash to buy books and leisure to read them; it also gave him "that greater Clearness of Head and quicker Apprehension which usually attend Temperance in Eating and Drinking."[28]

Franklin gives every indication that his youthful resolve to abstain from flesh was fervent. But some twenty pages later in his memoirs, he also tells us that he abandoned vegetarianism with hardly a second thought. On his first voyage from Boston, while becalmed off Block Island, Franklin's fellow passengers set themselves to catching cod. Franklin, the loyal disciple of Tryon, initially scorned the activity, condemning "the taking [of] every Fish as a kind of unprovok'd Murder, since none of them had or ever could do us any Injury that might justify the Slaughter." He remarks that this argument struck him as "very reasonable." But as he smelled the delectable aroma of the frying cod, Franklin, "formerly . . . a great Lover of Fish," found himself precariously balanced "between Principle and Inclination" until the following happy insight occurred to him: "when the Fish were opened, I saw smaller Fish taken out of their Stomachs: Then thought I, if you eat one another, I don't see why we mayn't eat you. So I din'd upon Cod very heartily." The moral of the story? "So convenient a thing it is to be a *reasonable Creature,* since it enables one to find or make a Reason for every thing one has a mind to do."[29]

As usually read (and, no doubt, as Franklin intended it to be read), this story comes across as a fable that offers up a saucy, worldly-wise maxim, the sort of thing that could have come straight out of *Poor Richard.* Moreover, it also paints Franklin as a lovable, avuncular storyteller, gracious and honest enough to tell an occasional joke against himself. But there is a much darker side to the fable's light appearance. It illustrates Franklin's conviction that reason is quite often misused in order to accommodate principle to self-serving inclination. Most of us rationalize, as in this case, when there may not be a great deal riding on our behavior, and we tend to downplay our falls, laughing them off in the way Franklin does here. But the deeper message is nonetheless clear: we are driven by avarice, greed, and gluttony, and we marshal all the skills of our much-lauded reason to whitewash motives.

The second illustration of Franklin's low esteem of moral reasoning is just as famous as the first. In the midst of telling the reader how difficult it was for him to cultivate the virtues of method and order, Franklin confesses that he "made so little Progress in Amendment, and had such frequent Relapses, that [he] was almost ready to give up the Attempt." Then he offers the following little story as an instructive analogy:

> Like the Man who in buying an Ax of a Smith my Neighbour, desired to have the whole of its Surface as bright as the Edge; the Smith consented to grind it bright for him if he would turn the Wheel. He turn'd while the Smith press'd the broad Face of the Ax hard and heavily on the Stone, which made the Turning of it very fatiguing. The Man came every now and then from the Wheel to see how the Work went on; and at length would take his Ax as it was without farther Grinding. No, says the Smith, Turn on, turn on; we shall have it bright by and by; as yet 'tis only speckled. Yes, says the Man; but—*I think I like a speckled Ax best.*[30]

This story, so much like one of Abraham Lincoln's "wheezes" in its dry humor and homespun grace, is normally read as a quaint warning about the sheer hard work it takes to achieve what we desire, and how tempting it is to settle for something less. And indeed that is the most obvious point of the story. But Franklin's message is deeper and grimmer than just that. Once again he is pointing out that inclination frequently vetoes principle, that "something that pretend[s] to be Reason" in fact may be nothing more than an eruption of laziness and self-will. We contrive rather than discover reasons for not following the course we know to be the best. As Franklin says elsewhere, we justify our lack of manners by telling ourselves that we wish to avoid foppery and affectation; that a perfect character is undesirable because it brings with it the envy and hatred of others; and that we should allow a few faults to remain in us in order to keep friends and acquaintances "in Countenance."[31] Of course all this is sheer hypocrisy. But such, Franklin thinks, is the nature of moral reason.

Given this bleak assessment of human nature, it is understandable that Franklin quickly regretted the amoralism he had defended in his *Dissertation* and he did his best to collect and destroy all copies of it. It is revealing that, in speaking of this great *erratum* years later, he remarked that the pamphlet's "doctrine, though it might be true, was not very useful."[32] This judgment certainly applies to Franklin's conviction that the abstract First Cause, although intellectually defensible, was unable to satisfy the natural inclination to devotion. But Franklin's concern also speaks to the fact that the *Dissertation*'s mechanistic view of reality, although perhaps true, was worse than useless as a check to the corrupt nature of humans. He became convinced, as he tells us, that "*Truth, Sincerity and Integrity* in Dealings between Man and Man" were essential, and that consequently his book was a little-needed corrosive.[33]

So in 1726 he took the plunge by scribbling the "Plan of Conduct" memorandum in his sea journal. Henceforth, he resolved, he would act *as if* corrupt human nature could be redeemed. Two years later, in his "Articles of Belief and Acts of Religion," he underscored this resolution by including moral reflections and injunctions as an integral part of his private devotions.[34] Finally, at about the same time he composed his "Articles," he "conceiv'd the bold and arduous Project of arriving at moral Perfection" by systematically training himself in the practice of virtue.[35] Although the system for "moral Perfection" he devised was originally for his own use, he never intended it to be merely a private strategy. He believed that a training course in virtue that worked for one person would work for all.

Franklin's basic idea is that humans cannot be *rationally* persuaded to pursue virtue. The pride that simmers in the heart of each individual, not to mention reason's convenient habit of contriving justifications for selfish inclinations, blocks that avenue. Instead, Franklin falls back on an Aristotelian recipe: train people to mimic virtuous behavior until what was once uncomfortable imitation eventually becomes ingrained habit.[36] In short, Franklin is aiming for the replacement of one set of habits—those that are exclusively self-serving—with another set of habits that are less corrupted. In doing so, he remains loyal to his earlier-cited endorsement of a Hobbesian psychology that maintains that people are basically driven by selfish desires and habits. We are easily habituated to vice, since it conforms with our corrupt inclinations. But "wrong Turns of the Mind when confirm'd by Time, are almost as little in our Power to cure, as those of the Body."[37] Moral failing is not so much a matter of "Ignorance of . . . Duty, as thro Inattention to [our] own faults, or thro strong Passions and bad Habits." It follows that "till that Inattention is cured . . . , *Advice* is rather resented as a Reproach."[38]

And what is the best way to cure the inattention that blinds the individual to both his duty and his particular shortcomings? Franklin here appeals to the traditional nostrum prescribed by his Calvinist forebears and discussed in Mather's *Essays to do Good:* introspection. In words that could have come straight out of Mather's book, Franklin insisted that "for the Acquirement of solid, uniform, steady Virtue, nothing contributes more, than a daily strict SELF-EXAMINATION."[39] He elected to examine his conscience on retiring for the night, and he recommended the same regimen to others. The self-examination was intended to evaluate the day's activities (not just once, but three times over); but just as important, it was a time set aside for questioning one's motives, those "*Thoughts and Intentions* which are the Original of . . . Actions."[40] In the absence of introspective scrutiny, Franklin feared, reason would cunningly contrive justifications for dubious behavior. But confronting one's intentions and motives in this headlong manner might provide insight into one's own character less easy to whitewash.

Still, self-examination, important as it is as a first step in the effort to habituate oneself to virtue, is a tricky business. The depravity of our moral faculties runs deep, and we are constantly in peril of deception—a deception that the baser self actually welcomes—when we attempt to clean the house of our conscience. Consequently, as an additional check to the passions and their wily inclinations, Franklin has this advice for the person who would cultivate virtue: "lest all this Diligence should be insufficient, as Partiality to himself will certainly render it, it is very requisite for him to *chuse* a FRIEND, or MONITOR, who must be allowed the greatest Freedom to advertise and remind him of his Failings, and to point out Remedies."[41]

For his own part Franklin, inspired partly by his youthful study of the Port Royal logic, chose a method rather than a person as his monitor. That method has been fulsomely described in the *Autobiography* and is probably the book's most famous and quoted section.[42] In brief, Franklin's monitor was a checklist of thirteen virtues, selected from the "various Enumerations of the moral Virtues [he] had met with in [his] Reading."[43] These were his targets, the habits he wished to cultivate in himself. He realized, acute student of human behavior that he was, the risk involved in going after all of them at once. Such a herculean task would almost inevitably prove impossible, thereby providing reason enough to forsake the cultivation of all of them. Instead, Franklin decided to "give a Week's strict Attention to each of the Virtues successively."[44] Each night during his self-examination period, he "confessed" his shortcomings to his checklist monitor by making a mark by the appropriate virtue for each time he had violated it during the course of the day.

> Proceeding thus to the last, I could go thro' a Course compleat in Thirteen Weeks, and four Courses in a Year. And like him who having a Garden to weed, does not attempt to eradicate all the bad Herbs at once, which would exceed his Reach and his Strength, but works on one of the Beds at a time, and having accomplish'd the first proceeds to a Second; so I should have (I hoped) the encouraging Pleasure of seeing on my Pages the Progress I made in Virtue, by clearing successively my Lines of their Spots, till in the End by a Number of Courses, I should be happy in viewing a clean Book after a Thirteen Weeks daily Examination.[45]

The garden analogy is particularly apt here. Cultivation of a garden is a task that gives clearcut, visible feedback. Gazing on the tract of land, one can clearly gauge success or failure. Similarly, the debit marks or pure blank spaces of Franklin's monitor provided him with a yardstick by which to measure his moral victories and setbacks. It provided him, in other words, with a mirror on his own behavior, thus serving the function that a flesh-and-blood monitor presumably would.

What Franklin found especially satisfying about his method for the habituation of virtues was its practicality. He had had a deep and abiding distrust of abstract reasoning in moral and metaphysical matters ever since his unhappy experience with the *Dissertation.* Moreover, in the worthy years since, both his own ruminations and his reading convinced him that rational discourse was of little if any use in dissuading people from following their innately corrupt inclinations. Learned arguments about why one should act virtuously only told people what they already knew but refused to follow. Like Saint Paul, they knew the better but pursued the worse. Consequently, convinced that "mere speculative Conviction that it was our Interest to be compleatly virtuous, was not sufficient to prevent our Slipping," Franklin sought a method that emphasized modification of concrete behavior rather than abstract rational appeals.[46] One *became* good by *doing* good: this was the only reliable way to deal with a human nature essentially egotistical and careless of the welfare of others. Henceforth this was Franklin's most steadfast normative intuition.[47]

If this point is overlooked, it is quite easy for critics like D. H. Lawrence to dismiss Franklin's scheme for moral improvement as merely a bookkeeper's uninspired calculus.[48] And, indeed, Franklin sometimes writes of it in terms that invite such responses. In a 1772 letter to Joseph Priestley, for example, he recommends what he calls a "*Moral* or *Prudential Algebra,*" a way of arriving at moral decisions by weighing the pros and cons of any contemplated course of action "with the Precision of Algebraic Quantities."[49] But Franklin resorts to such an apparently rigid method not because he has the soul of a shopkeeper, but because humans in his estimation have the souls of beasts and must be kept on short leashes lest they harm themselves. Taming a beast is a long and somewhat tedious chore. Rote learning is necessary in order to instill as habit what cannot be appreciated or acted upon as principle.

Nor was Franklin setting himself up as a paragon of virtue, somehow immune from the general corruption that characterizes human nature. When he took himself in hand in 1726 with his "Plan of Conduct," it was because he knew himself to be one of the barely tamed beasts, ready to break away from the straight and narrow at the slightest provocation. Even in old age he lamented that he had never been able to quite conquer his tendency to "disorderliness," Franklin's expression for lack of discipline. He tells us in his memoirs that "in truth I found myself incorrigible with respect to *Order;* and now I am grown old, and my Memory bad, I feel very sensibly the want of it."[50] One suspects that this is not a ploy on the old man's part to bask in admiring protests but an honest confession of failure. Franklin goes on to say, however, that even though he never succeeded to his satisfaction in habituating himself to the virtue of order, he is a "better and happier Man" for having tried.[51] Moral improvement is not measured in absolute terms. It is a matter of degrees. Any progress away from our natural egoism is a victory.

Franklin tells us that around 1732 he conceived the idea of sharing his method for moral improvement with the public by composing a little book he intended to call the *Art of Virtue.* (It's not difficult to see the influence of Defoe and Mather in this plan.) Although it remained a fond project for the rest of his life, he never actually got around to writing any of it except for the précis sketched out in the *Autobiography.* He excuses himself on the grounds that the demands first of private business and then public service denied him the leisure in which to compose.[52] But it could also be that Franklin, the inveterate experimenter, was never satisfied enough with the testing of his method to call an end to it.

In a letter to Lord Kames, he underscored the practicality of his contemplated *Art of Virtue.* Most people, he says, lead bad lives not because they do not know how to change but because they lack a method (or monitor). Virtue does not come naturally to humans. It is an art, and like all art demands an apprenticeship in which its skills are mastered through sheer hard work and application. Some persons, by virtue of their background and schooling, are better prepared than others to undertake the training, but all need it. The *Art of Virtue* was intended as their manual of instruction.[53]

Although Franklin admired and adopted many of deism's beliefs, particularly its endorsement of the Newtonian view of the physical universe, it is somewhat misleading to call him a deist. His thought was too fluid and too ambivalent to be locked into any single category. Probably nothing separates him more clearly from mainstream eighteenth-century deism than his disesteem of moral reason. Most of the American deists of his generation and afterward uncritically accepted reason as the failsafe foundation of not only natural philosophy but virtue as well.[54] Human reason, a reflection of the divine reason that set in motion the logical but providentially benevolent universe, was a reliable guide to the virtuous life. It erred only when hampered by the ignorance, fear, and superstition encouraged by church and state to subjugate people. Eliminate the "double despotism" of church and state, as the turn-of-the-century deist Elihu Palmer would put it, and reason will flourish, providing humans with adequate standards for personal and societal behavior.[55]

But Franklin didn't buy it. The deep distrust of human reason birthed by his boyhood Calvinism and probably reinforced by his acquaintance with works such as de Mandeville's *Fable of the Bees* and Hobbes's *Leviathan,* precluded his sharing the deists' rather naive trust in rationality as a sufficient foundation for virtue. He knew too much about the way humans behaved—about the ways *he* behaved—in the absence of normative checks and balances. Reason did not and could not serve in this capacity because reason, as David Hume later pointed out, is the slave of the passions and inclinations.[56]

Given Franklin's abiding skepticism about the likelihood that human reason can serve as a normative barometer, he also rejected the Enlightenment's Lockean presumption that humans, if just left alone by corrupting social institutions, will naturally cooperate with one another in ways that maximize everyone's best interest. Humans are selfish, egoistic creatures, motivated always by the desire to aggrandize their own positions. Any program for moral improvement that idealistically denies rather than faces and works with this deep-seated wolfishness is doomed from the start. Yet without some sort of normative regulation society is threatened and the possibility of individual well-being diminished.

The beauty of Franklin's art of virtue, so he thought, was that it addressed these rather ugly truths about human nature in a realistic way. Reason is incapable of leading persons to virtue. Well, then—what reason cannot do, rote habituation can. Humans are incapable of acting altruistically. Even if they were not, traditional moral injunctions to practice ascetic self-denial are beside the point: "Temperance, Justice, Charity, &c. Are Virtues, whether practis'd with or against our Inclinations."[57] In that case, an appeal must be made to their sense of self-interest. What is needed is a demonstration that virtue is a necessary condition for happiness, not an obstacle to it. The moral life doesn't call for sacrifice and self-renunciation but rather for cultivation of those qualities that make life really worth living.

For Franklin, enlightened self-interest and a behavioristic approach to the promotion of virtue provide incentive as well as method. But as a practical man who eschewed abstract moral speculation in favor of an appeal to the concrete, he also recognized that the incentive might not be strong enough for many, and perhaps most. "Enlightened self-interest" is a slippery category that can be rationalized in all sorts of ways, and where there is an opportunity there is a way for inclinations and passions to assert themselves. Consequently, Franklin realized that even stronger appeals, ones that played to human passions such as love, fear, and hope, were necessary. In short, the additional incentive of religious belief was usually necessary to induce persons to act virtuously.

In his "Articles of Belief," Franklin implicitly expressed his conviction that religious beliefs, although perspectival, are necessary conditions for promoting meaningful and purposeful lives. Now we see another function that religious useful fictions provide: they regulate human affairs by checking certain types of behavior and encouraging others.

Commentators on Franklin's scheme for the habituation of virtue often conclude that it is a completely secular plan, and that it goes out of its way to distance itself from religious belief. But in fact this is a misreading of Franklin's own description. True, Franklin did assert that he had "purposely avoided" tying his scheme to any particular religious tradition to ensure that it carried "no Mark of any of the distinguishing Tenets of any particular Sect." But this does not mean that he saw no role for religion in his scheme, for he goes on to remark that he wished it "might be serviceable to people in all Religions." He deliberately kept his description of it free of religious language not because he intended to separate it from religion, but rather because he wished to avoid "any thing in it that should prejudice any one of any Sect against it."[58] He presumed that whoever took his plan of conduct seriously would also have some set of religious beliefs as *additional* inducements to morality.

There is ample evidence to suggest that Franklin saw the promotion of virtue as one of religion's most useful functions. He tells us in his *Autobiography,* for example, that one of the reasons he forsook regular church attendance as a young man was because of the absence of edifying moralizing and an overabundance of abstruse theologizing in the typical Presbyterian sermon.[59] Religious instruction should provide enough theology to orient the worshipper in his or her world, but it should never become so ethereal that it neglects the equally important task of normative regulation.[60] Religious perspectives that tended to put good works at a low premium were frequently the butt of Franklin's scorn, as in this 1753 letter:

> I wish [Calvinism] were more productive of Good Works than I have generally seen it: I mean real good Works. Works of Kindness, Charity, Mercy, and Publick Spirit; not Holiday-keeping, Sermon-Reading or Hearing, performing Church Ceremonies, or making long Prayers, fill'd with Flatteries and Compliments, despis'd even by wise Men, and much less capable of pleasing the Deity. The Worship of God is a Duty, the hearing and reading of Sermons may be useful: but if Men rest in hearing and Praying, as too many do, it is as if a Tree should value itself on being water'd and putting forth Leaves, tho' it never produc'd any Fruit.

In short, God prefers "the Doers of the Word to the meer Hearers."[61] Religious perspectives are fictions, but those that use organized worship to encourage righteousness—production of "Fruit"—in the congregation are especially useful ones. "Without that effect," warns Franklin, "the Pre[acher or the] Priest, in my Opinion, is not merely sounding Brass or a tinkling Cymbal, which are innocent Things; he is rather like the Cunning man in the Old Baily, who conjures and tells Fools their Fortunes to cheat them out of their Money."[62]

These are telling criticisms of many conventional styles of worship in eighteenth-century America, but they by no means suggest that Franklin thought religion worthless. Bad as it may at times be, organized religion, of whatever sect, was necessary. That this is Franklin's position is clear from a 1786 letter to an unknown correspondent, referred to in the previous chapter. In it, Franklin comments on a manuscript sent to him for his consideration. The manuscript appears to have been a defense either of atheism or at least of a deism very much along the lines defended years earlier in the *Dissertation.* Franklin strongly urges the manuscript's author to "burn this Piece before it is seen by any other Person," partly because doing so will save the author "a great deal of Mortification" from critics, but also (and more significantly) because its destruction will forestall a great deal of harm.

> You yourself may find it easy to live a virtuous Life without the Assistance afforded by Religion; you having a clear Perception of the Advantages of Virtue and the Disadvantages of Vice, and possessing a Strength of Resolution sufficient to enable you to resist common Temptations. But think how great a Proportion of Mankind consists of weak and ignorant Men and Women, and of inexperienc'd and inconsiderate Youth of both Sexes, who have need of the Motives of Religion to restrain them from Vice, to support their Virtue, and retain them in the Practice of it till it becomes *habitual,* which is the great Point for its Security; And perhaps you are indebted to her originally[,] that is to your Religious Education, for the Habits of Virtue open which you now justly value yourself.

In short, concludes Franklin, "if Men are so wicked as we now see them *with Religion* what would they be if *without it?*"[63]

The doctrine of religious perspectivism, then, is crucial not only for infusing one's daily life with purposefulness, but also for holding in check the self-serving passions and inclinations that otherwise would render humans even more wolfish than they normally are. Lord Shaftesbury may or may not have spoken correctly when he wrote that "the Perfection and Height of VIRTUE must be owing to *the Belief of a GOD,*" but the sentiment, in Franklin's view, is an extremely useful fiction for regulating behavior.[64]

But how does it do so? By providing a supreme monitor of one's conduct. It will be recalled that Franklin had urged a monitor of some kind in his scheme for the habituation of virtue, one who could insist on honesty, gauge progress, and provide censure, praise, and encouragement. What better entity to fill this regulatory role than God? Mortal monitors are fallible and untrustworthy, but the Supreme Monitor is not. Moreover, God inflames our deepest passions, and hence provides inducements to virtue and disincentives to vice in an ultimately profound way. The thought of God restrains certain behavior by acting on our fear of divine displeasure and eternal damnation. Conversely, it encourages other behavior by acting on our love of doing that which is pleasing to God, and our hopes for eternal reward. In a word, religious belief does what reason or social sanctions cannot: it checks human passion until, as Franklin said to his unknown correspondent, controlled behavior becomes habitual.

Franklin, of course, knew that the religious beliefs that check our wolfish inclinations are but useful fictions, cultural artifacts that, at best, dimly reflect objective truth. Thus the only monitor available to him personally was the daily self-accounting on his checklist, not the great heavenly monitor feared and loved by the unsuspecting majority. He recognized that others (such as his unknown correspondent) might also be able to strain toward virtue without the supervision of the Monitor, but his dreary assessment of human nature convinced him that their numbers would always be small. Consequently, when writing to all but a select handful of individuals, and especially when writing for public consumption, Franklin typically recommended piety and devotion as habits particularly conducive to good works. For him, virtue was the highest form of worship; he shared at least this much with more conventional deists.

John Adams always dismissed Franklin as a theoretical rather than a practicing moralist.[65] But to insinuate that Franklin preached virtue without practicing it, or that his reflections on morality were speculative rather than practical, is dead wrong. Regardless of what personal foibles and shortcomings Franklin the person may have suffered from, he learned his lessons in morality early and well, and spent most of his life striving to do good in the civic mode of Mather and Defoe. His first concern when it came to morality was an immensely practical one: how to tame *homo lupus* enough to establish a modicum of individual happiness and social well-being. Given the course he set for himself with the great insight of 1728, it is not surprising that his answer rested in large part on his conviction that religious fictions can serve as useful normative regulators.

6 Sugar and Paper

BENJAMIN FRANKLIN loved France. Everything about it (or at least those parts of it in which he moved) suited him: its urbane worldliness, its musical and literary salons, its enlightened appreciation of natural philosophers. The French, he decided, were a "delightful people." Long afterward, when he was an old man, Franklin fondly remembered his years in France as some of the happiest of his life.[1]

And France loved Franklin. When he paid his first visit there in the early autumn of 1767 he was gratified to discover that he was a celebrity. Feted by both learned and courtly society, honored by no less a figure than Louis XV, Franklin was swept up in a whirlwind of acclaim. By his second visit two years later, the acclaim had become an adulation, which only intensified with time. In 1772 he was enthusiastically elected to the French Academy of Sciences; the next year saw the publication of his *Oeuvres,* the very first collection of his writings to appear. Franklin could not have failed to be struck by the fact that it was the French, not the English or Americans, who so honored him. When the Second Continental Congress appointed him a commissioner to the court of France in September 1776, his heart must have bounded. Philadelphia seemed insufferably drab and provincial when measured against glittering memories of Paris.

Franklin arrived in France in late December accompanied by two grandsons, sixteen-year-old William Temple Franklin and seven-year-old Benjamin Franklin Bache. He took up temporary quarters in Paris but by early spring had settled in Passy, a village about half a mile outside of the city. His digs were luxurious. They were part of the Hôtel Valentinois, the estate of Donatien Leray de Chaumont, an ardent and wealthy supporter of the American cause. The high living suited Franklin, who had always appreciated life's creature comforts. But his fellow commissioner, the more straitlaced Bostonian John Adams, expressed dismay and then disgust over what he considered his senior colleague's untoward love of French wine, food, and festivity.[2]

What particularly irked the prudish Adams was Franklin's easy relations with those members of the fairer sex—and there were many of them—who doted on the *philosophe distingué.* Franklin had always been something of a sensualist. Even though over half a century separated the elderly commissioner from the callow youth who in London had pursued intrigues with several "low" women, the fires of passion still smoldered and occasionally blazed.[3] The pervasive atmosphere of coquettishness and erotic innuendoes characteristic of French high society delighted Franklin. As he contentedly wrote to a niece in 1779, French ladies had a thousand ways of "making themselves agreeable."[4] He was soon flirting with an ardor all the more *charmant* because of his age and ungrammatical French.

One of the French ladies whom Franklin found especially intriguing was Madame Brillon de Jouy, née Anne-Louise d'Hardancourt. In her mid-thirties when Franklin met her in 1777, Madame Brillon was wife to a wealthy nobleman almost twenty-five years her senior and mother to a couple of young girls. She was also an extraordinary musical talent. An eighteenth-century critic described her as "one of the greatest lady-players on the harpsichord in Europe."[5] A student of Boccherini, she also composed music. Apparently content to amuse her circle of friends with marches and quadrilles, she never desired—or at least never sought—public recognition. She was also skilled with charcoal and watercolors.[6]

Franklin's friendship with Madame Brillon lasted until the end of his life, continuing by correspondence after he returned to America in 1785. What began as a flirtation in which Franklin, half-playfully, half-seriously, tried to seduce his young admirer, matured into a relationship of mutual esteem and affection in which Franklin acquiesced to the more mundane but less demanding role of *cher papa.*[7] By 1781, the erstwhile suitor had forsworn his own romantic hopes in order to push those of his grandson William Temple Franklin. He wanted the young man to marry Monsieur and Madame Brillon's daughter Cunegonde, and he had no qualms about playing on their sympathies to press his suit. "Having almost lost my own daughter because of the wide distance between us," he wrote Madame Brillon with heavy-handed pathos, "I hoped to find another one in you, and still another in your daughter, to take care of my old age."[8]

Franklin's strategy was clever, but it proved unsuccessful. Monsieur Brillon remained singularly unimpressed by the prospects of welcoming the rather dissolute William Temple into his family. But in order to spare the elderly Franklin's feelings, he fixed on the youth's Protestantism as an excuse for declining the offer: Cunegonde could not possibly marry outside the Catholic faith. Franklin wasn't willing to give up without one last effort. In April 1781 he drafted a letter to Madame Brillon , responding to her husband's objection to William Temple's suit. It contains one of his most revealing reflections on religion.

Franklin remarks that he himself is not bothered by the difference in the young couple's religious backgrounds because "in each Religion there are some essential things, & others which are only Forms & Fashions; As a piece of Sugar which can be wrapped up in brown or white or blue Paper, & tied with flaxen or wool string, red or yellow; it is always the Sugar which is the essential thing."[9]

This is as transparent an analogy as Franklin would ever pen to convey his fundamental insight, arrived at fifty years earlier, of theistic perspectivism. Most of the credos, scriptures, and doctrines associated with specific religious traditions are the products ("Forms & Fashions") of historical context and hence come and go as times and needs change. But carefully peel them away, layer by layer, and the true core (or "Sugar") of religious belief, a core shared to one degree or another by all traditions, is revealed. This is the essential thing. The rest is string and paper.

But what, more precisely, is this *chose essentielle*? The earlier Franklin, the Franklin of the *Dissertation,* would have replied that the only rock-bottom essential of religious belief is the stark postulation of a divine Prime Mover. As we have seen in earlier chapters, however, intellectual doubts as well as existential crises in his life gradually convinced him that this quasi-deistic approach was both emotionally unfulfilling and morally bankrupt. Humans needed a personal religion, not abstract metaphysics. They needed "gods," not just an aloof, impassable God. Hence what Franklin came to consider as the necessary conditions or "essentials" of religious belief included those perspectival doctrines that both steered individuals through life and encouraged social stability. Moreover, as we saw in chapter 4, Franklin himself so felt the need for these beliefs that he tended at times to forget his conviction that they were perspectival. By 1781, he had no reservations about enumerating for Madame Brillon five characteristics of essential religion:

> 1st. That there is a God who made the World, & who Governs it by his Providence.
>
> 2nd. That he should be adored, & served[.]
>
> 3rd. That the best service to God is doing good to men.
>
> 4th. That the human soul is immortal &
>
> 5th. That in a future Life if not in the present one, vice will be punished, & Virtue rewarded.[10]

Franklin concludes that "these Essentials one finds in your Religion & in ours," and repeats that "the Differences are but Paper & String."[11]

Two related points follow from Franklin's division of religious belief into sugar and paper. The first is that there is great room for divergence from one sect to the next, and hence a correspondingly great need for mutual toleration. The championing of religious toleration is one of Franklin's intellectual and ethical mainstays, and it is a direct consequence of his perspectival conviction that most religions have the same basic intuitions about God, even if they express them in a multiplicity of idioms.[12] This does not mean, as we will shortly discover, that Franklin judged all sectarian beliefs to be equally acceptable, but only that mere doctrinal disagreement was no warrant for rejection, much less persecution, of dissenting opinions. The tragedy of religion in general and Christianity in particular, Franklin thought, was that "every sect believing itself possessed of *all truth,* and that every tenet differing from theirs was *error,* conceived that when the power was in their hands, persecution was a duty required of them by that God whom they supposed to be offended with heresy."[13]

Second, the fact that the sugar of essential religion is always wrapped in the paper and twine of fashion served, in Franklin's estimation, as a caution against the perils of religious smugness and pride. The paper is often wrapped so tightly around the sugar that the two become well-nigh indistinguishable; the paper's tint bleeds into the sugar, the sugar's sweetness is absorbed by the paper. Consequently, just as the wise religionist ought not take offense at the differences in sectarian idioms, so she ought also to acknowledge that she may be guilty of confusing paper and sugar in her own set of "essential" religious beliefs. This points to the need to recognize one's own convictions as provisional and always open to modification—not because one's faith in them is lukewarm but because one is all too aware, given the immense human capacity for self-deception, rationalization, or simple honest confusion, of the ever-present possibility of error.

Franklin explicitly sounds this theme as early as 1738 in response to a letter from his parents in which they expressed concern that he had "imbib'd some erroneous [religious] Opinions." He grants that "God only knows whether all the Doctrines I hold for true, be so or not." For his part, he suspects that some in fact are not: like everyone else, he is a "weak, ignorant Creature," prone to mistakes in reasoning and liable to be led astray by bad books and arguments. Thus it would be "great Vanity," he concedes, to assume that he has been lucky enough to select only true opinions from the enormous range of available ones. "No," he writes, "I am doubtless in Error as well as my Neighbours, and methinks a man can not say, *All the Doctrines that I believe, are true; and all that I reject, are false,* without arrogantly claiming to himself that Infallibility which he denies to the Pope."[14]

Up to this point in his letter, Franklin appears to be bowing to his parents' disapproval of his heterodox religious beliefs. But the conclusion he proceeds to draw from his admission of fallibility shows not only that he is not at all apologetic about his position, but also that he is gently chastising Abiah and Josiah for their uncritical assumption that the "piously dissenting" way is the only one pleasing to God. "From such Considerations as these it follows, that I ought never to be angry with any one for differing in Judgment from me. For how know I but the Point in dispute between us, is one of those Errors that I have embrac'd as Truth. If I am in the Wrong, I should not be displeas'd that another is in the right. If I am in the Right, 'tis my Happiness and I should rather pity than blame him who is unfortunately in the Wrong."[15]

Franklin probably intended this letter's discussion of human fallibility to deflect his parents' concern that he had fallen from grace. But regardless of his immediate motive, it is undoubtable that his caution against religious smugness is sincere. Similar sentiments crop up throughout his writings.[16] Like all his condemnations of sectarian intolerance, they are natural consequences of the great insight of theistic perspectivism he arrived at in 1728.

It is against this backdrop that Franklin's lifelong aversion to religious enthusiasm needs to be viewed. True, his youthful reading of authors such as Addison, Locke, and Shaftesbury had predisposed him to look on zealotry as an affront to the dispassionate dictates of reason. But after the ardor of his ten-year affair with rational religion cooled, Franklin's nascent Calvinism reasserted its ancient accusation that reason, moral as well as intellectual, was irremediably suspect. Consequently, Franklin's subsequent condemnation of enthusiasm had to rest on some other foundation than the typical Enlightenment charge that it violated reason. That foundation was his perspectival conviction that it was necessary to separate the sugar from the paper in religious beliefs, and that this in turn entailed toleration of dissenting positions as well as humility in arriving at one's own. Enthusiasts violated both of these principles. They cocooned themselves within "imaginary Satisfactions and Pleasures" and refused to countenance any alternative doctrine that might disrupt their own contrived contentment.[17] Such intransigence inevitably led to recrimination and hatred, thereby gravely damaging the reputation of religion. "Indeed when religious People quarrel about Religion, or hungry People about their Victuals, it looks as if they had not much of either among them."[18]

It will be recalled that in his developmental account of faith James Fowler characterizes the fifth, "conjunctive," stage as one in which the believer sheds his earlier dogmatism and comes to accept the inevitability of alternative religious opinions. Far from trying to eliminate these alternatives, he now adopts an attitude of live-and-let-live when it comes to God-belief, recognizing that religious traditions are colored by place and time and hence necessarily speak different dialects. Just as he grows in his willingness to tolerate dissenting perspectives, so he likewise learns to maintain an "ironic" attitude toward his own faith tradition. Committed to it as he is, he also acknowledges that it, no more than any other religious perspective, is the final word when it comes to the pursuit of God. Sectarian truths are always relative to the Absolute that is their target. Consequently, they are always and everywhere provisional.[19]

It is this fifth stage of religious development that Franklin entered into around the time he drafted his "Articles of Belief and Acts of Religion." After successive periods of religious naivete, anger, dogmatism, and confusion, his doctrine of theistic perspectivism finally reconciled him to the ambivalence in his personal beliefs and the ambiguity inherent in religious aspirations in general. It is this realization that grounded his subsequent advocacy of freedom of conscience.

What might have sparked the worried 1738 letter from Josiah and Abiah about their son's infidelity? We will never know. Perhaps it was no specific event. Perhaps their worries had accumulated over the years, beginning as early as Benjamin's youthful reluctance to attend church, until the two finally felt duty-bound to voice them. It is unlikely that Josiah and Abiah knew of their son's freethinking *Dissertation.* That, at least, they were spared. But they could hardly have been insulated from the unabashedly public and suspiciously heterodox cry for freedom of conscience Benjamin sounded in the notorious Hemphill affair of 1735. When word reached them about their son's furious battle with Philadelphia's Presbyterian establishment, the piously dissenting couple must have recoiled in horror. Truth to tell, the blatant way in which he strutted his religious dissension probably alarmed Franklin a little as well, even if only afterward, when passions on either side had cooled. At any rate, he never again attacked either traditional Calvinism or the clergy quite so openly.

The Hemphill scandal is well known.[20] In 1734, a young Presbyterian minister named Samuel Hemphill arrived in Philadelphia from Ireland and presented his credentials to the local synod. He had been called as a much-needed assistant to the Reverend Jedediah Andrews, probably the most influential Presbyterian clergyman in the Philadelphia Synod.[21] Andrews was a no-nonsense New Englander who took his Calvinism seriously. (He was also one of those Harvard men mercilessly lampooned by Silence Dogood.) He proselytized zealously, appearing to go out of his way to antagonize his Anglican competition, and his sermons never veered from the straight and narrow of the Westminster Confession.[22]

Although Andrews was a star in the Presbyterian firmament, Franklin had little use for him. In the late 1720s and early 1730s Franklin largely stayed away from conventional church services, resorting instead to the liturgy he had written for himself in his "Articles of Belief and Acts of Religion." But it would have been awkward for an up-and-coming man of business to dissociate himself completely from the religious establishment. So Franklin, a cradle Presbyterian, willingly "paid [his] annual Subscription for the Support of the only Presbyterian Minister or Meeting . . . in Philadelphia." Understandably, Andrews was uncomfortable with one of his flock trying to buy a way out of active worship, and he frequently visited Franklin to "admonish" him for his failure to attend services. Franklin appears finally to have made a good-faith effort to comply, actually interrupting his private studies to go to church for five consecutive Sundays. But a month of Andrews's orthodoxy was all Franklin could stomach. He dismisses the sermons as "chiefly either polemic Arguments, or Explications of the peculiar Doctrines of our Sect, and were all to me very dry, uninteresting and unedifying." They inculcated no moral principles, Franklin complained, "their Aim seeming to be rather to make us Presbyterians than good Citizens." That Andrews sought to make his congregants good Presbyterians seems a reasonable goal for a Presbyterian minister, but Franklin grew "disgusted, and attended his Preaching no more." He returned to his private devotions, convinced that Presbyterianism—or at least Andrews's version of it—was beyond reform.[23]

The arrival of young Reverend Hemphill revived Franklin's interest in attending church. Hemphill had a "good Voice" and spoke extemporaneously with a cadence and intensity all the more welcome after years of Andrews's sermons. Franklin tells us that Hemphill's "most excellent discourses . . . drew together considerable Numbers of different Persuasions, who join'd in admiring them." He himself, delighted that Hemphill's sermons "inculcated strongly the Practice of Virtue" while avoiding theological complexities, became one of the new minister's "constant Hearers."[24]

The situation quickly, and predictably, exploded. Andrews had brought in Hemphill to assist, not upstage, him. Scarcely six months passed before a ruffled Andrews pressed formal charges against the younger man, asserting that he preached sermons that, among other things, claimed that Christianity was just a "new Edition" of natural philosophy, chastised the church for representing God "as stern and inexorable, and fit only for Tyrants to impose and Slaves to obey," denied the doctrines of original sin and atonement, and on at least one occasion "appeared to me and others as designing to open the Door of the Church wide enough to admit all honest Heathens." This final transgression especially exercised Andrews since it seemed to raise up "freethinkers, Deists, [and] nothings" to the level of loyal Christians.[25] Briefs were prepared and witnesses rounded up. The trial opened in mid-April 1735 and dragged out through the entire summer. By September it was all over, with the synod finding Hemphill guilty of heterodoxy and unworthy to preach.

Andrews's accusations as well as the subsequent synodical verdict galvanized Franklin into action. It is clear from the stridency of his words that the issue wasn't just an intellectual one for him. Franklin's personal dislike of Andrews, coupled with a long-standing disdain of Presbyterian doctrine, infused his perspectival aversion to sectarian dogmatism with a passion that delighted liberal and infuriated conservative religionists. Just as earlier his response to Wollaston's defense of liberal Christianity was in effect an attack on all religious belief, so now his rush to Hemphill's aid was a broader assault on religious intolerance in general.

Between the beginning of April and the end of October Franklin wrote and published no fewer than four public defenses of Hemphill.[26] The first piece appeared even before the synodical trial began; the final one continued the fray a month after the verdict was handed down. Ultimately they did Hemphill no good.[27] But the pieces were a welcome emotional release for Franklin: in them he vented his contempt for Andrews, his rage at religious intolerance, and his scorn for arcane theological subtleties. He also gave public expression for the first time, albeit in an indirect way, to his theistic perspectivism.

Certainly the most striking theme in Franklin's published defenses of Hemphill is their unrelenting attack on the clergy. All the resentment the young Franklin had once directed toward the Boston clerical establishment is now unleashed, magnified many times over, at the members of the Philadelphia Synod. He calls them "*Rev. Asses,*" guilty of "Enthusiastick Cant" and "contemptible Stupidity."[28] They are "grave and dull Animals" who, constitutionally incapable of rational thought, habitually resort to "Passages of the sacred Scriptures to prove... their Opinion."[29] Possessed by a "Spirit of Persecution," these "Reverend Gentlemen" arrogantly presume that in condemning all religious opinions that differ from theirs they are maintaining doctrinal purity. But in fact their actions are profoundly contrary to the original spirit of the faith. Franklin reminds them that "in the two or three first Centuries of Christianity, those acquainted with the History of those Times, tell us, they can find no Signs, no Footsteps of such Confessions of Faith, or Tests of Orthodoxy." The persecution of Hemphill is no more justifiable than the "hellish Tribunal of the *Inquisition.*"[30]

The Reverend Asses thus come across as the villains in Franklin's version of the Hemphill melodrama. Their primary fault is arrogance. Anticipating the theme he would sound in the 1738 letter to his parents, Franklin wrote that "Infinite Wisdom" had not chosen either to reveal its secrets to humankind or to appoint any "infallible Interpreters" of itself. Consequently, any "Pretence to Infallibility is absurd."[31] All personal interpretations of ultimate religious truth are worth considering, and certainly ought to be beyond the reach of inquisitorial persecution. "I do assert," Franklin wrote, "our own spiritual Liberty."[32]

This declaration was as autobiographical as philosophical. Franklin had written his own private liturgy in 1728 because he found himself unable in all good conscience to assent to the idioms, metaphors, and doctrines of either orthodox Christianity or deistic rational religion. Then, he had invited the gods to come forth in his own spiritual life. Now he defended the right of others to do likewise. "No Man ought to resign his Liberty" in religious matters, he thundered. "Let him make Choice of his Minister as his Judgment and Conscience direct him."[33] Some may prefer a conservative such as Andrews, others a liberal like Hemphill, others still no minister save their own good sense and intuition. But each must find his or her own path to the essentially unknowable.

The obvious objection to this radical defense of freedom of conscience, Franklin acknowledges, is that it threatens to shatter the "Unity of the Church" into a thousand creeds and sects, thereby leaving "little or no Hopes of a Coalition or Re-Union of the Christian Sects into one Body." The proverb "As many Men as Many Minds" is already woefully descriptive of religious sensibilities. If the authority of institutional creeds and traditional doctrines is further subverted, what is to prevent spiritual liberty from reducing the already fragile church to spiritual anarchy?[34] And if spiritual anarchy becomes the order of the day, can social and political anarchy be far behind?

It is noteworthy that Franklin reflected on these possibilities as early as his defense of Hemphill. As we saw in preceding chapters, he became more concerned as the years passed that the dark, broken side of human nature would lose what minimal restraints the church placed on it were popular religiosity to lose its authority.[35] The ambiguity of his own religious convictions asserted itself, then, even as early as the Hemphill affair. On the one hand, he accepted the enlightened ideal of religious liberty as a given. All persons should have the freedom, as he did, to discover that religious perspective best able to enhance the meaning and value of their lives. But many people, on the other hand, are simply not ready for such autonomy. Their lives revolve around the credal traditions into which they were born, and to cast doubt upon them is to create a psychological and spiritual vacuum in which, as Yeats later warned, "things fall apart; the centre cannot hold."[36] How to reconcile the two?

Franklin offered two solutions in his writings on the Hemphill case. Neither completely resolved the tension between the spiritual imperative of religious autonomy and the social imperative of moral order, but both are predictable consequences of Franklin's theistic perspectivism. Moreover, he would invoke both throughout the rest of his life as justifications for religious toleration.

In the first place, Franklin argued that there is no "Unity of the Church" to be protected. The hysterical charge on the part of Reverend Andrews and the synodical judges that Hemphill's preaching represented a danger to the integrity of the Christian faith was in fact a straw man because the "Church Universal" is a chimera. In Philadelphia alone, wrote Franklin, "we have half a Dozen, for aught I know half a Score, different Sects." Moreover, there is dissent within each one of the sects; it is rare to discover a believer who does not disagree with at least some of his denomination's doctrines. "Many a Man who in Appearance is of this or that Profession, entertains many Notions quite opposite to it, or to the Notions of others of the same Denomination." Consequently, "Creeds or Confessions" may give rise to an "external Show" of "Unanimity in religious Sentiments," but do not thereby reflect any substantive agreement. Since there is no Church Universal to worry about, then, there can be no harm in encouraging believers to declare "their Minds or Opinions to one another in publick and private."[37]

In the second place, frank exchanges of religious differences may in fact lead to a more profound appreciation of what is essential and inessential in religious matters, thereby helping all believers better distinguish paper from sugar. In Christianity, for example, there can be no doubt that the sugar is the supreme commandment upon which hangs "all the law and the prophets"

(Matthew 22:37): love of God and one's fellows.[38] To honor the God who created and governs the world by doing good to humans is, as Franklin would later write to the Brillons, the *chose essentielle.* Sectarian staples such as the immaculate conception or a reformation emphasis on justification by faith are historical idiosyncrasies—tissue and string—that may be forsworn without damaging the sugar. In preaching doctrine that focused on the principles of morality, then, Hemphill was not guilty of heresy. His error (if error it be) consisted in stripping away sectarian idiom in order to go straight to the heart of the Christian message, thereby shocking those who were unable to do without the familiar religious metaphors in which they were raised.

The Hemphill affair allowed Franklin the opportunity to state publicly some of the consequences, even if not the core, of his theistic perspectivism: that "private Judgment" in religious matters cannot "without Injustice [be] den[ied] to another"; that there is a common essential religious intuition at the heart of sectarian disagreement that can be revealed by open and unafraid dialogue; and that this dialogue is impeded by "our suffering the Clergy to get upon our Backs, and ride us, as they do their Horses, where they please."[39] In truth, poor Reverend Hemphill was more occasion than cause for Franklin's attack on Presbyterian intolerance. The disgraced minister soon disappeared from both Philadelphia and history. But the championing of religious toleration that Hemphill's trial focused remained with Franklin to the end of his days. His later condemnations of intolerance would be more tempered but no less sincere.

The Hemphill affair was also a personal catharsis for Franklin. It made public once and for all his break with the piously dissenting religion of his boyhood. Henceforth he would overtly align himself with the Church of England while privately resorting from time to time to his "Articles of Belief and Acts of Religion."[40] Despite his disingenuously soothing attempt to calm his parents' fears about his orthodoxy, Josiah and Abiah had good cause for worry. Their son had traveled far from Boston Calvinism and would never return. In Franklin's mind, Calvinism would always espouse doctrines that promoted "Enthusiasm, Demonism, and Immorality in the World."[41]

Franklin's public defense of Reverend Hemphill—or, more to the point, his public battle against Presbyterian intolerance—taught him two things. The first was that sectarian dogmatism was unlikely to be defeated by head-on assaults. Franklin had succeeded in venting his personal indignation over the depredations of religious bigotry, and even scored some telling points in the process. But in spite of all his efforts, Hemphill still had been convicted, deprived of his license to preach, and run out of town in disgrace. An unsavory personal corollary was that Franklin's own reputation had also been tarnished in the eyes of his orthodox fellow-citizens. For a businessman, this was an unacceptable state of affairs.

Franklin also learned that the anger stirred up by the Hemphill affair tended only to render religious battle lines even more inflexible. The conflict stiffened both liberal and conservative in their mutual dislike of one another's beliefs, further retarding the open dialogue and spirit of toleration Franklin the perspectivist saw as the ideal.[42] Recrimination became the order of the day, and by the time the dust settled, zealous Presbyterians and liberal Christians (not to mention freethinkers) were more polarized than ever.

Henceforward Franklin would avoid public disputations about religious matters. Discretion rather than frontal attack became his strategy. As he had Poor Richard say in the edition of the almanac that immediately followed the Hemphill trial, "In a discreet man's mouth, a publick thing is private."[43] Instead of seeking to demolish sectarian intolerance by overt polemics, Franklin in the future tried to undermine it by more gently defending an ecumenical spirit of religious inclusiveness. His contempt for sectarian bigotry remained as strong as ever, but his public responses to it would by and large be indirect and constructive rather than explicit and destructive.

As a first move, Franklin distanced himself from the Presbyterian establishment by dropping his subscription to Andrews's church and becoming a pewholder in the city's more congenial Anglican Christ Church. Doubtless Franklin the businessman felt the practical need for a public display of allegiance to some form of organized Christianity. Moreover, as we saw earlier, he appears even during these early years to have thought that institutional religion was an important guardian of social morality, and that he ought to observe public proprieties for the sake of the common as well as his own good. Finally, it is certainly the case that he found the Church of England's theology and liturgical style less grating than that of the zealous Presbyterians. In spite of its formal acceptance of key Calvinist articles such as predestination, the spirit of early eighteenth-century Anglicanism, at least in religiously pluralistic Pennsylvania, was relatively latitudinarian. It placed a high premium on morality and allowed for (even if it didn't actually advertise) a certain degree of liberty of conscience. Josiah and Abiah's concerns over their son's orthodoxy could just as well have been sparked by his throwing in his lot with the Anglicans as by his taking on Philadelphia's Presbyterian establishment.

Thus ensconced in a denominational tradition he could live with, all the while periodically returning to the private devotions spelled out in his "Acts of Religion," Franklin went about his business and bided his time. Then, in

November 1739, the British revivalist George Whitefield blew into town, preaching salvation and (as always) collecting monies to support the orphanage he had established in Savannah, Georgia.

Franklin had printed announcements of Whitefield's impending arrival in his newspaper, the *Pennsylvania Gazette.* The revivalist's reputation was already well known, and excitement mounted as the day of his arrival drew near. His first night in Philadelphia Whitefield preached from the courthouse gallery, speaking to "near 6000 People before him in the Street, who stood in an awful Silence to hear him." The preaching (and money gathering) continued for three more days before ever larger crowds.[44] Whitefield excited so much interest that Franklin, ever the enterprising businessman, promptly negotiated to print a collection of his journals and sermons and solicited subscriptions at four shillings a set.[45] When Whitefield returned to Philadelphia after a week-long sortie to New York, the *Gazette* breathlessly reported that he drew "a Multitude, computed at not less than 10,000 People."[46]

Over the next couple of years, Franklin's *Gazette* would publish more favorable pieces on Whitefield than did any other paper in America.[47] This is not to say that its endorsement of the revivalist was unequivocal; as the Great Awakening that Whitefield helped launch picked up steam, Franklin printed a number of items critical of its alleged excesses. But what is remarkable, given Franklin's disdain for Christian orthodoxy, was not that he ran pieces unfavorable to Whitefield, but that he printed so few.

Even more remarkable is the fact that Franklin and Whitefield actually became and remained friends until the latter's death in 1770. On the surface of things, the two could not have been less alike. Franklin was coolly contemptuous of orthodox mainstays such as original sin and saving grace; Whitefield preached both continuously. Since his early reading of Locke and Shaftesbury, Franklin had carried a suspicion bordering on outright hostility of any display of religious enthusiasm; Whitefield's preaching was deliberately orchestrated to appeal to the emotions.[48] Whitefield's orthodox eyes discerned little distinction between liberal religion and atheism; Franklin considered them as different as chalk and charcoal.[49] Throughout the years of their friendship, Whitefield continued praying for Franklin's conversion and urged him to give himself over to Jesus; Franklin just as stalwartly resisted, and not only dissented but frequently disapproved of Whitefield's fundamental religious beliefs. Yet in spite of all these differences, Franklin willingly admitted that Whitefield was a "perfectly *honest Man,*" and when he heard of his death years later fondly referred to him as "my dear old Friend."[50]

How to understand Franklin's friendship with Whitefield, one that clearly went beyond the merely pecuniary affection a publisher has for a best-selling author? The explanation lies largely in Franklin's perspectival conviction that the marrow of true religion is in doing good and pursuing one's own god with courage and sincerity, and in his eagerness to promote an ecumenical spirit of religious tolerance. Notwithstanding their obvious differences, Franklin saw Whitefield as fundamentally sympathetic to these ideals.[51]

For all his fidelity to the reform doctrine of *sola fide,* George Whitefield was a tireless advocate of good works. His campaigns for social reform and moral improvement would have gladdened the heart of Cotton Mather, dead in his grave some eleven years before Whitefield arrived on the American shore, because they perfectly exemplified the old puritan's conviction about the importance of morality in the Christian ethos. Whitefield spent the better part of his adult life collecting funds for his pet project, the Georgia orphanage he named "Bethesda." Early in his career, even before ordination, he had ministered to the wretches in London jails and prisons. He helped establish a number of schools in both England and the colonies and was always ready to lend his talents as a preacher to raise money for charitable causes, be they persecuted German Protestants or victims of the great Boston fire of 1760. Although Whitefield never denounced the institution of slavery, he fearlessly castigated owners for treating their dogs better than their slaves, warning them that should the tables ever be turned "all good men must acknowledge the judgment would be just." In 1740, he wrote (and Franklin printed) a scathing indictment of southern slaveowners in which he spelled out the abuses he had observed in his travels through Maryland, Virginia, and the Carolinas. The pamphlet brought down a predictable firestorm of recrimination on Whitefield's head, but he refused to be cowed. Come what may, he told the slaveowners, it was his duty to "inform you in the meekness and gentleness of Christ, that God has a quarrel with you for your cruelty to the poor negroes."[52]

Franklin could not but have been impressed by the energetic way Whitefield threw himself into the cause of moral reform. Just prior to the Hemphill affair, Franklin's main criticism of Jedediah Andrews—and, by implication, most other mainstream Presbyterian ministers—was that he was long on theology and short on good works. But in Whitefield Franklin found a man who reversed the relationship. Like many of the revivalists who emerged during the Great Awakening years, Whitefield professed a relative indifference to doctrines and dogmas; as he once admitted to Wesley, "I never read any thing that *Calvin* wrote," claiming instead that his beliefs were derived from "CHRIST and his apostles."[53] If this suspicion of theologizing tended to place a premium on the heart rather than the head—a move that Franklin deplored as leading to enthusiasm—it also liberated Whitefield from a dogmatic fidelity to incomprehensible (in Franklin's estimation) Calvinist doctrines that discounted the efficacy of good works. The consequence was that Franklin could ignore Whitefield's enthusiasm and conventional religious language while applauding his good works. Andrews and other mainstream Presbyterians had buried Christianity's moral message under tons of arcane theology; Whitefield tended to place virtue centerstage, convincing Franklin that the revivalist placed as high a premium on doing good as he himself did. Reminiscing less than a year after Whitefield's death, Franklin summed up his admiration for his friend. "I knew him intimately upwards of thirty years," Franklin wrote. "His Integrity, Disinterestedness, and indefatigable Zeal in prosecuting every good Work, I have never seen equalled, I shall never see exceeded."[54]

Whitefield's relative disregard of orthodox theologizing accounted for another characteristic noticed and approved by Franklin the perspectivist: a tolerance of other Christian sects highly unusual in most of the clergy, much less revivalist preachers. Whitefield's tolerance of dissent did not stretch as far as Franklin's; he had no use for non-Christian religious belief, and he was wary of liberal Christianity.[55] But Whitefield's primary concern was that persons become Christians rather than good members of one or another Christian sect. Denominational affiliation was accidental and relatively unimportant compared to the centrality of a heartfelt commitment to Christ. As Whitefield wrote in 1739, "I long for professors to leave off placing religion in saying 'I am a Churchman,' 'I am a Dissenter.' My language to such is, 'Are you of CHRIST? If so, I love you with all my heart.'"[56]

On at least one occasion Whitefield publicly echoed Franklin's conviction that sectarian allegiance was paper rather than sugar. On the very night that Whitefield preached in Philadelphia for the first time, delivering his remarks from the balcony of the Court House, he recounted the following imaginary conversation:

> "Father Abraham, who have you in heaven? any Episcopalians?" "No." "Any Presbyterians?" "No." "Any Baptists?" "No." "Have you any Methodists, Seceders, or Independents there?" "No, no!" "Why, who have you there?" "We don't know those names here. All who are here are Christians, believers in Christ—men who have overcome by the blood of the Lamb, and the word of his testimony." "Oh, is that the case? then god help me, God help us all, to forget party names, and to become Christians, in deed and in truth."[57]

One can hardly imagine a Jedediah Andrews urging that religious "party names" be forgotten.

Franklin heard Whitefield's parable that night, and it so accorded with his own disregard of sectarian divisions that it lodged in his memory for the rest of his life. A generation after he first heard it, Franklin himself wrote a "*Conte,*" or "Tale," that bears a striking similarity to Whitefield's parable. A French officer by the name of Montresor is ill. A priest, believing Montresor's illness mortal, entreats him to make his peace with God while he still has the opportunity. The implication is that Montresor has fallen away from orthodoxy (in this case, Catholicism) and, consequently, in the eyes of the church, is in danger of damnation. Revealingly, Franklin makes a point of assuring us that Montresor, although not a good churchman, is an "*homme de bien.*"

Montresor rebuffs the priest by telling him of a dream he had the night before. "I was at Heaven's gate," says Montresor, along with a crowd of other souls, all clamoring for admission. Saint Peter asked each in turn his religious profession. Some were Catholics, others Quakers, still other Anglicans (perhaps not surprisingly, none were Presbyterians). Peter admitted each, telling him to go to the part of heaven reserved for his specific denomination. Then came Montresor's turn. When Saint Peter asked him his religion, he confessed that he had none. "What a pity!" Peter responded. "I do not know where to place you; *but enter anyway; find yourself a place wherever you can.*"[58] For Franklin, Montresor's predicament is everyone's. All must find a religious place for themselves as best they can; all must invite the gods to come forth; and all must allow others the same freedom.

The ecumenical spirit of religious toleration that attracted Franklin to Whitefield in the first place progressively convinced him that sectarian styles of worship frequently represented stumbling blocks to those who craved communion with the divine. For Franklin, the essence of religious belief was its ability to enhance personal meaning and promote virtue. It followed that liturgical practices ought to maximize opportunities for both rather than smothering participants in creeds and rituals as unedifying as they are arcane. Communal worship should strive for a clearing in the forest that allows the gods to come forth, rather than cluttering up the already tangled undergrowth with so much liturgical rigamarole that their emergence is stifled. The aim of public acts of worship should be to invite in as many persons as possible, and this meant toning down idiosyncratic idioms or narrow credos.

As we have seen, Franklin threw in his lot with the Anglican communion shortly after the Hemphill controversy. Although he never forsook the private devotionals of his "Articles," he adopted the Church of England's liturgical framework when it came to public worship. But on at least two occasions in later life he sought to reform the Anglican service in order to make it more palatable to as many different tastes as possible. Neither effort caught on, but both illustrate Franklin's conviction that good works ought not to be overshadowed by theology.

Sometime (probably) in the late 1760s Franklin revised the Lord's Prayer in order to eliminate infelicities of language or style that might repulse or bewilder an eighteenth-century mind.[59] In rewriting the Pater Noster, Franklin tells us, he sought to render it "more concise" but "equally expressive." The ultimate editorial standard he invoked was his perspectival conviction that there is no one correct way of speaking about the divine that categorically excludes all others. As he revealingly states in his justifications for the revision, "We have in our Language no *proper name* for God; the Word *God* being a common or general Name, expressing all chief Objects of Worship."[60] Franklin's point is not merely a semantic one about whether the word "God" is a name or a noun. More substantively, it is that no particular sect has a monopoly on God-talk, no religious tradition a legitimately exclusivistic claim to designate its "chief Object of Worship" *God*.

Just as no sect can authentically claim its notion of God as the only true one, so no sect can expect modern worshippers to derive meaning from antiquated religious idioms that have lost their ability to convey meaning. For Franklin, the metaphors and symbols that convey religious beliefs—and these certainly include theological and credal expressions—are historical constructs, fashions and forms that reflect the aims and needs of the periods in which they arose. This means that each generation needs to rethink its religious imagery. Metaphors that were pregnant with meaning for our ancestors may now ring hollow. Accordingly, Franklin suggests in his revision of the Lord's Prayer that traditional religious language must be adapted to meet new needs. "Christians in these Times have other Ideas" than their ancestors when they intone familiar lines about, for instance, the Kingdom of Heaven, and those ideas should be expressed in credal reformulations.[61] The being to whom the prayer is addressed remains the same; what changes is the manner in which each generation thinks about, images, and expresses that being.

Some five years after his revision of the Lord's Prayer, Franklin again sought to encourage breadth in the Church of England's liturgy by collaborating with Lord Le Despencer (Francis Dashwood) in his abridgment of the Book of Common Prayer. Both men were convinced that the service prescribed in the prayer book was too lengthy and its accompanying catechism too filled with meaningless theologisms (such as the Athanasian Creed) to speak meaningfully to the modern mind. Accordingly, they radically edited the prayer book until all arcane references, archaic language, and allusions (especially in the psalms) to unvirtuous behavior fell away. Long, repetitious prayers in which "the mind wanders and the fervency of devotion is slackened" were also edited, "not to lessen or prevent the Practice of Religion, but to honour and promote it." These changes served, as the editors noted in their preface, to shorten the service "near one half, without the omission of what is essentially necessary."[62] The new version of the prayer book was published in September 1775 but fell stillborn from the press. As Franklin later said, "Some were given away, very few sold, and I suppose the bulk became waste paper."[63]

Most of the revisions to the Book of Common Prayer originated with Le Despencer. By Franklin's own admission, his contributions were limited to an abridgment of the catechism and the psaltry, and collaboration on the preface to the whole. But once again Franklin's interest in distinguishing between paper and sugar clearly comes across. The catechism, that "compendium of systematic theology, which learned divines have written folio volumes to explain" and which still remains largely unintelligible to most worshippers, he reduces to "those plain answers . . . which express our duty towards God, and our duty towards our neighbour."[64] The belief in God and a sense of responsibility to our fellow humans: these are the essentials. Denominational frills are important if they provide comfort or enrich an individual's sense of purposefulness, but they ought neither to serve as stumbling blocks for persons struggling to live within a particular faith tradition nor as truncheons to intimidate dissenters.

Franklin's attempted reformation of the Church of England's style of worship, as well as his championing of liberty of conscience, was based on the conviction that each religious tradition possessed a morsel of sugar buried beneath all the layers of sectarian wrapping. Theological inflections and liturgical accents may vary from one faith community to the next, but all were perspectival efforts to express the same religious aspirations and intuitions. As Franklin wrote in one of his parables, "are we not all of one blood?"[65]

But his perspectivist-inspired openness to alternative religious traditions was not indiscriminate. Notwithstanding his ecumenical eagerness to live and let live, Franklin was unwilling to embrace all sects as equally benign or valuable. Although believing that even "the worst had some good Effects," Franklin clearly felt that some faith traditions were better able than others to provide personal nourishment to their adherents and moral direction to society.[66] All denominations to one degree or another endorsed what Franklin considered to be the *choses essentielles.* But they also "more or less mix'd [them] with other Articles which without any Tendency to inspire, promote or confirm Morality, served principally to divide us and make us unfriendly to another."[67] For Franklin, then, the ultimate concern was the extent to which a sectarian tradition honestly and humbly acknowledged its own theological fallibility and accordingly concentrated its efforts not on unyielding apologetics but on good works. Such an unarrogant approach not only abstractly admitted that all human effort to express God necessarily falls short. It also practiced the concrete corollaries of such a confession: tolerance and compassion.

In short, Franklin was a minimalist when it came to institutionalized religion: the less emphasis on formal doctrine and ecclesial structure, the more opportunity for the gods to come forth. His concerns over social stability and public morality prevented him from advocating the complete collapse of organized religion into private devotions, but his general intuition was that a spirit of tolerance *within* sects was just as important as one *between* them. As he wrote to his parents in 1738 and repeated many times afterward, no individual or church has a monopoly on religious truth. Consequently, the better part of wisdom is to avoid arrogantly exhaustive theologies and credos, lest they breed dogmatism and persecution.

Franklin's aversion to the piously dissenting Presbyterianism of his parents stemmed in part from the fact that he saw it as antithetical to his ideal of religious openness. The strict Calvinism of his boyhood had brooked no opposition. All that was necessary for salvation was summarized in the Westminster Confession, and dissent served only to seduce the unregenerate away from the path of righteousness. But Franklin had no patience with this mentality. Sectarians, he insisted, had nothing to fear from the open give-and-take of religious opinion. Anticipating John Stuart Mill's position in *On Liberty* (1859) that the value of beliefs are best tested in the free marketplace of ideas, Franklin argued that "the Cause of Religion . . . will be best serv'd by Stopping the Prosecution" that censors dissent. Allow religious perspectives to be publicly aired. If there is "any evil Tendency" in them, it will soon be apprehended.[68] Those sects whose members acknowledge their unavoidable fallibility in things divine have nothing to lose from such public intercourse, because it provides them with an opportunity for self-examination and reassessment of their central beliefs.

Without some such sense of humbleness in the face of the great mystery, religious sects too frequently cry "Philosophical Heresy" when confronted with the slightest dissent.[69] They invent religious tests by which to separate the orthodox sheep from the theologically suspect goats, even though the appeal to such dogmatic standards is antithetical to the spirit of early Christianity.[70] They condemn and sometimes even harshly persecute non-Christian religionists.[71] And in their arrogance they invoke the authority of scripture to justify intolerance and cruelty: "With the Scriptures in their Hands and Mouths, they can set at nought that express Command, *Thou shalt do no Murder;* and justify their Wickedness, by the Command given Joshua to destroy the Heathen. Horrid Perversion of Scripture and of Religion! to father the worst of Crimes on the God of Peace and Love!"[72]

One of the reasons Franklin held Quakers in high esteem was because of their refusal to dogmatize internally or condemn outsiders who disagreed with them. Their "Equity and Moderation" in spiritual matters made them, in Franklin's eyes, a model of how an institutionalized religion ought to comport itself.[73] Similarly, Franklin came to admire the Brethren sect, or "Dunkers," as they were called in eighteenth-century Philadelphia, for their practice of what Fowler would call ironic imagination. Franklin went out of his way in his memoirs to describe and praise the Brethren's religious openness.

One of the founders of the Brethren, Michael Welfare, had complained to Franklin that he and his co-worshippers "were grievously calumniated by the Zealots of other Persuasions, and charg'd with abominable Principles and Practices to which they were utter Strangers." Franklin suggested that the sect set the record straight by drawing up and publishing a credo. Welfare replied that such a strategy had been considered by the Brethren but ultimately rejected because they did not wish to chisel their beliefs in stone. Recognizing that some of the convictions they once held were erroneous, they were not presumptuous enough to suppose that all their present beliefs were impeccable. The danger, Welfare told Franklin, was "that if we should once print our Confession of Faith, we should feel ourselves as if bound and confin'd by it, and perhaps be unwilling to receive farther Improvement."[74]

Franklin was thrilled when he heard these words. Here was a sect that displayed the same spirit of openness to private devotion and differing religious perspectives as his own "Articles of Belief." Franklin praised the Brethren in the highest terms, describing them as unique in the "History of Mankind" in their refusal to suppose that they possessed the truth and that all who disagreed with them were necessarily in error. When compared to them, most other sectarians were like "a Man travelling in foggy Weather: Those at some Distance before him on the Road he sees wrapt up in the Fog, as well as those behind him, and also the People in the Fields on each side; but near him all appears clear." But such apparent clarity was deceptive, of course, because "in truth he is as much in the Fog as any of them."[75]

Franklin's point here is obvious: no human can hope to penetrate the cloud of unknowing to any great extent; each of us gropes through an ultimately impenetrable fog in search of the divine. This person stumbles across and seizes one landmark in the fog, that person another. Each landmark may point to something on the other side, but neither is more than a metaphor, a symbol—a perspective. The earnest seeker of God never forgets this, no matter how pellucid her own perspective may at times appear to her.

In an often-cited letter written five weeks before his death, Franklin responded to Ezra Stiles's request for a summary of his religious opinions. True to the theistic perspectivism he had adopted over sixty years earlier, Franklin told

Stiles that he believed the essence of religion consisted in loving God and in doing good to one's fellow humans. These, he concluded, were the "fundamental Principles of all sound Religion." Other religious tenets (such as, for example, the divinity of Jesus) were best left to individual consciences. As for himself, he saw no evidence that "the Supreme" marked out for special disfavor those individuals who avoided the straits of orthodoxy, and he was content to do the same: "I have ever let others enjoy their religious Sentiments."[76]

Some of Franklin's contemporaries interpreted his refusal to endorse specific doctrinal beliefs as a sign of religious indifference. His old enemy John Adams spoke for many of them when he sneered that "the Catholics thought him almost a Catholic. The Church of England claimed him as one of them. The Presbyterians thought him half a Presbyterian, and the Friends believed him a wet Quaker."[77] But just the contrary was the case. Franklin regarded the human search for God too highly to insist dogmatically that there was only one correct way to go about it. Any perspective is necessarily relative to the Absolute it attempts to express. Consequently, no perspective is sacrosanct, even if all to one degree or another point in the right direction. In a parable written sometime around 1779, Franklin instructed his readers: "Trust not a single person with the government of your state." But the political language is allegorical and was intended to point to a more fundamental truth: trust not a single religious perspective with the governance of your soul.[78]

That's the negative way of putting it. The more constructive way is that almost any religious perspective, whether institutional or private, can serve as an opportunity for spiritual growth. The fact that there is a diversity of perspectives is something to be celebrated rather than deplored, because such a multiplicity enhances the chance of arriving at one or another that truly allows the gods to come forth.

After his years of wandering in the wilderness first of cradle Calvinism and then bloodless deism, Franklin finally came to the conclusion that religious conviction rides more upon mythos than the logos of either scholastic theology or natural philosophy. This means that human attempts to express the divine will always be couched in loose terms and hence open to charges of ambiguity. But the great lesson that Franklin learned—even though it is one he sometimes forgot—is that, in religious matters, ambiguity is more desirable than dogmatic certainty. It makes for a clearing in that great forest of the human soul that invites forth the symbols, the metaphors, and the tales with which we strive to touch God.

In one of his own tales, Franklin wonderfully conveyed this message, and it is a good story with which to conclude this book. The story recounts the adventures of a young Christian captured and raised by the Seneca Indians.

After the Indians spent some years sharing their religious traditions with him and listening with great interest to his, the youth dogmatically informed them that the Christian story—*his* story—is the only true one. It was "written down by direction of the great spirit himself," he said, "and preserved carefully in a book, which was never altered, but had ever remained the same, and was undoubtedly, the truth."

The Indians listened politely to the youngster. Then, gently, they chided him for his rudeness: "When young, it seems you were not well taught, you did not learn the civil behaviour of men. We excused you: it was the fault of your instructors. But why have you not more improved, since you have long had the opportunity from our example?" The young man's face reflected his confusion, so one of the Indians patiently tried to explain.

"You see," he said, "I always believed your stories, why do you not believe mine?"[79]

Notes

Introduction

1. Franklin's interest in religious questions remained with him throughout his life, but his writings on them for the most part tend to be concentrated in his early and later years. He does speculate on religion occasionally in the 1760s and 1770s, but the bulk of his writings and concerns in these years focus on the burdens of public service, the war with England, and his ministerial duties in France.

2. Quoted by Alfred Owen Aldridge, *Benjamin Franklin and Nature's God* (Durham: Duke University Press, 1967), p. 233. From Claude Fauchet, *Éloge civique de Benjamin Franklin* (Paris, 1790).

3. James Parton, *Life and Times of Benjamin Franklin* (New York: Mason Brothers, 1864), vol. 2, p. 646. Parton, like most other nineteenth-century commentators on Franklin, was heavily influenced by Mason Locke Weems's *Life of Benjamin Franklin. With Many Choice Anecdotes and Admirable Sayings of This Great Man, Never before Published by Any of His Biographers* (Hagerstown, Md.: Printed by the author, 1818). In this highly creative rewriting of Franklin's autobiography (see n. 21 of this chapter) Weems overshadowed the real Franklin with a mythical one who died a good Christian, gazing devoutly at a painting of the Crucifixion. Weems thus gave birth to a distorted image of Franklin, which, like his equally false portrait of George Washington, became an enduring part

of American iconography. For more on the Weems fabrication that Franklin was a Christian, see Sheldon Sloan, "Parson Weems on Franklin's Death," *Pennsylvania Magazine of History and Biography* 37 (July 1973): 369–76. Twentieth-century treatments that buy into Weems's baptism of Franklin include James M. Stifler, "The Religion of Benjamin Franklin," *Benjamin Franklin Gazette* 3 (May 1940): 11–14, and Albert Hyma, *The Religious Views of Benjamin Franklin* (Ann Arbor, Mich.: George Wahr Publishing Co., 1958). For a particularly pious—and influential—treatment of Franklin-as-Christian written for young people, Helen Nocolay's *The Boy's Life of Benjamin Franklin* (New York: D. Appleton–Century, 1935) is to be recommended. Even many commentators who cannot quite accept Parson Weems's extreme claims typically argue that Franklin was a Christian in spirit if not letter. See, for example, Burton Hanson, "Benjamin Franklin," *Case and Comment* 24 (February 1918): 701–13.

4. *Diary and Autobiography of John Adams,* ed. L. H. Butterfield (Cambridge, Mass.: Belknap Press of Harvard University Press, 1961), vol. 2, p. 391. In this entry of his diary, dated Wednesday, 23 June 1779, Adams records a conversation about Franklin between himself and one Monsieur Marbois. Adams insinuates that Franklin has no religion, belongs to the same infidel camp as Voltaire or Hume, and may possess great "Merit as a Philosopher" but is not much of a statesman. Adams questions Franklin's sexual morality and justifies all of these rather shameful slanders by concluding the entry with a memorandum to himself saying that it would be "worse than Folly to conceal my Opinion of [Franklin's] great Faults." For more on Adams's appraisal of Franklin's character, see chap. 5, n. 65.

5. Letter from William Robertson to William Strahan, 18 February 1765, *The Papers of Benjamin Franklin,* ed. Leonard W. Labaree et al. (New Haven: Yale University Press, 1959–), vol. 11, p. 70. Hereafter cited as *Papers.* Robertson's remark was prompted by Franklin's recommendation of someone for an honorary divinity degree.

6. Recorded by Benjamin Rush, 3 July 1794, *Autobiography and Commonplace Book* (Princeton: American Philosophical Society/Princeton University Press, 1948), p. 231. The standard and too simplistic interpretation of Franklin's religion, of course, is that it is a blend of moderate deism and humanism. See, for example, Ernest Sutherland Bates, *American Faith* (New York: Norton, 1940), pp. 226–31; Daniel Walden, "Benjamin Franklin's Deism: A Phase," *Historian* 26 (May 1964): 350–61; Harold E. Taussig, "Deism in Philadelphia in the Age of Franklin," *Pennsylvania History* 37 (July 1970): 217–36; and Cecil B. Currey, "Benjamin Franklin's Religion," *Mankind* 5 (August 1975): 22–27.

7. *The American Annual Register . . . for the Year 1796* (Philadelphia, 1797), p. 222.

8. Quoted in Alfred Owen Aldridge, *Franklin and His French Contemporaries* (New York: New York University Press, 1957), p. 61. Flamaren's remarks are from a letter dated 15 January 1777. More recent commentators who concur that Franklin was basically indifferent to religion include Kenneth Murdock, "Jonathan Edwards and Benjamin Franklin," in *The Literature of the American People: An Historical and Critical Survey,* ed. Arthur Hobson Quinn (New York: Appleton-Century-Crofts, 1951), pp. 116–23, and Richard Boyd Hauck, *A Cheerful Nihilism* (Bloomington, Ind.: Indiana University Press, 1971), pp. 32–39, who typecasts Franklin as a "confidence man" in religious matters.

9. Aldridge, *Benjamin Franklin and Nature's God,* p. 231.

10. Ernest Renan, *Oeuvres complètes,* ed. Henriette Pschari (Paris: Calmann-Lévy, 1947), vol. 3, p. 981.

11. Ralph L. Ketcham, *Benjamin Franklin* (New York: Washington Square Press, 1965), pp. 183–84. Ketcham devotes his entire tenth chapter to Franklin's religion.

12. Brian M. Barbour, "Franklin and Emerson," in *Benjamin Franklin: A Collection of Critical Essays,* ed. Brian M. Barbour (Englewood Cliffs, N.J.: Prentice Hall, 1979), pp. 25–29.

13. D. H. Lawrence, *Studies in Classic American Literature* (London: Martin Secker, 1933), p. 16.

14. Ibid., p. 17. Elsewhere, Lawrence says: "Benjamin had no concern, really, with the immortal soul. He was too busy with social man" (p. 19).

15. Ibid., p. 22. Lawrence goes on to decry the ideal of human perfectability he sees as the ultimate goal of Franklin's player piano ethics: "The perfectibility of man, dear God! When every man as long as he remains alive is in himself a multitude of conflicting men. Which of these do you choose to perfect, at the expense of every other?" (p. 15).

16. Ibid.

17. Aldridge, *Benjamin Franklin and Nature's God,* p. 252.

18. Aldridge is almost alone in this regard. To my knowledge, only one earlier study of Franklin's religious beliefs appreciates the importance of a developmental approach: Charles Lyttle's, "Benjamin Franklin's Change from Radicalism to Conservatism in Religious Thought," *Meadville Theological School Quarterly Bulletin* 22 (January 1928): 3–20.

19. Aldridge, *Benjamin Franklin and Nature's God,* p. 144.

20. For a discussion of these letters, dated 13 April 1738, see chap. 6.

21. *The Autobiography of Benjamin Franklin,* ed. Leonard W. Labaree, Ralph L. Ketcham, Helen C. Boatfield, and Helene H. Fineman (New Haven: Yale University Press, 1964), p. 157. Hereafter cited as *Autobiography.*

Chapter 1: Between Worlds

1. *Autobiography,* p. 63. In 1748, Poor Richard commemorated the anniversary of Addison's death by saying that his "writings have contributed more to the improvement of the minds of the British nation, and polishing their manners, than those of any other English pen whatever." *Papers,* vol. 3, p. 254.

2. See below in this chapter for a fuller discussion of Addison and Steele's influence on Franklin.

3. *The Spectator,* no. 531 (Saturday, 8 November 1712). Addison in turn got the story from Cicero's *De Natura Deorum* (I.xxii.60): "Roges me quid aut quale sit deus, auctore utar Simonide, de quo cum quaesivisset hod idem tyrannus Hiero, deliberandi sibi unum diem postulavit; cum idem ex eo postridie quaereret, biduum petivit; cum asepius duplicaret numerum dierum admiransque Hiero requireret cur ita faceret, 'Quia quan-

to diutius considero,' inquit, 'tanto mihi res videtur obscurior.'" Simonides of Ceos (ca. 556–467 BC), a poet whose work is all but lost, comes in for some rough treatment at the hands of Socrates in the *Protagoras* (339a–347a). Socrates twists a few lines from one of Simonides' fragments to show (speciously) that he contradicts himself, and therefore that poets ought not be accepted as reliable teachers of virtue. For a fairer treatment, see W. J. H. F. Kegel's *Simonides* (Groningen: J. B. Wolters, 1962).

4. Carl Van Doren's broad claim that "the more you study Franklin the more lines you find running out from him in all directions" ("Meet Doctor Franklin," in *Meet Dr. Franklin* [Philadelphia: Franklin Institute, 1943], p. 6) perfectly captures the complexity of Franklin's religious beliefs.

5. Carl Bridenbaugh, *Cities in the Wilderness: The First Century of Urban Life in America, 1625–1742* (New York: Ronald Press, 1938), p. 143. Bridenbaugh offers a good account of Boston at the turn of the century, as does Walter Muir Whitehall, *Boston: A Topographical History* (Cambridge, Mass.: Belknap Press of Harvard University Press, 1968), pp. 1–46, and G. B. Warden, *Boston, 1689–1776* (Boston: Little, Brown, 1970), pp. 3–79.

6. In 1635, for example, Massachusetts passed a law requiring church attendance. Three years later, a ministry tax was enacted, imposed on all citizens regardless of whether or not they were full (i.e., communicating) church members, much less members of dissenting sects. The same year another law was passed requiring all excommunicated members to make a good faith endeavor for reinstatement within six months. And in 1653, fed up with the persistent godlessness in town, the Boston General Court proclaimed the following blue law: "Upon information of sundry abuses and misdemeanors committed by several persons on the Lord's Day, not only by children playing in the streetes and other places, but by youthes, maydes, and other persons, both straungers and others, uncivilly walkinge the streetes and feildes travilling from towne to towne, goeing on ship-board, frequentinge common houses and other places to drinke, sport, and otherwise to misspend that precious time, which thinges tend much to the dishonor of God, the reproach of religion, and the prophanation of his holy Sabbath . . . ; it is therefore ordered by this Court and the authoritie, that no children, youths, maydes, or other persons shall transgress in the like kind on penalty of beinge reputed great provokers of the high displeasure of Almighty God." Violaters were also promised more mundane consequences in the form of civil penalties. Quoted in Herbert W. Schneider, *The Puritan Mind* (New York: Henry Holt, 1930), p. 84.

Two generations later, a youthful Franklin would also condemn unruly behavior on the streets of Boston, not because it violated the sabbath or his religious convictions, but because it offended his sense of propriety. See the twelfth and thirteenth Silence Dogood letters (1722) in *Papers*, vol. 1, pp. 39–42. In general, Franklin was contemptuous of blue laws. See, for example, his letter to Jared Ingersoll, written in Franklin's middle years. Although it refers to the religious laws of Connecticut, it could easily apply to Massachusetts: "When I travelled in Flanders, I thought of your excessively strict Observation of Sunday; and that a Man could hardly travel on that day among you upon his lawful Occasions, without Hazard of Punishment; while, where I was, every on[e] travell'd, if he pleas'd, or diverted himself in any other way; and in the Afternoon both high and low went to the Play or the Opera, where there was plenty of Singing, Fiddling and Dancing. I look'd around for God's Judgments but saw no Signs of them. The Cities were well built and full of Inhabitants, the Markets fill'd with Plenty, the People well favour'd and well clothed, the Fields well till'd; the Cattle fat and strong, the Fences, Houses, and Windows all in Repair." Letter to Jared Ingersoll, 11 December 1762, *Papers,* vol. 10, pp. 176–77.

7. Increase Mather, *A Discourse Concerning the Danger of Apostacy* (Boston, 1685), p. 87.

8. John Winthrop, "A Modell of Christian Charity," quoted in Robert C. Winthrop, "Boston Founded," in *The Memorial History of Boston Including Suffolk County, Massachusetts, 1630–1880,* ed. Justin Winsor (Boston: James R. Osgood, 1880), vol. 1, p. 111.

9. *John Dunton's Letters from New-England* (Boston: Publications of the Prince Society, 1867), vol. 4, pp. 74, 65, 70. The list of "Laws for Reformation of Manners" provided by Dunton indicates the city elders' determination to extirpate godlessness from the environs. Drunkenness is punished with "either Whip or . . . a Fine of Five shillings"; cursing or swearing by boring through the offending tongue with a hot iron; for public kissing and single fornication, whipping or a fine; for adultery and witchcraft, death; scolds are gagged and "set . . . at their own Doors, for certain hours together, for all comers and goers to gaze at." (Dunton approves of this, and wishes England imposed a similar penalty.) Stealing is punished with a fourfold recompense. Miscegenation is particularly abhorrent: "An English Woman suffering an Indian to have carnal knowledge of her, had an Indian cut out exactly in red cloth, and sewed upon her right Arm, and enjoyned to wear it Twelve Months" (pp. 70–71). Still, for all their laws, Dunton concluded that Bostonians were chronic drunkards, could "out-vye Judas and all the false other Cheats in Hell" in "Lying and Cheating" and in general constituted a moral "Dunghill of Filth" (pp. 72, 73, 74). One of the capital crimes Dunton mentions is witchcraft. In 1754 Franklin, then an established Pennsylvanian, cosponsored a motion in the Assembly to eliminate any mention of witchcraft from the colony's penal code. *Papers,* vol. 5, p. 202.

10. *Magnalia Christi Americana* (I.iv.2). Mather sadly adds, "Truly 'twere to have been wished, that something more excellent had been the *main End* of the *Settlements* in that brave Country." Harry S. Stout, in his masterful *The New England Soul: Preaching and Religious Culture in Colonial New England* (New York: Oxford University Press, 1986), is particularly good at tracing the conviction among the orthodox that each generation had slipped farther away from the original purity of the founders. See also Joseph Haroutunian's excellent theological and social analysis of Puritanism's decline in *Piety versus Moralism: The Passing of the New England Theology* (New York: Henry Holt, 1932).

In spite of Cotton's coming close to the realization that the good old days may not have been all that good, he continued to preach jeremiads in which he lamented his generation's fall. For representative examples, see Cotton Mather, *Days of Humiliation, Times of Affliction and Disaster: Nine Sermons for Restoring Favor with an Angry God,* ed. George Harrison Orians (Gainesville, Fla.: Scholars' Facsimiles and Reprints, 1970).

11. There are many good analyses of seventeenth-century efforts to ameliorate the harshness of New England Calvinism. Three are especially noteworthy: Schneider, *The Puritan Mind,* chaps. 2–3; Perry Miller, *The New England Mind: From Colony to Province*

(Cambridge, Mass.: Harvard University Press, 1981), pp. 95–104, 240–58; and Stout, *The New England Soul,* pp. 58–61, 136–38. The quotation, cited by Stout (p. 130), is from Nathanael Appleton, *A Great Man Fallen in Israel* (Boston, 1724), p. 31.

12. The phrase "New Learning" was favored in the colonies and suggests, as James Turner nicely points out, "something of [the] exciting freshness" of enlightened thought for the New England mind. *Without God, Without Creed: The Origins of Unbelief in America* (Baltimore: Johns Hopkins University Press, 1985), p. 275, n. 1.

13. Bridenbaugh, *Cities in the Wilderness,* pp. 129–30; David Lundberg and Henry F. May, "The Enlightened Reader in America," *American Quarterly* 28 (Summer 1976): 262–93; Benjamin W. Labaree, *Colonial Massachusetts: A History* (Millwood, N.Y.: KTO Press, 1979), p. 81; Kenneth Silverman, *The Life and Times of Cotton Mather* (New York: Harper and Row, 1984), p. 281.

14. Herbert A. Morais, *Deism in Eighteenth-Century America* (New York: Columbia University Press, 1934), p. 60.

15. Herbert W. and Carol Schneider, eds., *Samuel Johnson, President of King's College: His Career and Writings* (New York: Columbia University Press, 1929), vol. 1, pp. 6, 23.

16. Morais, *Deism in Eighteenth-Century America,* p. 83.

17. *The American Weekly Museum,* no. 824 (October 9–16, 1735).

18. For more on the Hemphill affair, see chap. 6. In addition to Morais's *Deism in Eighteenth-Century America* (especially pp. 3–27), the other standard work on American deism is G. Adolf Koch, *Republican Religion: The American Revolution and the Cult of Reason* (New York: Henry Holt, 1933). Although both works are dated, and there is a crying need for a new study of deism in colonial America and the early Republic, they are still well worth consulting. More recent discussions may be found in Henry F. May's classic *The Enlightenment in America* (New York: Oxford University Press, 1976); Ernest Cassara, *The Enlightenment in America* (Lanham, Md.: University Press of America, 1988), pp. 116–44; and Kerry S. Walters, *Rational Infidels: The American Deists* (Durango, Colo.: Longwood Academic, 1992) and *The American Deists: Voices of Reason and Dissent in the Early Republic* (Lawrence: University Press of Kansas, 1992). Although not dealing specifically with deism, the essays in a special issue of *American Quarterly* ["An American Enlightenment," ed. Joseph Ellis] 28 (Summer 1976), provide excellent studies of the religious and intellectual climate during the American Enlightenment years. Especially instructive are the essays by Ellis, D. H. Meyer, and David Lundberg and Henry F. May. See also S. P. Sherman's "Franklin and the Age of Enlightenment," in *Americans* (New York: Scribner, 1922), pp. 28–62.

19. Perhaps no other single turn captures the intellectual spirit of the Enlightenment as well as its emphasis on secondary causation rather than direct divine intervention in the affairs of nature and history. This move both minimized the importance of divine agency (as Laplace would shortly say, the astronomer no longer had need of the God-hypothesis) and brought forth naturalistic explanations in all arenas of human inquiry. Adam Smith in political economy, Voltaire in ethics, Lavoisier in chemistry, Hume in religious history, Montesquieu in sociology, and Diderot in the arts, for example, naturalized their domains by insisting on the sufficiency of explanations utilizing

secondary causes. The word "providence," if it was retained at all, soon designated little more than that uniform system of secondary causation which underlay physical, social, and psychological events.

20. In saying this, I part with Bruce Kuklick, who somewhat extravagantly asserts that the Calvinists were "extraordinary optimists," hoping as they did for the ecstasy of regeneration. While that hope was certainly present, I think it too strong to interpret it as a mark of optimism. To *hope,* after all, is not necessarily to *expect.* See his frequently insightful *Churchmen and Philosophers: From Jonathan Edwards to John Dewey* (New Haven: Yale University Press, 1985), p. 8.

21. Many clergy flirted with deism for at least a period during their student days. Yale's Samuel Johnson and Ezra Stiles, and Ebenezer Gay, are the three foremost divines who came close to apostasy, but there were others as well. Joseph Hawley (1723–88), one of Jonathan Edwards's cousins, discovered deism while studying at Harvard and soon became so infected by it that he refused to accept "any Doctrine upon the mere authority of God's word." Similarly, William Bliss (1728–1808) was "deeply plunged in [deism] for many years" after a youthful encounter. Both men re-embraced orthodoxy only in their middle years. Ezra Stiles, *Literary Diary,* ed. R. B. Dexter (New York: Scribner, 1901), vol. 1, p. 566. See Schneider and Schneider, *Samuel Johnson,* vol. 1; Edmund S. Morgan, *The Gentle Puritan: A Life of Ezra Stiles, 1727–1795* (New York: Norton, 1983); and Robert J. Wilson, *The Benevolent Deity: Ebenezer Gay and the Rise of Rational Religion in New England, 1686–1787* (Philadelphia: University of Pennsylvania Press, 1984).

22. The colonies' eagerness in the eighteenth century to absorb British learning and make it their own has been referred to by some scholars as "anglicization." For more extended discussions, see John Clive and Bernard Bailyn, "England's Cultural Provinces: Scotland and America," *William and Mary Quarterly* 11 (1954), pp. 200–213; Silverman, *Life and Times of Cotton Mather,* pp. 138–90; and Stout, *The New England Soul,* pp. 127–47.

23. Kenneth Ballard Murdoch, *Increase Mather: The Foremost American Puritan* (Cambridge, Mass.: Harvard University Press, 1926), pp. 147–49; and Bridenbaugh, *Cities in the Wilderness,* p. 129. Cotton Mather, whose consuming ambition to become a member of the Royal Society may have been sparked by his attendance at the meetings of the Boston circle, described it as "a *Philosophical Society* of Agreeable Gentlemen, who met once a Fortnight for a Conference upon Improvements in *Philosophy* and Additions to the Stores of *Natural History.*" He goes on to claim that one Wolferdus Senquerdius, professor at Leyden, had benefited from the society's correspondence, and he ends by writing that "the Calamity of the Times, anon gave a fatal and a total Interruption in this Generous Undertaking." *Parentator: Memoirs of Remarkables in the Life and the Death of the Ever-memorable Dr. Increase Mather* (Boston, 1724), p. 86. The "Calamity of the Times" referred to is undoubtedly the revocation of the old Massachusetts Bay charter in 1684, an act that sent Increase to London four years later as a lobbyist for its restoration (accomplished in 1692).

24. *The Christian Philosopher,* ed. Winton U. Solberg (Urbana: University of Illinois Press, 1994), p. 308. Mather goes on to crow that he has now beyond any doubt

"dispatc'd the *Atheist,* with bestowing on him *not many* Thoughts, yet *more* than could be deserved by such an *Idiot*" (p. 309). (When one contrasts this characteristically coarse piece of prose with the usual urbane grace of Franklin's, one appreciates just how far Franklin traveled from his Calvinist boyhood.) Mather, good Calvinist that he was, also interpreted history—especially the history of the Puritans—as a demonstration of divine purposefulness. As he says in the *Magnalia* ("General Introduction," p. 4), a consideration of the "*Persons* and *Actions*" of the elect so points to the existence of a Supreme Designer that "'Tis nothing but *Atheism* in the Hearts of Men, that can perswade them otherwise."

25. *Bonifacius: An Essay Upon the Good,* ed. David Levin (Cambridge, Mass.: Belknap Press of Harvard University Press, 1966). For a fuller discussion of Mather's influence on Franklin, see chap. 5 of the present book. For more on Mather's relationship to the New Learning, see Silverman, *Life and Times of Cotton Mather,* pp. 40–42, 93–94, 167–68, 243–54, 405–10; and Robert Middlekauff, *The Mathers: Three Generations of Puritan Intellectuals, 1596–1728* (New York: Oxford University Press, 1971), especially pp. 279–304. Possibly the best study of Mather as natural philosopher is Jeffrey Jeske, "Cotton Mather: Physico-theologian" in *The American Enlightenment,* ed. Frank Shuffelton (Rochester, N.Y.: University of Rochester Press, 1993), pp. 61–72, but see also Pershing Vartanian, "Cotton Mather and the Puritan Transition into the Enlightenment," *Early American Literature* 7 (1973): 213–24.

26. *Magnalia Christi Americana,* I, "The Boston Ebenezer," II.

27. Entry for 30 April 1721, *Diary of Cotton Mather* (Boston: Massachusetts Historical Society, 1911), vol. 2, p. 615. The occasion for this outburst was Mather's fury at a schism in North Church.

28. Somewhat like Franklin, Cotton Mather straddled the worlds of Calvinist piety and Enlightenment rationalism. Unlike Franklin, however, he tilted toward the Calvinist rather than the Enlightenment side. Even in those books such as *The Christian Philosopher* that claim to be natural philosophy one finds disparate carry-overs from his Calvinism unconcernedly sandwiched in between descriptions of physical phenomena. Interjections on special providences, for example, frequently find their way into sober accounts of nature. This passage from a discussion of comets is typical: "When I see a vast Comet, blazing and rolling about the unmeasurable *Ether,* I will think: 'Who can tell, but I now see a wicked World *made a fiery Oven in the Time of the Anger of GOD! The Lord swallowing them up in his Wrath, and the Fire devouring them!*'" *The Christian Philosopher,* p. 53. Franklin would write frequently about comets, but in a straightforward Enlightenment manner, with no suggestions of divine wrath. See, for example, *Papers,* vol. 2, p. 393; vol. 3, p. 452; vol. 4, pp. 488–89; vol. 7, pp. 90–91.

29. The expression "schizophrenic conception of God" is James Turner's. I find it particularly descriptive. The first two chapters of his *Without God, Without Creed* offer a judicious analysis of the worldview clash in eighteenth-century American religious sensibilities.

30. As Perry Miller has exhaustively demonstrated, a tension between heart and head, will and intellect, was always characteristic of New England's brand of Calvinism, giv-

en its insistence on utter depravity and, at the same time, its high regard for learning. "In certain aspects," Miller writes, "the Puritan appears an antirationalist, but in others he is exceedingly rational; he attacks with fury those misguided zealots who jump to the conclusion that religion can dispense with learning, ministers with education, saints with knowledge, or converts with the fullest possible understanding, not only of theology, but of science and philosophy. Puritan writers can pity the insignificance of human reason, and in the next breath sing the praises of the human mind." *New England Mind,* p. 66. See also his "The Marrow of Puritan Divinity" in *Errand into the Wilderness* (New York: Harper and Row, 1964), pp. 48–98.

31. See Hamilton Andrews Hill, *History of the Old South Church, Boston 1669–1884* (Boston: Houghton, Mifflin, 1890), for a description of the church during the time Franklin and his parents attended services there.

32. *The Diary of Samuel Sewall, 1674–1729,* ed. M. Halsey Thomas (New York: Farrar, Straus and Giroux, 1973), vol. 2, pp. 941, 960, 975, 874, 886; vol. 1, p. 603; vol. 2, pp. 712, 813, 859, 921. Carl Van Doren curiously judges Josiah Franklin as an "orthodox but not too devout man" (*Benjamin Franklin* [New York: Viking, 1952], p. 7), but the testimony of both Samuel Sewall and Benjamin suggests otherwise. In his history of Old South, Hamilton Hill quotes a funeral elegy commending the piety of Josiah's brother Benjamin. The elder Benjamin died 17 March 1727 and was a member (probably a full one) of Old South. The elegy describes him as "a rare and exemplary Christian. . . . His presence in the house of God was always solemn and affecting; and though he courted not the observation of men, yet there were many that could not but take notice, and admire the peculiar excellences that so visibly adorned him." Hill goes on to comment (vol. 1, p. 420) that Josiah was very much like his brother in both piety and character. I'm inclined to take this as a more accurate appraisal than Van Doren's.

33. *Autobiography,* p. 58.

34. Ibid., pp. 55, 54. Franklin also notes (p. 55) that at meals Josiah "always took care to start some ingenious or Useful Topic for Discourse, which might tend to improve the Minds of his Children. By this he turn'd our Attention to what was good, just, and prudent in the Conduct of Life."

35. Ibid., p. 113.

36. Ibid., p. 63. Two additional tales illustrate Franklin's impatience even as a child with prolonged periods of public worship. One comes from his grandson's collection of "Anecdotes relative to Dr. Franklin." "Dr. Franklin, when a child, found the long graces used by his father before and after meals very tedious. One day after the winter's provisions had been salted,—'I think, Father,' said Benjamin, 'if you were to say *grace* over the whole cask—once for all—it would be a vast *saving of time.*'" William Temple Franklin, ed., *Memoirs of the Life and Writings of Benjamin Franklin,* 2d ed. (London: Henry Colburn, 1818), vol. 2, p. 296. The other is from Benjamin Rush, that inveterate compiler of anecdote and gossip. In the summer of 1789, Franklin confessed to Rush that as a boy he taught himself geography during his father's interminable prayers by studying the four large maps that hung in the family parlor. "Excerpts from the Papers of Dr. Benjamin Rush," *Pennsylvania Magazine of History and Biography* 29 (1905): 15–30; the

geography anecdote is on p. 27. Later in life, Franklin would advocate a radical editing of the lengthy liturgical service in the Book of Common Prayer. See chap. 6 for a discussion of Franklin's revisions of the Book of Common Prayer.

37. Harry Stout has authoritatively traced the progress of a new "aesthetics of the infinite" in the preaching of this period. As the Newtonian model of the cosmos gained general acceptance, religious metaphors compatible with its mechanism began to replace more traditional ones. God, for example, was increasingly referred to from the pulpit as the "Supreme Architect" or the "Great Governor of the Universe." *The New England Soul,* p. 133.

Joseph Sewall, son of Samuel, was minister at Old South, along with Thomas Prince, throughout Franklin's boyhood and youth. The younger Sewall was rather unremarkable, but his associate was not. Although Prince was a true son of traditional Calvinism, described while under Increase Mather's tutelage as a genuinely "praying student" and later an enthusiastic champion of George Whitefield, he was also a great bibliophile, student of language, and amateur logician, natural philosopher, and mathematician. At his death in 1758, he left behind fifteen hundred volumes, comparable in size to the libraries of only Cotton Mather and Governor Hutchinson.

38. *Autobiography,* p. 58. It is a pity we have no information about specific titles in Josiah's collection of "polemic Divinity."

39. Ibid., pp. 52–53.

40. For example, in a letter to his sister Jane Mecom, when Franklin was sixty-five years of age, he describes Josiah as a "very wise man." Letter, 17 July 1771, *Papers,* vol. 18, p. 185.

41. See, for example, Essays no. 185 (Tuesday, 2 October 1711) and 201 (Saturday, 20 October 1711), in *The Spectator,* ed. G. Gregory Smith (New York: Scribner, 1897), vol. 3, pp. 62–65, 122–25.

42. Essay no. 465 (Saturday, 23 August 1712). See also Essay no. 459 (Saturday, 16 August 1712). Thomas Paine was so impressed by Addison's quasi-deistic paraphrase of Psalm 19 in *Spectator* 465 that he included it in his own *Age of Reason.*

43. The growing anticlericalism in turn-of-the-century Boston is chronicled in Miller, *New England Mind,* pp. 324–44. The squib on Old South's door is quoted on p. 331, the Mather response on p. 336. Given James Franklin's strident opposition to New England Calvinism in general, one cannot help wondering if it might have been his hand that nailed the broadside on the church of Josiah and Abiah Franklin.

44. Essay no. 10 (Monday, 12 March 1711), *The Spectator,* vol. 1, pp. 38–39.

45. Given his angry feelings of inadequacy, Franklin must have been especially gratified when Harvard awarded him an honorary M.A. in 1753, and again when the college officially thanked him in 1774 for a copy of "a French Translation of his Philosophical Works," which "is a Testimony of the Sense Forreigners have of the Merit of those Writings, which must do honor to the Country that gave him Birth." *Papers,* vol. 21, p. 226.

46. Antoine Arnauld and Pierre Nicole, *Logic or the Art of Thinking,* trans. and ed. Jill Vance Buroker (Cambridge: Cambridge University Press, 1996), p. 29.

47. Ibid., pp. 8–9.

48. In his "Proposals Relating to the Education of Youth in Pennsylvania" (1749), written some thirty years after he read the Port Royal Logic, Franklin unintentionally reveals what may be another, less noble reason for his boyhood zest for Arnauld and Nicole. He writes that in the instruction of history, questions of right and wrong, justice and injustice, will arise and excite in the young scholars a desire for debate. "When they ardently desire Victory, for the Praise attending it, they will begin to feel the Want, and be sensible of the Use of *Logic,* or the Art of Reasoning to *discover* Truth, and of Arguing to *defend* it, and *convince* Adversaries." It is not difficult to imagine that the young Franklin, headstrong, ambitious, and a lover of disputation, took up logic at least in part to "*convince* Adversaries" in debate. *Papers,* vol. 3, p. 413–14. See also ibid., vol. 4, p. 325.

49. John Locke, *An Essay Concerning Human Understanding* (New York: Valentine Seaman, 1824), I, 1, 2, p. 51.

50. *Papers,* vol. 3, p. 259.

51. Locke, *Essay,* IV, 19, 12, p. 222.

52. "Our *Geese* are but *Geese,* tho' we may think 'em *Swans.*" *Papers,* vol. 1, p. 71. See discussion in chap. 2.

53. *Autobiography,* pp. 113–14.

54. Anthony Ashley Cooper, Lord Shaftesbury, "A Letter Concerning Enthusiasm," in *Characteristics of Men, Manners, Opinions, Times* (London[?], 1714), I, 7, p. 54.

55. Ibid., I, 3, p. 22. Shaftesbury returns to the theme of bantery and ridicule as effective weapons against enthusiasm in the second treatise of *Characteristics,* "*Sensus Communis:* An Essay on the Freedom of Wit and Humour." The best analysis of Shaftesbury's philosophy is Stanley Grean, *Shaftesbury's Philosophy of Religion and Ethics: A Study in Enthusiasm* (Columbus: Ohio University Press, 1967). The subtitle suggests the novelty of Grean's approach. Lawrence E. Klein, *Shaftesbury and the Culture of Politeness: Moral Discourse and Cultural Politics in Early Eighteenth Century England* (Cambridge: Cambridge University Press, 1994), examines Shaftesbury's use of stylistic humor and irony as substantive weapons. Robert Voittle, *The Third Earl of Shaftesbury, 1671–1713* (Baton Rouge: Louisiana State University Press, 1984), is an informative biography. Curiously, for all his admiration of Shaftesbury, Franklin was not convinced by the former's case for a moral faculty, even though Shaftesbury's arguments for it clearly struck at the core of Calvinism's doctrine of moral depravity.

56. Collins asserts, for example, that the story of Jesus' virgin birth is paralleled in the Siamese myth of a certain Sommonocondon who "was born of a virgin, and was the god expected by the universe." *A Discourse on Free-Thinking* (London, 1713), pp. 52–53.

57. Ibid., p. 109. For examples of the Paine and Palmer varieties of anticlericalism, consult appropriate chapters in my *The American Deists* and *Rational Infidels.* Franklin himself also adopted anticlerical language in his defenses of Reverend Samuel Hemphill. See chap. 6 for further discussion of the Hemphill affair.

58. *Autobiography,* p. 64. It is unknown whether Franklin read Collins's subsequent *A Discourse on the Ground and Reason of the Christian Religion* (1724), published eleven years after *Free-Thinking.* The second book, although still polemical, is much better than

the first. Its primary thesis is an elaborate argument that centers on the nature of prophecy in the Old Testament. He maintains that prophecy should be interpreted allegorically, intending thereby to undercut the supernatural claims of the New Testament.

59. See chap. 2 for further discussion of Franklin's religious ambivalence.

60. See, for example, Jean Piaget, *Judgment and Reasoning in the Child,* trans. Marjorie Gabain (London: Kegan Paul, 1928) and *Genetic Epistemology,* trans. Eleanor Duckworth (New York: Columbia University Press, 1970); Erik Erikson, *Childhood and Society* (New York: Norton, 1963) and *Identity, Youth, and Crisis* (New York: Norton, 1968); and Lawrence Kohlberg, *The Philosophy of Moral Development: Moral Stages and the Idea of Justice* (San Francisco: Harper and Row, 1981) and *The Psychology of Moral Development: The Nature and Validity of Moral Stages* (San Francisco: Harper and Row, 1984). Kohlberg's 1958 doctoral dissertation has been published by Garland Press (1994) as *The Development of Modes of Moral Thinking and Choice in the Years 10 to 16.*

61. James W. Fowler, *Stages of Faith: The Psychology of Human Development and the Quest for Meaning* (San Francisco: Harper and Row, 1981), pp. 4–5; see also pp. 2–15. Other works in which Fowler explores his developmental account of faith include *Trajectories in Faith: Five Life Stories* (Nashville: Abingdon, 1980) and *Becoming Adult, Becoming Christian: Adult Development and Christian Faith* (San Francisco: Harper and Row, 1984). For a collection of critical responses to Fowler's development theory, see Craig Dykstra and Shawn Parks, eds., *Faith Development and Fowler* (Birmingham, Ala.: Religious Education Press, 1986). The volume includes an overview of faith development theory written by Fowler himself: "Faith and the Structuring of Meaning," pp. 15–42. Tillich discusses faith as "ultimate concern" in *Dynamics of Faith* (New York: Harper, 1957).

62. Fowler, *Stages of Faith,* pp. 122–34. Quotations are from pp. 133, 134.

63. Ibid., pp. 135–50.

64. Ibid., pp. 151–73. Quotations are from pp. 172–73.

65. Ibid., p. 134.

66. *Autobiography,* p. 57.

67. For an interesting account of the early *Courant,* see Worthington Chauncey Ford, "Franklin's *New England Courant,*" *Proceedings of the Massachusetts Historical Society* 57 (1923–24): 336–53.

68. The influence of Addison's *Spectator* essays on the Dogood letters is obvious. For example, Addison has his spectator provide autobiographical information in the first essay (Tuesday, 1 March 1711) because "I have observed, that a Reader seldom peruses a Book with Pleasure 'till he knows whether the Writer of it be a black or a fair Man, of a mild or choleric Disposition, Married or a Batchelor, with other Particulars of the like nature, that conduce very much to the right Understanding of an Author." Franklin has Mistress Dogood say in her first letter: "It is observed, that the Generality of People, now a days, are unwilling either to commend or dispraise what they read, until they are in some measure informed who or what the Author of it is, whether he be *poor* or *rich, old* or *young,* a *Schollar* or a *Leather Apron Man,* &c. and give their Opinion of the Performance, according to the Knowledge which they have of the Author's Circumstances, it may not be amiss to begin with a short Account of my past Life." *Papers,* vol. 1, p. 9.

For more on Addison's influence, see George F. Horner, "Franklin's Dogood Papers Reexamined," *Studies in Philology* 37 (1940): 501–23, and Jeanette S. Lewis, "'A Turn of Thinking': The Long Shadow of *The Spectator* in Franklin's *Autobiography*," *Early American Literature* 13 (Winter 1978–79): 268–77.

69. So Kenneth Silverman speculates (p. 339) in the commentary to his *Selected Letters of Cotton Mather* (Baton Rouge: Louisiana State University Press, 1971).

70. Silence Dogood, no. 3; see also the defense of women in nos. 5 and 10. *Papers*, vol. 1, pp. 13–14, 18–21, 32–36. This was not the only occasion on which Franklin was to use a female character as a prick to social conscience. In 1747, Franklin published "The Speech of Miss Polly Baker." Polly, the mother of five natural children, defends her honor on both moral and utilitarian grounds. Along the way, she also underscores the hypocrisy of a society that persecutes unwed mothers but winks at the shenanigans of the fathers. (Unfortunately, not much has changed in social attitudes since Polly's time.) This piece proved to be one of Franklin's most popular writings, widely translated and embraced by liberal thinkers as a magnificent statement of human rights. John Adams thought otherwise, characteristically lambasting it as yet another instance of Franklin's "Outrages" against public decency. *Papers*, vol. 3, pp. 120–26.

71. Silence Dogood, no. 2, *Papers*, vol. 1, pp. 11–13.

72. Silence Dogood, no. 1, ibid., p. 10

73. Silence Dogood, no. 4, ibid., pp. 14–18.

74. Silence Dogood, nos. 6, 7, 8, 10, 12, 13, ibid., pp. 21–23, 23–26, 27–30, 32–36, 39–41, 41–42.

75. Silence Dogood, no. 9, ibid., pp. 30–32: "A notoriously profane Person in a private Capacity, ruins himself, and perhaps forwards the Destruction of a few of his Equals; but a publick Hypocrite every day deceives his betters, and makes them the Ignorant Trumpeters of his supposed Godliness: They take him for a Saint, and pass him for one, without considering that they are (as it were) the Instruments of publick Mischief out of Conscience, and ruin their Country for God's sake" (p. 30).

76. Silence Dogood, no. 14, ibid., pp. 43–45. A good half of this piece is an extended quotation from Addison (*Spectator* 185) on zealotry.

77. Silence Dogood, no. 4, ibid., pp. 14–18. Mistress Dogood's attack on Harvard scholars was directed against class privilege as much as arcane theology—the Leather Aprons against the wealthy. This was immediately recognized by Samuel Mather, who responded in print, under the name "John Harvard," to the Dogood letter. His attack was based almost entirely on class distinction. He marvels, for example, that an unlettered (that is, nonwealthy) person would presume to talk about such matters in the first place. "[W]ho ever heard of entering a Temple and ascending the Magnificent Steps of a Throne with a Plough in hand! O rare Allegory! Well done Rustic Couranto!" As befitted a genuine man of letters, Mather then went on to ridicule Dogood's style and counteraccused her of plagiarism. Miller, *New England Mind*, pp. 342–43.

78. "On Titles of Honor" (18 February 1723), *Papers*, vol. 1, pp. 51–52. This piece, which appeared in the *New-England Courant*, just as closely mimics three pages of William Penn's *No Cross, No Crown* (1669), as the opening Dogood letter does *Spectator* 1. Al-

though the editors of the *Papers* describe it as a "parody" of Penn, it strikes me more as simply a benign borrowing of Penn's style in order to make a similar point. Franklin also poked fun at titles in *Poor Richard* for 1751 (*Papers*, vol. 4, pp. 97–98) and in a letter (26 January 1784) to his daughter Sarah Bache (*Writings*, vol. 9, pp. 161–68).

79. *Autobiography*, p. 71.

80. Ibid., pp. 70, 71.

81. From C. W. Shaeffer, trans., *Hallische nachrichten, Reports of the United States Evangelical Lutheran Congregations in North America* (Reading, Pa., 1882), vol. 1, p. 26. Cited in Aldridge, *Benjamin Franklin and Nature's God*, p. 145.

82. *Autobiography*, p. 82. Keith is an interesting character whose reputation is probably undeserved. Feckless he may have been, but not, it seems, dishonest or manipulative. As governor, he was a good friend to Pennsylvania. When the Proprietors dismissed him in 1726, he was promptly elected to the Assembly. See Charles P. Keith, "Sir William Keith," *Pennsylvania Magazine of History and Biography* 12 (April 1988): 1–33, and Tom Wendel, "The Life and Writings of Sir William Keith, Lieutenant-Governor of Pennsylvania and the Three Lower Counties, 1717–1726" (Ph.D. diss., University of Washington, 1964).

Chapter 2: A False Start

1. *Autobiography*, pp. 93–94, 95, 98–99. For more on the subsequent adventures of the roguish Ralph, see Robert W. Kenny, "James Ralph: An Eighteenth-Century Philadelphian in Grub Street," *Pennsylvania Magazine of History and Biography* 64 (1940): 218–42.

2. The *Dissertation* is essential to understanding the development of Franklin's thought, so it is extraordinary that Albert Henry Smyth chose not to publish it in his edition of Franklin's collected works. Smyth writes, "The work has no value, and it would be an injury and an offence to the memory of Franklin to republish it." *The Writings of Benjamin Franklin*, ed. Albert Henry Smyth (New York: Macmillan, 1907), vol. 2, p. vi. Hereafter cited as *Writings*. Smyth's (religiously inspired?) delicacy had a far-reaching impact, since his edition was the standard collected works until Yale University Press began publication of the *Papers* in 1959.

3. *Autobiography*, p. 96.

4. Ibid.

5. Ibid., pp. 61–62. Franklin's accounts of his youthful attempts to teach himself style are deservedly famous. He would rewrite essays he had read in *The Spectator* and then compare them with the originals to discover and correct his faults. Frequently he also turned prose into verse or composed long lists of synonyms in order to cultivate fluidity. "Sometimes," he tells us, "I had the Pleasure of Fancying that in certain Particulars of small Import, I had been lucky enough to improve the Method or the Language" of *The Spectator* essays (*Autobiography*, p. 62). Given the grace of Franklin's later writings, it can hardly be denied that his method succeeded.

6. *The Religion of Nature Delineated* was published privately in 1722, and a second, corrected edition appeared shortly before Wollaston's death in late 1724. Ten thousand

copies had been sold by the time of the sixth edition in 1738, a quite extraordinary run for the eighteenth century. By 1759 the reading public had gone through no fewer than eight English editions. French and German translations, in addition to a number of pirated editions, were also published. By the day's standards, Wollaston's book was a best-seller. Enthusiasm on the American side of the Atlantic was also high. Yale adopted it as a textbook in the 1740s and in 1750 Samuel Johnson advised Franklin to make it required reading at the proposed Philadelphia Academy. Letter from Samuel Johnson, 14 [?] December 1750, *Papers*, vol. 4, p. 79. One can only imagine Franklin's unspoken reaction to the request.

7. See, for example, Thomas Jefferson's letter (13 June 1814) to Thomas Law: "Of all the theories on [moral principle], the most whimsical seems to have been that of Wollaston, who considers *truth* as the foundation of morality. The thief who steals your guinea does wrong only inasmuch as he acts a lie, in using your guinea as if it were his own. Truth is certainly a branch of morality, and a very important one to society. But, presented as its foundation, it is as if a tree, taken up by the roots, had its stem reversed in the air, and one of its branches planted in the ground." *The Writings of Thomas Jefferson* (Monticello Edition), ed. Andrew A. Lipscomb (Washington, D.C.: Thomas Jefferson Memorial Association, 1903), vol. 14, p. 139. Jonathan Edwards also criticized Wollaston's thesis, although less harshly. See Norman Fiering, *Jonathan Edwards's Moral Thought and Its British Context* (Chapel Hill: University North Carolina Press, 1981), pp. 132–38. I cannot resist quoting Leslie Stephen's deliciously acerbic evaluation of Wollaston: "Thirty years' profound meditation had convinced Wollaston that the reason why a man should abstain from breaking his wife's head was, that it was a way of denying that she was his wife. All sin, in other words, was lying." *History of English Thought in the Eighteenth Century* (London: Smith, Elder, 1876), vol. 1, p. 130.

8. See Gerald R. Cragg, *Reason and Authority in the Eighteenth Century* (Cambridge: Cambridge University Press, 1964), and R. W. Harris, *Reason and Nature in the Eighteenth Century* (London: Blandford, 1968). John Redwood's *Reason, Ridicule and Religion: The Age of Enlightenment in England, 1660–1750* (Cambridge: Cambridge University Press, 1976) is also helpful. For an excellent discussion of the physico-theological roots of eighteenth-century British liberal Christianity, see Richard S. Westfall, *Science and Religion in Seventeenth-Century England* (Ann Arbor: University of Michigan Press, 1973), especially pp. 162–92.

9. *Autobiography*, p. 145. See Franklin's 9 November 1765 letter to his wife, Deborah, in which he contemptuously says that howsoever his "pious Presbyterian Countrymen" may revile him, they at least do "not charge me (as they do their God) with having plann'd Adam's Fall, and the Damnation of Mankind." *Papers*, vol. 12, p. 360. For similar sentiments, see *Papers*, vol. 2, p. 114. But see also Franklin's letter to his sister Jane Mecom (17 July 1771) in which he says that the "Doctrine of Pre-existence . . . seems to have been invented with a good Intention, to save the Honour of the Deity, which was thought to be injured by the Supposition of his bringing Creatures into the World to be miserable, without any previous misbehaviour of theirs to deserve it." *Papers*, vol. 18, p. 184. It is not clear how to interpret this. Is it another example of Franklin's religious

ambivalence? Is it a reflection of his perspectival notion that religious fictions are useful and hence ought to be recommended to the uneducated populace? Or is this simply a piece of sarcasm?

One thing is clear: Franklin disliked what he took to be the "Old Testament" tendencies of New England theology. These included the belief in an angry and avenging God as well as divinely sanctioned actions that strike the moralist as suspect. As late as 1784 he expressed such reservations: "there are several Things in the Old Testament, impossible to be given by *divine* Inspiration; such as the Approbation ascribed to the Angel of the Lord, of that abominably wicked and detestable Action of Jael, the wife of Heber, the Kenite [Judges 4]. If the rest of the Book were like that, I should rather suppose it given by Inspiration from another Quarter, and renounce the whole." Letter to Joseph Priestley, 21 August 1784, *Writings,* vol. 9, p. 267.

10. Although most of his contemporaries read Wollaston as a Christian, albeit a liberal one, there have been recent scholarly attempts to argue that in fact he was a deist. See, for example, Ernest Tuveson, "Shaftesbury and the Age of Sensibility," in *Studies in Criticism and Aesthetics 1660–1800,* ed. Howard Anderson and John S. Shea (Minneapolis: University of Minnesota Press, 1967), pp. 73–93; Redwood, *Reason, Ridicule and Religion;* and Ernest Gordon Rupp, *Religion in England: 1688–1791* (Oxford: Clarendon Press, 1986). I remain unconvinced, however. As Chester Chapin points out in "Was William Wollaston (1660–1724) a Deist?" (*ANQ: A Quarterly Journal of Short Articles, Notes, and Review,* n.s., 7 [April 1994]: 72–76), Wollaston never criticizes any accepted doctrine of orthodox Christianity, nor does he deny revelation. But either, surely, is a sine qua non for designation as a deist.

11. In fact, Wollaston thinks that standard arguments for the existence of God based on inferences from the physical order have been so "beaten and exhausted" that they have become standard fare ("are no one's property") and have left little "new" to say. *The Religion of Nature Delineated* (London: Sam. Palmer, 1724), p. 6. How much of this is meant as praise, and how much is irony, is not clear (to me, at least).

12. Ibid., p. 7.

13. Ibid., pp. 15, 26.

14. Ibid., p. 202.

15. Ibid., p. 203.

16. Ibid., p. 202.

17. Ibid., p. 203.

18. For a twentieth-century defense of Wollaston's ethical theory, see Stanley Tweyman, "Truth, Happiness and Obligation: The Moral Philosophy of William Wollaston," *Philosophy* 51 (1976): 35–46.

19. Franklin's entire *Dissertation* has been reprinted twice in recent years: *Papers,* pp. 57–71, and Walters, *The American Deists,* pp. 55–66.

20. *Papers,* vol. 1, p. 59.

21. Ibid.

22. Ibid., p. 60.

23. Ibid.

24. Ibid., p. 62.

25. Ibid. There is a superficial resemblance between Franklin's separation of freedom of the will and liberty and that of Jonathan Edwards in his later (1754) *Enquiry into . . . Freedom of Will.* (Modern edition: *The Works of Jonathan Edwards,* vol. 1, ed. Paul Ramsey [New Haven: Yale University Press, 1957].) I am not suggesting that Edwards was influenced by Franklin's *Dissertation.* I doubt very much if he ever saw a copy. I am merely pointing out an interesting parallel of thought that is perfectly compatible with the metaphysics of either man. If God is absolutely sovereign (from either Calvinist or mechanical first principles), then human freedom is necessarily rendered problematic.

26. *Papers,* vol. 1, p. 62.

27. Ibid., pp. 62–63.

28. In a 9 November 1779 letter to Benjamin Vaughan, Franklin recollects burning copies of the *Dissertation. Papers* vol. 31, p. 59. Franklin's zeal and the ravages of time were so effective that only four copies are known to have survived: one each in the British Museum, the Library of Congress, the John Carter Brown Library, and Yale University Library. Vaughan was editor of Franklin's *Political, Miscellaneous, and Philosophical Pieces* (London, 1779).

29. *Papers,* vol. 1, p. 63.

30. Ibid., p. 64.

31. No commentator has done a better job of analyzing Franklin's intellectual debt to Newton than I. Bernard Cohen. See especially his *Benjamin Franklin: His Contribution to the American Tradition* (Indianapolis: Bobbs-Merrill, 1953), *Franklin and Newton: An Inquiry into Speculative Newtonian Experimental Science and Franklin's Work in Electricity as an Example Thereof* (Philadelphia: American Philosophical Society, 1956), and *Benjamin Franklin's Science* (Cambridge, Mass.: Harvard University Press, 1990).

32. *Papers,* vol. 1, p. 64.

33. Ibid., p. 65.

34. Ibid.

35. Ibid.

36. Ibid., pp. 66, 68.

37. Ibid., p. 68.

38. Ibid., p. 66.

39. Ibid., pp. 69, 70.

40. Ibid., p. 71.

41. This expression, of course, is coined by Willey in his magisterial *The Eighteenth-Century Background* (London: Chatto and Windus, 1940). For sheer grace and erudition, Willey's essays in the history of seventeenth- and eighteenth-century ideas are unparalleled.

42. James's psychological reflections on the temperamental origins of philosophizing (or theologizing) run throughout his corpus, appearing as early as the *Principles of Psychology*'s 1891 analysis of reasoning and the emotions. Other obvious treatments include "The Will to Believe" and "The Sentiment of Rationality," in *The Will to Believe and Other Essays in Popular Philosophy* (1897); "On a Certain Blindness in Human Beings,"

in *Talks to Teachers on Psychology* (1899); "The Sick Soul," in *The Varieties of Religious Experience* (1902); "The Present Dilemma in Philosophy," in *Pragmatism* (1907); "The Types of Philosophic Thinking," in *A Pluralistic Universe* (1909); and "The Place of Affectional Facts in a World of Pure Experience," in *Essays in Radical Empiricism* (1912).

43. Franklin later considered his love of dispute a handicap. Early on, he recounts in his *Autobiography* (pp. 64–65), he discovered the Socratic method through Xenophon's *Memorabilia*, "was charm'd with it, adopted it, dropt my abrupt Contradiction, and positive Argumentation, and put on the humble Enquirer and Doubter." But it becomes clear that Franklin came to regret his earlier disputatious approach not because he considered it morally questionable, but because it was not as successful in debate as the Socratic style: "I found this Method safest for my self and very embarassing to those against whom I used it, therefore I took a Delight in it, practis'd it continually and grew very artful and expert in drawing People even of superior Knowledge into Concessions the Consequences of which they did not foresee, entangling them in Difficulties out of which they could not extricate themselves, and so obtaining Victories that neither my self nor my Cause always deserved." In spite of this last bit of self-deprecation, Franklin comes across rather badly here.

44. *Autobiography*, p. 114. In his 9 November 1779 letter to Benjamin Vaughan (see n. 28 of this chapter), Franklin says this: "The Great Uncertainty I found in Metaphysical Reasonings, disgusted me, and I quitted that kind of Reading & Study, for others more satisfactory."

45. Regardless of how much firsthand knowledge of Bacon Franklin had, he was enough of a child of the Enlightenment to adopt the seventeenth-century natural philosopher as a hero. Poor Richard characterizes him as "*great* in his prodigious genius, parts and learning." But he goes on to say that Bacon was also "*little*, in his servile compliances with a *little* court, and submissive flattery of a *little* prince." *Papers*, vol. 3, p. 337. The rebellious author of the Dogood letters admired the scientist but deplored the sycophant.

Franklin's contemporary Pierre Jean Georges Cabanis once said that Franklin was fond of quoting Bacon's claim that "a little philosophy inclineth man's mind to atheism; but depth in philosophy brings the man's mind about to religion." (Cited in Aldridge, *Benjamin Franklin and Nature's God*, p. 226.) Perhaps. But there is no evidence in Franklin's written works that he had more than a passing acquaintance of Bacon.

46. See especially Edwards's *A Treatise on the Nature of Religious Affectations*, ed. John Smith (New Haven: Yale University Press, 1959 [first published 1746]), and Schleiermacher's *On Religion: Speeches to its Cultured Despisers*, trans. John Oman (New York: Harper and Row, 1958 [first published in 1799]).

47. I hasten to add that I do not intend these remarks to call into question the value or even the veracity of religious belief. Contrary to Freud's claim in works such as *The Future of an Illusion* (1927), I fail to see how the aetiology of a belief says much about its truth-value. As Plato pointed out, we frequently may be right for the wrong reasons. It follows that psychological accounts of religious beliefs do not thereby invalidate them.

48. *Autobiography*, pp. 97, 103–4. Alehouses and coffee houses were the hubs of intellectual life in eighteenth-century London, and the youthful Franklin's publication of the *Dissertation* gained him entrance to both. He met Bernard de Mandeville at a Cheap-

side tavern called the Horns. He also frequently discoursed with men of science at Batson's Coffee House. There, a Dr. Pemberton promised to introduce him to Isaac Newton (see chap. 3, n. 31). But the meeting, as Franklin ruefully says, "never happened." Although not a habitué, Franklin also specifically mentions visiting Saltero's coffee house and museum in Cheyne Walk, Chelsea.

49. Ibid., p. 96. But Franklin admits that "the principles of my Pamphlet" also "appeared abominable" to Palmer.

50. Ibid., p. 115.

51. Ibid., p. 157. For more detailed discussion of this planned book, see chap. 5.

52. Elizabeth Flower and Murray G. Murphey, *A History of Philosophy in America* (New York: Putnam, 1976), vol. 1, p. 101.

53. Parts of this paragraph are taken from my *Rational Infidels,* pp. 56–57.

54. *Autobiography,* p. 114. Clearly, however, many of Franklin's later acquaintances knew of the treatise and its general subject matter, even if they had not actually read it. On 8 May 1779, for example, Joseph Priestley wrote Franklin about a pamphlet he had just read "in favour of the doctrine of Necessity." Priestley thought it had been published in 1729 and asked Franklin if it was the one he wrote. *Papers,* vol. 29, pp. 453–54. Benjamin Vaughan wrote a couple of months later asking the same question. Letter to Franklin, 30 July 1779, *Papers,* vol. 29, pp. 175–76. The treatise both men referred to is probably Anthony Collins's *A Dissertation on Liberty and Necessity . . . and an epistle dedicatory to truth* (London, 1729). It will be recalled that Franklin's *Dissertation* was published four years earlier.

55. *Papers,* vol. 3, pp. 88–89, letter to Thomas Hopkinson (?), 16 October 1746. In a marginal note written later by Franklin, he says that this passage is an explicit reference to his youthful *Dissertation.* The immediate occasion for Franklin's reminiscence was his reflections on Andrew Baxter's aprioristic *An inquiry into the Nature of the Human Soul, wherein its Immateriality is evinced,* 2d ed. (London, 1737).

56. "To the Royal Academy of Brussels," in *Franklin's Wit and Folly: The Bagatelles,* ed. Richard E. Amacher (New Brunswick, N.J.: Rutgers University Press, 1953), pp. 68–69. Some marginalia that Franklin scribbled in his copy of Joseph Tucker's *A Letter from a Merchant in London to His Nephew in North America* (London, 1766) are pertinent here. Franklin writes at one point, "The difference between a Fool and a Madman is said to be, that the Fool reasons wrong from right Premises, the Madman right but from wrong Premises." *Papers,* vol. 17, p. 356. By this assessment, the *Dissertation* was the product of a Fool: the aloof distance of God is a correct premise, but the necessitarian and amoralistic conclusions spun from it are harmful. In any case, metaphysical reason is either foolish or insane.

57. In a 1771 letter to his sister Jane Mecom, Franklin also suggests, in a protopositivist vein, that speculative reason cannot stretch far enough to generate theological conclusions: "Where [God] has thought fit to draw a Veil, our Attempting to remove it may be deem'd at least an offensive Impertinence. And we shall probably succeed little better in such an Adventure to gain forbidden Knowledge, than our first Parents did when They ate the Apple." *Papers,* vol. 18, p. 185.

58. *Autobiography,* p. 114.

Chapter 3: The Great Insight

1. *Autobiography,* p. 105.

2. There were other reasons for a bad conscience as well, not the least of which was Franklin's shabby treatment of Deborah Read, a young Philadelphia maid he had courted and with whom he had "interchang'd some Promises." Once in London, Franklin forgot "by degrees" his "Engagements" with the poor girl and sent her but one letter, "and that was to let her know I was not likely soon to return." Despairing over her faithless Ben, Deborah married another during his absence, but the union proved a miserable one. Franklin eventually married Deborah after she was widowed, but his cavalier treatment of her is surely, as he himself admits, one of the "Great Errata" of his life. *Autobiography,* pp. 92, 96, 106–7.

3. Part of the reason Denham had returned to England involved honor. Franklin tells us (*Autobiography,* pp. 104–5) that Denham, before his immigration to America, had gone bankrupt in Bristol and accumulated huge debts. Once in America he made his fortune. "Returning to England in the Ship with me, He invited his old Creditors to an Entertainment. . . . And when they expected nothing but the Treat, every Man at the first Remove, found under his Plate an Order on a Banker for the full Amount of the Unpaid Remainder with Interest." (A similar culinary surprise is the climax of Arthur Conan Doyle's "The Naval Treaty." Could Doyle have been inspired by Franklin's memoirs?)

Frederick Tolles is correct when he says that Thomas Denham is "one of the most shadowy" figures to walk across the pages of Franklin's *Autobiography. Quakers and the Atlantic Culture* (New York: Macmillan, 1960), p. 57. Almost nothing is known of him apart from Franklin's sketchy treatment. But it is possible to locate him within the wider ethos of mid-Atlantic Quaker mercantilism in the early eighteenth century, and Tolles does this admirably. See his "Benjamin Franklin's Business Mentors: The Philadelphia Quaker Merchants," *William and Mary Quarterly,* 3d ser., 4 (January 1947): 60–69; *Meeting House and Counting House: The Quaker Merchants of Colonial Philadelphia, 1682–1763* (Chapel Hill, N.C.: University of North Carolina Press, 1948), especially chap. 3 and appendix A; and *Quakers and the Atlantic Culture,* especially chap. 4.

4. *Autobiography,* p. 107.

5. Ibid. An interesting study of Denham as Franklin's "savior" is Hugh J. Dawson, "Fathers and Sons: Franklin's 'Memoirs' as Myth and Metaphor," *Early American Literature* 14 (1979–80): 269–78.

6. Fowler, *Stages of Faith,* p. 173.

7. *Autobiography,* p. 96.

8. Ibid., pp. 98–99.

9. For Franklin's description of de Mandeville, see ibid., p. 97.

10. Ibid., p. 114.

11. Ibid.

12. Ibid., pp. 102–3.

13. Compare the young Franklin's admiration for the London saint with his son

William's description of Bruges nuns as "Cross Old Maids who had forsakin The World becaus the World had first forsaken them." Letter of William Franklin to Sarah Franklin, 10 October 1761, *Papers,* vol. 9, p. 366.

14. Fowler, *Stages of Faith,* pp. 173, 182–83.

15. *Autobiography,* p. 107.

16. There are few figures in early eighteenth-century America as colorful as Keimer. The *Dictionary of American Biography* entry on him provides a bare-bones resumé of his astounding career, but two articles help to flesh out the fascinating story: Stephen Bloore, "Samuel Keimer: A Footnote to the Life of Franklin," *Pennsylvania Magazine of History and Biography* 54 (July 1930): 255–87, and C. Lennart Carlson, "Samuel Keimer: A Study in the Transit of English Culture to Colonial Pennsylvania," *Pennsylvania Magazine of History and Biography* 61 (1937): 357–86. Moore's essay is somewhat limited because he considers Keimer primarily as a "footnote" to Franklin. Carlson's essay, on the other hand, treats at some length Keimer's literary and religious interests. For a treatment of Keimer that treats him (somewhat too strongly) as a deist, see C. E. Jorgenson, "A Brand Flung at Colonial Orthodoxy: Samuel Keimer's 'Universal Instructor in All Arts and Sciences,'" *Journalism Quarterly* 12 (September 1935): 272–77.

17. Although in later life more publisher than author, Keimer did write, prior to his emigration to America, three pamphlets that fairly well express his typically protestant quest for religious purity. The pamphlets were composed in a burst of energy in 1718: *A Search after Religion,* in which Keimer attacks both established church and dissenting sects; *A Brand pluck'd from the Burning,* a spiritual autobiography; and *The Platonick Courtship,* a Bunyanesque denunciation of worldliness and sectarian error.

18. *Autobiography,* p. 88. Keimer first publicly espoused both of these points in *A Search after Religion.*

19. Fowler, *Stages of Faith,* p. 198.

20. Ibid., pp. 197, 186, 198. The Ricoeur texts Fowler cites are *The Symbolism of Evil,* trans. Emerson Buchanan (Boston: Beacon Press, 1967), pp. 351–52, and "The Hermeneutics of Symbols and Philosophical Reflection," in *The Philosophy of Paul Ricoeur,* ed. Charles E. Reagan and David Stewart (Boston: Beacon Press, 1978), pp. 36–58.

21. "Articles of Belief and Acts of Religion," *Papers,* vol. 1, p. 102. Franklin always retained this mechanistic notion of God as First Cause. Later in life, he would describe the deity as "notoriously the greatest mechanic in the universe." W. T. Franklin, *Memoirs of the Life and Writings of Benjamin Franklin,* vol. 2, p. 298.

22. "Articles of Belief and Acts of Religion," *Papers,* vol. 1, p. 102.

23. Ibid.

24. Avid reader of *The Spectator* that he was, Franklin would have run across the idea of the great Chain of Being in its pages. References to the cosmic chain run through the essays, with explicit discussions in numbers 519 (1712) and 621 (1714), among others. But the idea was in the air, and he probably encountered it elsewhere as well. As Arthur Lovejoy said of the eighteenth century, "there has been no period in which writers of all sorts—men of science and philosophers, poets and popular essayists, deists and orthodox divines—talked so much about the Chain of Being, or accepted more implicit-

ly the general scheme of ideas connected with it, or more boldly drew from these their latent implications, or apparent implications." *The Great Chain of Being: A Study of the History of an Idea* (Cambridge, Mass.: Harvard University Press, 1936), p. 183. The Enlightenment savants accepted the metaphor, as did their Calvinist counterparts. Franklin would have absorbed the idea by cultural osmosis, and its influence clearly shows up in his later "An Arabian Tale" (*Papers,* vol. 31, pp. 308–9), in which Franklin has one of his angelic characters say: "Contemplate the scale of beings, from an elephant down to an oyster. Thou seest a gradual diminution of faculties and powers, so small in each step that the difference is scarce perceptible. There is no gap, but the gradation is complete. . . . [I]n ascending from an elephant to the infinitely Great, Good, and Wise, there is also a long gradation of beings, who possess powers and faculties of which thou canst yet have no conception." The date of this bagatelle is contested. See A. Stuart Pitts, "The Sources, Significance, and Date of Franklin's 'An Arabian Tale,'" *Publication of the Modern Language Association of America* 57 (1942): 155–68.

25. *Papers,* vol. 1, p. 102.

26. Ibid., pp. 102–3.

27. Ibid., p. 103.

28. Ibid., pp. 103–4.

29. Aldridge, *Benjamin Franklin and Nature's God,* pp. 29–33. Aldridge apparently still accepts the polytheism thesis. He repeats it, for example, in his recent "Enlightenment and Awakening in Edwards and Franklin," in *Benjamin Franklin, Jonathan Edwards, and the Representation of American Culture,* ed. Barbara B. Oberg and Harry S. Stout (New York: Oxford University Press, 1993), p. 31.

30. The Newton quotation is taken from a conversation the mathematician supposedly had with his nephew John Conduitt in 1725, which was subsequently recorded in a memorandum entitled "A Remarkable and Curious Conversation between Sir Isaac Newton and Mr. John Conduitt." Quoted by Parton, *Life and Times,* vol. 1, p. 175. The memorandum originally appeared in David Brewster's 1855 biography of Newton.

31. One of the men Franklin met in London was Dr. Henry Pemberton (1694–1771). As noted earlier, the two were introduced at Batson's Coffee House (*Autobiography,* p. 97). Pemberton, who James Parton tells us was an intimate of Newton's, and who in fact edited the third edition of the *Principia,* promised to introduce Franklin to Newton, but the meeting never came off. Parton surmises that Newton may have shared with Pemberton the polytheistic views transcribed by his nephew John Conduitt (see n. 19, above), and Pemberton in turn passed them on to Franklin. We know Franklin was also familiar with John Ray's *The Wisdom of God manifested in the Works of the Creation* (London, 1691) because Franklin mentioned it in the "Articles" and recommends it as required reading in his 1749 "Proposals Relating to the Education of Youth in Pennsylvania." *Papers,* vol. 3, p. 417. In that treatise Ray likewise suggests the possibility of planetary spirits. Finally, Franklin may have read Plato's *Timaeus,* which distinguishes between the Demiurge and intermediate gods. How familiar Franklin was with Plato is unclear, although he certainly knew his Xenophon. C. M. Walsh offers a circumstan-

tial argument in "Franklin and Plato," *Open Court* 20 (March 1906): 129–33, which concludes Franklin knew Plato's dialogues well. I find his case unconvincing.

32. Aldridge's interpretation of the later Franklin texts as expressions of continuing allegiance to polytheism are in *Benjamin Franklin and Nature's God,* pp. 31–32.

33. Elizabeth E. Dunn, "From a Bold Youth to a Reflective Sage: A Reevaluation of Benjamin Franklin's Religion," *Pennsylvania Magazine of History and Biography* 111 (October 1987): 512. It is worth pointing out that Dunn rather uncritically accepts Aldridge's polytheism thesis, both in this essay and in her later "'A Wall between Them Up to Heaven': Jonathan Edwards and Benjamin Franklin," in Oberg and Stout, *Benjamin Franklin, Jonathan Edwards, and the Representation of American Culture,* pp. 61–62. This is strange, since she also argues that the "Articles" is an irreverent joke.

34. Dunn, "From a Bold Youth," p. 513. Curiously, Dunn remarks that "the document clearly reflects [Franklin's] efforts to arrive at a socially presentable creed." But a less socially acceptable statement of belief can hardly be imagined.

35. On Newton's religious views, see David Brewster, *Memoirs of Sir Isaac Newton* (Edinburgh: Thomas Constable, 1855), vol. 2, pp. 313–59; Herbert Drennon, "Newtonianism: Its Method, Theology, and Metaphysics," *Englische Studien* 68 (1933–34): 397–409; Alexandre Koyre, *From the Closed World to the Infinite Universe* (Baltimore: Johns Hopkins University Press, 1957), pp. 155–89, 206–72; Frank E. Manuel, *The Religion of Isaac Newton* (Oxford: Clarendon Press, 1974); the essays in James E. Force and Richard H. Popkin, *Essays on the Context, Nature, and Influence of Isaac Newton's Theology* (Dordrecht: Kluwer Academic, 1990), especially Popkin's "The Crisis of Polytheism and the Answers of Vossius, Cudworth, and Newton" (pp. 9–26) and "Polytheism, Deism, and Newton" (pp. 27–42); and J. E. McGuire's "Force, Active Principles, and Newton's Invisible Realm," in his *Tradition and Innovation* (Dordrecht: Kluwer Academic, 1995), pp. 190–238.

36. For an excellent treatment of Franklin as protopragmatist, see James Campbell, "The Pragmatism of Benjamin Franklin," *Transactions of the Charles S. Peirce Society* 31 (Fall 1995): 745–92.

37. Letter to Henry Bouquet, 14 April 1757, *Papers,* vol. 7, p. 182.

38. Letter to Pierre Samuel du Pont de Nemours, 28 July 1768, *Papers,* vol. 15, pp. 181–82.

39. Letter to Joseph Priestley, 7 June 1782, *Writings,* vol. 8, pp. 452–53.

40. Letter to Abbé Soulavie, 22 September 1782, *Writings,* vol. 8, p. 599.

41. Letter to Sir Joseph Banks, 21 November 1783, *Writings,* vol. 9, pp. 117–18.

42. *Papers,* vol. 3, p. 348.

43. Ibid., vol. 1, p. 101. Franklin was so impressed by these lines that he later used them again as one of the epigraphs to his daily record of self-examination in virtue. See chap. 5 for a discussion of this record.

44. *Cato, A Tragedy,* in *Miscellaneous Works of Joseph Addison,* ed. A. C. Guthkelch (London: G. Bell and Sons, 1914), vol. 1, pp. 411–12. In the scene (V, i) Cato sits alone, in a "thoughtful posture," with a copy of "Plato's book on the Immortality of the Soul" (the *Phaedo?*) in his hand and a drawn sword on a nearby table. His soliloquy is quite moving, particularly to someone in Franklin's state of religious indecision:

It must be so—*Plato,* thou reason'st well!—
Else whence this pleasing hope, this fond desire,
This longing after immortality?
Or whence this secret dread, and inward horror,
Of falling into nought? why shrinks the soul
Back on her self, and startles at destruction?
'Tis the divinity that stirs within us;
'Tis heaven it self, that points out an Hereafter,
And intimates eternity to man.
Eternity! thou pleasing, dreadful, thought!
Through what variety of untry'd being,
Through what new scenes and changes must we pass!
The wide, th' unbounded prospect, lyes before me;
But shadows, clouds, and darkness, rest upon it.
Here will I hold. If there's a pow'r above us,
(And that there is all nature cries aloud
Through all her works) he must delight in virtue;
And that which he delights in, must be happy.
But when! or where!—This world was made for *Caesar.*
I'm weary of conjectures—This must end 'em.

45. At one point in his *Autobiography* (p. 115) Franklin thanks providence for preserving him from "*wilful* gross Immorality or Injustice that might have been expected from my Want of Religion." In the original manuscript the sentence concludes with this qualification, which Franklin subsequently crossed through: "some foolish Intrigues with low Women excepted, which from the Expence was rather more prejudicial to me than to them." But Franklin is dissembling at least thrice here: first in crossing out the confession; second, in minimizing his shortcoming in its final clause; third, by conveniently forgetting his knavish treatment of Deborah Read.

46. I believe this is the point Franklin hints at in a computational brainteaser included in the 1757 *Poor Richard.* The teaser, entitled "Paradoxes," has two parts. In the first, Franklin claims that a Christian, a Jew, and a Turk, who all worship on different days of the week, can sail to a specific place on the globe where the differences will converge such that "they shall all keep their Sabbath on one and the same Day." The second part has it that if a Jew, a Christian, and a Turk leave separately on different courses from a particular point on earth, when they return to that point their days of worship will be identical, even though each is not aware of the fact. Franklin is not simply offering a puzzle here. More fundamentally, he is hinting that sectarian distinctions are illusory, that in fact apparent doctrinal differences ultimately, if looked at from a certain perspective (or "point") converge. *Papers,* vol. 7, pp. 85–86.

47. Franklin's position here is similar to that of the theologian Paul Tillich. The claim that discourse about God can never be fully descriptive is an ancient one. Throughout the centuries, Christian and non-Christian theology has held that God-talk is necessarily symbolic, metaphorical, analogous, evocative, even though there is also the con-

stant temptation to forget this and treat the symbols as if they were literal descriptions. Neither Franklin nor Tillich, then, is making an extraordinary claim when he insists on the symbolic nature of God-talk. But in order to get across the point, Tillich, like Franklin before him, distinguishes between "gods" and "God." The former are our symbolic representations of God in which we think of the deity as *a* being that, subsequently, can be experienced, named, and defined in the same way all other beings can. But God as the Ground of being is not *a* being but being itself, and hence immune to classification and description. Tillich's God as the Ground of being is very much like Franklin's First Cause, while his gods-as-beings correspond to Franklin's artifactual sectarian gods. See Tillich's *Systematic Theology,* vol. 1 (Chicago: University of Chicago Press, 1953), especially pp. 211–41.

48. Although Hobbes and Hume tend to be rather coy in their remarks on religious belief, it is relatively clear they think it ultimately stems from fear—in Hobbes's mind, a "perpetual fear" of "death, poverty, or other calamity" that allows man "no repose, nor pause of his anxiety, but in sleep" (*Leviathan,* 1651), while in Hume's mind, a fear of the unknown, which prompts humans to postulate divine explanations, thereby invidiously splitting their allegiance between "invisible, intelligent power[s]" and "sensible, visible objects" (*The Natural History of Religion,* 1757). Feuerbach argues that humans deplete themselves by ascribing their best virtues and talents to an omni-attributed deity who in fact is simply an anthropomorphic projection (*The Essence of Christianity,* 1841), and Freud famously argues that God-belief is an "obsessive infantile neurosis," a cultural defense mechanism by which humans invent a supernatural parent to protect them from the anxiety of living. All four of these skeptics deplore such projections and long for an age in which humans can do without them. Franklin obviously does not concur.

49. The expression "useful fiction" is taken, of course, from Hans Vaihinger's *The Philosophy of "As If,"* trans. C. K. Ogden (New York: Harcourt, Brace, 1925). Vaihinger, a neo-Kantian, argues that our explanatory patterns and conceptual grids are useful fictions that construct more than describe the world. Much of his thought anticipates the twentieth-century social constructivism of figures such as Norwood Hansen, Wittgenstein, Foucault, and Derrida. The failure to appreciate the fact that Franklin evaluated religious beliefs in terms of their existential usefulness has led commentators on his religion astray. For example, in his discussion of Franklin's religion, Paul K. Conkin claims Franklin dismisses religious beliefs as merely "subjectively true" (*Puritans and Pragmatists: Eight Eminent American Thinkers* [New York: Dodd, Mead, 1968], pp. 73–108). Charles Mabee, in his "Benjamin Franklin's Literary Response to Dogmatic Religion" (*American Journal of Theology and Philosophy* 3 [May 1982]: 60–68), confuses Franklin's perspectivism with mere relativism. Erika Seipp, in her *Benjamin Franklins Religion und Ethik* (Giessen: L. C. Wittichlische Hofbuchdruckerei, Darmstadt, 1932), notes the apparently abrupt transition between the *Dissertation* and the "Articles" but fails to explain it.

50. Nietzsche, who endorsed a much more radical perspectivism than did Franklin, makes a similar point in a frequently cited passage from "On Truth and Falsity in the Ultramoral Sense," in *Early Greek Philosophy and Other Essays,* trans. Maximilian A.

Mügge (New York: Macmillan, 1911), when he says that human beliefs can become "worn-out metaphors which have become powerless to affect the senses; coins which have their obverse effaced and now are no longer of account as coins but merely as metals" (p. 180). For Franklin, religious beliefs are invariably expressed in one or another idiom that in time loses currency.

51. The meaning and purposefulness of an individual's religious perspective are dependent on that perspective's usefulness in orienting him or her in the world, and this in turn is partly founded, as explained in the text, on the perspective's social currency. An endearing illustration of this point can be found in an exchange of letters in 1779 between Franklin and his grown daughter Sarah Bache. Sarah writes that her son, William, after listening to "a foolish Girl" talk about death, awoke in the night screaming that death was coming for him. As Sarah recalls, "I was so frightened says he that I sweat all over and I jump'd out of Bed and pray'd up to Herculas." When Sarah asked the lad what he prayed, "down he went on his knees with uplifted hands, I think I never saw such a picture of devotion, and repeated the lords prayer." Sarah asks her father's advice: "wether tis best to instruct him in a little religion or let him pray a little longer to Herculas." Letter to Franklin, 17 January 1779, *Papers,* vol. 28, p. 391. Franklin responds with the good-natured humor of an affectionate grandfather, but there is also seriousness in the reply: "teach [Will] . . . To direct his worship more properly, for the deity of *Hercules* is now quite out of fashion." Letter to Sarah Bache, 3 June 1779, *Papers,* vol. 29, p. 614. Franklin is not at all upset, as his more orthodox contemporaries might have been, that young Will prays to Hercules. The one God, after all, wears many faces and has many names. But Franklin thinks it well to instruct the child in a more conventional religious perspective because Hercules worship, being "quite out of fashion," lacks social currency and hence utility.

Elsewhere, Franklin recommends that another grandson, Benjamin Franklin Bache, be educated while in Europe as a good Presbyterian (and republican). *Papers,* vol. 29, pp. 351, 358, 614. Again, this is not because Franklin is sympathetic with Presbyterianism, but rather because it, and not Roman Catholicism, is the predominant religious currency of the America to which young Ben will eventually return.

52. For the source and content of Ricoeur's "second naivete" see n. 20 of this chapter.

53. Aldridge, *Benjamin Franklin and Nature's God,* p. 219. Aldridge characteristically calls the incident "a direct link, of course, to the polytheism of Franklin's youthful 'Articles of Belief.'"

54. Franklin had lived in London since his 1764 appointment by the Province of Pennsylvania to serve as a lobbyist for a change from proprietary to royal government. Six years later the Massachusetts Assembly appointed him to serve as its London agent. Franklin pursued his political missions, performed experiments in natural philosophy, met and conversed with royalty and men of letters, traveled to the Continent, and in general enjoyed himself immensely for close to ten years. But in the final days of 1772 he set in motion events that would render him persona non grata at the Court of Saint James. He sent to Thomas Cushing, speaker of the Massachusetts House of Representa-

tives, a bundle of eighteen letters written by Boston officials between 1767 and 1769. Some of the letters came from the pen of Thomas Hutchinson, then the seated governor of Massachusetts, and lieutenant-governor at the time the letters were written. In them, Hutchinson deplores the mood of sedition in the colonies and urges the British government to take harsh measures before things get out of hand. He even suggests that such measures may include an "abridgement of what are called English liberties." Letter from Hutchinson, 20 January 1769, *Papers,* vol. 20, p. 550. Franklin warned Cushing not to publish the letters but somewhat disingenuously gave him permission to show them to so many others that their eventual publication was inevitable. They appeared in the *Boston Gazette* in June 1773 under the accusatory banner "Born and Educated among Us."

The uproar on both sides of the Atlantic was immediate. Although the letters revealed little about Hutchinson's politics that wasn't already well known, Bostonians were furious. Moreover, the scandal caused by the purloining and publication of official private correspondence enraged the British government. In late 1773, one John Temple, an American-born official in the British customs service, was accused of stealing the letters and smuggling them to Massachusetts. He naturally denied the charge but was challenged to a duel, fought it to a stalemate, and was challenged again. Franklin stepped in at this point, and on Christmas Day he published a statement in the London *Public Advertiser* confessing his guilt. He took the secret of how he actually obtained the letters to his grave.

On 29 January 1774 Franklin was summoned before a Privy Council already furious over the recently arrived news of the Boston Tea Party and pilloried there as a common thief for over an hour. Franklin wisely remained silent. The next day he was dismissed from the position of Deputy Postmaster General of North America, a royal appointment he had held since 1753.

It is not at all clear what Franklin's motives were in sending the stolen letters to Thomas Cushing. He always insisted that his primary intention was merely to make public the shoddy counsel men like Hutchinson were giving the British government, not to exacerbate the increasingly tense relationship between the colonies and London. If this was really his purpose, he failed miserably. See Bernard Bailyn, *The Ordeal of Thomas Hutchinson* (Cambridge, Mass.: Belknap Press of Harvard University Press, 1974), for more on the affair and its aftermath. The complete packet of letters is reprinted in *Papers,* vol. 20, pp. 539–80. For Franklin's attempts to exonerate himself, see, for example, *Papers,* vol. 21, pp. 86–96, 112–15, 147, and especially his "Tract Relative to the Affair of Hutchinson's Letters," pp. 414–35.

55. Pertinent extracts from Williams's 57-page memoirs dealing with his recollections of Franklin appear in an article by a twentieth-century author of the same name, David Williams, "More Light on Franklin's Religious Ideas," *American Historical Review* 43 (1938): 803–13. The editors of volume 21 of the *Papers* doubt the eighteenth-century Williams's account that Franklin sought refuge in his Chelsea home. They reject the circumstantial evidence Williams presents to defend his claim, arguing that it was given only toward the end of Williams's life, and that "the uncorroborated recollections

of the old are shaky evidence" (p. 120). Moreover, they can discover no contemporary support for Williams's claim. Still, the editors do not deny Franklin's acquaintance with Williams, nor his description of Franklin's religious beliefs. Nicolas A. Hans discusses The Thirteen in his "Franklin, Jefferson, and the English Radicals," *Proceedings of the American Philosophical Society* 98 (1954): 406–26. Background information on Williams, as well as specific commentary (pp. 8–13) on the founding of The Thirteen and its liturgical manifesto, may be found in E. V. Lucas, *David Williams: Founder of the Royal Literary Fund* (London: John Murray, 1920). Lucas claims Franklin was one of the club's founding members. See also Thomas Morris, *General View of the Life and Writings of the Reverend David Williams* (London, 1791), and *Papers*, vol. 21, pp. 119–21; vol. 22, pp. 173–74, 595–96; vol. 27, pp. 354–55; vol. 30, p. 623; vol. 31, p. 193.

56. Williams, "More Light on Franklin's Religious Ideas," p. 810.

57. Ibid., p. 812. A few years earlier, in June 1768, Franklin published a little piece in the *London Chronicle* entitled "The Captivity of William Henry." (There is some question about the document's canonicity. See the long introduction to it in *Papers*, vol. 15, pp. 145–48.) The essay purports to be a synopsis of a book written by one William Henry recounting his captivity and six-year sojourn among the Seneca Indians. No such book has ever been discovered. But Franklin uses his imaginary summary as a vehicle to voice his opinions about religion. One section in particular anticipates the remark in The Thirteen's credo about "local Gods." Canassatego, the Seneca chief, says, "White man, . . . Hear me! You say there is but one great good [god]. You know of no more. If there were but one, how unhappy must be he, without friends, without companions, and without that equality in conversation, by which pleasure is mutually given and received." Instead, continues Canassatego, there are "more than a hundred" gods: "Every country has its great good [god], who first peopled that country." *Papers*, vol. 15, p. 152.

58. James's essay "The Will to Believe" first appeared in *The Will to Believe and Other Essays in Popular Philosophy* (1897) and has been republished many times since. Three recent excellent treatments of his religious views are Henry Samuel Levinson, *The Religious Investigations of William James* (Chapel Hill, N.C.: University of North Carolina Press, 1981), James C. S. Wernham, *James' Will-to-Believe Doctrine: A Heretical View* (Kingston, Ontario: McGill-Queen's University Press, 1987), and Bennett H. Ramsey, *Submitting to Freedom: The Religious Vision of William James* (New York: Oxford University Press, 1993).

59. This is a point that clearly escapes those critics who argue that religious belief is false because frequently born of fear (see n. 34, above). But surely believing in God for bad reasons is no argument against the existence of God.

60. Letter from George Whitefield, 17 August 1752, *Papers*, vol. 4, p. 343. Several commentators have pointed out that there are striking similarities between Puritan conversion accounts and Franklin's autobiographical descriptions of his retreat from the necessitarianism of the *Dissertation*. See, for example, William Breitenbach, "Religious Afflictions and Religious Affectations: Antinomianism and Hypocrisy in the Writings of Edwards and Franklin," in Oberg and Stout, *Benjamin Franklin, Jonathan Edwards, and the Representation of American Culture*, pp. 13–26; David Levin, "The *Autobiography* of Benjamin Franklin: The Puritan Experimenter in Life and Art," *Yale Review* 53 (1964): 261–75; David

L. Parker, "From Sound Believer to Practical Preparationist: Some Puritan Harmonics in Franklin's *Autobiography,*" in *The Oldest Revolutionary: Essays on Benjamin Franklin,* ed. J. A. Leo Lemay (Philadelphia: University of Pennsylvania Press, 1976), pp. 67–75; and Karl T. Weintraub, "The Puritan Ethic and Benjamin Franklin," *Journal of Religion* 56 (July 1976): 223–37.

61. This problem is one that confronts many present-day historicists. For example, Richard Rorty argues that we need to abandon traditional "metaphysical" assumptions that our knowledge of the world is or can be an accurate reflection of its nature, and instead adopt a postmodernist "ironical" stance. The ironist, as described by Rorty, recognizes the contextuality of his descriptions, values, and theories, and hence accepts that no vocabulary (or, à la Wittgenstein, "language game") is "closer to reality than others." The ironist, in short, is a "nominalist and a historicist. She thinks nothing has an intrinsic nature, a real essence." Richard Rorty, *Contingency, Irony, and Solidarity* (Cambridge: Cambridge University Press, 1989), pp. 73, 74. At the same time, however, Rorty insists on the normative importance of a commitment to eradicate cruelty and promote fellow-feeling ("solidarity"). Thus he calls for an "ironic commitment"—that is, a commitment toward certain goals which recognizes itself as merely contingent, contextual. This strangely dissonant conclusion—namely, that one can be contingently committed—is disconcerting, and parallels the tension within Franklin's theistic perspectivism. I should point out, however, that Franklin's position is not as radical a deconstruction as Rorty's. Franklin allows for a reality—the First Cause—outside of religious language games and believes that those language games, in rough and ready ways, all point to God. Rorty, in what I take to be a misreading of Wittgenstein, refuses to take such discourse seriously and hence would confine us inescapably to our various contextual language games.

62. "A Parable against Persecution," July 1755, *Papers,* vol. 6, p. 123.

63. One of the ironies of Franklin's life is that in spite of his repudiation of the *Dissertation,* he would continue to be either vilified or adulated as a deist until his death. The reputation of infidelity had sunk too deeply in the popular mind, as evidenced by the charges of freethinking cited in the introduction to the present book. Two more examples: in 1768, Jacques Barbeu-Dubourg writes to Franklin in order to solicit his aid in the English (and, he hoped, uncensored) publication of his deistic *Code de l'humanite. Papers,* vol. 15, p. 115; see also Alfred Owen Aldridge, "Jacques Barbeu-Dubourg: A French Disciple of Benjamin Franklin," *American Philosophical Society Proceedings* 95 (1951): 331–92. In 1786, an unknown correspondent, possibly Thomas Paine, sends Franklin a manuscript defense of deism and asks for his comments. *Papers,* vol. 7, p. 294; *Writings,* vol. 9, p. 522.

Chapter 4: A Comfortable Belief

1. *Autobiography,* p. 116. The designation of themselves as "leather aprons" was a proudly rebellious acknowledgment that they were working tradesmen rather than socially and economically privileged gentlemen.

2. Ibid., p. 130.

3. "Rules for a Club Established for Mutual Improvement" (1727), *Papers,* vol. 1, p. 257. These rules, intended as regulatory principles for the Junto's members, consisted of twenty-eight questions that members were to ask themselves at each meeting. Questions typically fell into two categories: prudential ones ("Hath any citizen in your knowledge failed in his business lately, and what have you heard of the cause?" "Have you lately heard of any citizen's thriving well, and by what means?") and moral ones ("What unhappy effects of intemperance have you lately observed or heard; of imprudence, of passion, or of any other vice or folly?" "Hath you lately observed any encroachment on the just liberties of the people?"). The two categories sometimes bled into one another ("Have you lately heard any member's character attacked, and how have you defended it?"). What is noteworthy about the Junto's principles is its strong emphasis on self-examination, public confession, and good works. Although the idiom was different, meetings of the Junto must at times have carried the ambience of a Congregationalist service.

4. See chap. 5 for a detailed discussion of these two books.

5. Bernard Fay, "Learned Societies in Europe and America in the Eighteenth Century," *American Historical Review* 37 (1932): 255–66. Fay claims that the American Philosophical Society, which eventually sprang from the Junto, had "Masonic leanings" from its inception, and that "all the activities of its great 'star,' Benjamin Franklin, were of Masonic inspiration" (p. 258).

6. Chester E. Jorgenson and Frank Luther Mott, "Introduction," *Benjamin Franklin: Representative Selections,* rev. ed. (New York: Hill and Wang, 1962), p. xxxiv.

7. *Autobiography,* p. 117.

8. *Papers,* vol. 1, pp. 260, 264.

9. Ibid., pp. 264–69. The *Papers'* editors claim 1732 as the year Franklin delivered his address, but Alfred Owen Aldridge disputes the date in a review essay of volume 1 in *American Literature* 32 (May 1960): 208–10. Aldridge cites several reasons for his alternative claim that the paper was read in 1730, but his primary argument rests on a letter to Benjamin Vaughan (9 November 1779, *Papers,* vol. 31, pp. 57–60) in which Franklin, after discussing the repudiated *Dissertation,* goes on to say that in 1730 he "wrote a piece on the other side of the question." Aldridge thinks that Franklin's subsequent description of that piece shows it to be "On Providence." Aldridge's reasoning makes sense to me, although he himself admits that Franklin "may well have been mistaken by two years in his letter to Vaughan."

10. John Calvin, *Corpus Reformatorum,* vol. 32, p. 359. Quoted in Wilhelm Niesel, *The Theology of Calvin,* trans. Harold Knight (Philadelphia: Westminster Press, 1956), p. 70.

11. Ibid.

12. John Calvin, *Institutes of the Christian Religion,* book 1, chap. 16, sec. 4, trans. John Allen (Philadelphia: Presbyterian Board of Publishers, 1843), vol. 1, pp. 186–88.

13. Ibid., book 1, chap. 16, sec. 17 (vol. 1, pp. 190–91).

14. The literature on the clash between proponents and detractors of Calvin's doctrine of election is vast, but consideration of the works of Calvin's primary theological

opponent, Jacobus Arminius (1560–1609), is a must. The standard English edition is *The Writings of James Arminius,* ed. James Nichols and W. R. Bagnall (Grand Rapids, Mich.: Baker Book House, 1956). The selections in volume 3 deal especially with the Calvinist doctrines of election and predestination. The essays in Gerald O. McCulloh, *Man's Faith and Freedom: The Theological Influence of Jacobus Arminius* (Nashville: Abingdon Press, 1962), are instructive, particularly McCulloh's own "The Influence of Arminius on American Theology," pp. 64–87. See also Francis Albert Christie, "The Beginnings of Arminianism in New England," *Papers of the American Society of Church History,* ser. 2, 3 (1910–11): 151–72; and Gerald J. Goodwin, "The Myth of 'Arminian-Calvinism' in Eighteenth-Century New England," *New England Quarterly* 41 (1968): 213–37.

15. Calvin, *Institutes of the Christian Religion,* book 1, chap. 16, sec. 3 (vol. 1, p. 185).

16. Ibid., book 1, chap. 16, sec. 1 (vol. 1, p. 183).

17. John Winthrop, *Journal: History of New England, 1630–1649,* ed. James Kendall Hosmer (New York: Scribner, 1908), vol. 2, p. 276.

18. William Bradford, *Of Plymouth Plantation, 1620–1647,* ed. Samuel Eliot Morison (New York: Knopf, 1952), p. 58.

19. Increase Mather, *An Essay for the Recording of Illustrious Providences* (Boston, 1684), preface (preface pages unnumbered). Mather's book, like so many of his son Cotton's, illustrates the claim made in chapter 1 that turn-of-the-century Calvinists frequently found themselves caught between two worlds. Mather's *Essay* intends primarily to discuss the supernatural phenomenon of special providences. But in doing so, it also provides the reader with meticulously detailed and frequently accurate descriptions of the physical phenomena on which the divine interventions presumably ride. Mather's observations of the natural world are made with all the loving care of a natural philosopher. At times he seems almost to forget that they are not ends in themselves, and that he has a theological purpose for cataloging them.

As a youth, Franklin had read Mather's book (although in recalling it toward the end of his life he misremembered the title as *Remarkable Providences*). He has nothing to say about its argument, focusing instead on the "very obscure Hand"—that is, style—of its "eminent" author. Letter to Noah Webster, 26 December 1789, *Writings,* vol. 10, p. 76.

20. See chap. 1, n. 28.

21. *Papers,* vol. 1, pp. 264, 265.

22. Ibid., pp. 265–66.

23. Ibid., p. 266.

24. Ibid., p. 267.

25. Ibid., pp. 267–68.

26. Ibid., p. 268.

27. It will be recalled from chapter 2 that the reductio ad absurdum is the argument of choice in the *Dissertation.* Franklin's lifelong employment of reductios is not unusual, since they are the best kind of argument for the satirist who wishes to make a serious point humorously.

28. *Papers,* vol. 1, p. 269.

29. Ibid.

30. Ibid.

31. See chap. 3 for a discussion of James.

32. See my *Rational Infidels,* chap. 2.

33. *Papers,* vol. 7, p. 295; *Writings,* vol. 9, p. 522. Few of Franklin's letters are as controversial as this one. The three surviving manuscript versions of it have different dates, and the name of the addressee has been obliterated. The traditional date assigned the letter is 3 July 1786, but the editors of the *Papers* think the authentic date some thirty years earlier, 13 December 1757. (See their explanation, vol. 7, p. 293.) The recipient of the letter, who seems to have asked Franklin's opinions about a deistic manuscript, was long thought to have been Thomas Paine. The earlier letter date would effectively rule out that possibility. Although I am uncertain to whom Franklin wrote his letter, I'm not convinced by the claim that it was drafted in the late 1750s. For an early discussion of the letter's authenticity, see the anonymous "Dr. Franklin and Thomas Paine," *Religious Inquirer* 9 (August 1826): 157.

34. A rather unpleasant example of one of Franklin's own invocations of Christian fiction as a palliative to popular discontent is to be found in his 1768 essay "On the Labouring Poor." Decrying those political agitators who would stir up the masses to insurrection, he counsels laborers to be content with their lot and to give an honest day's work for an honest day's wage. In chiding them he invokes scripture: "SIX *days shalt thou labour.* This is as positive a part of the commandment as that which says, *the* SEVENTH *day thou shalt rest.* But we remember well to observe the indulgent part, and never think of the other. St. Monday is generally as duly kept by our working people as Sunday; the only difference is, that, instead of employing their time, cheaply, at church, they are wasting it expensively at the alehouse." *Papers,* vol. 15, p. 107.

35. Ibid., vol. 7, p. 294; *Writings,* vol. 9, p. 520.

36. Letter to John Franklin, [May?] 1745, *Papers,* vol. 3, pp. 26–27.

37. Letter to James Hutton, 7 July 1782, *Writings,* vol. 8, p. 561. This is one of the most anguished letters Franklin ever penned. Scarcely any other document, except his "Articles of Belief," reveals so much emotion. He is stunned by the waste of innocent life—"Some of the Indians may be suppos'd to have committed Sins, but one cannot think the little Children had committed any worthy of Death"—and maddened with rage at the thought that the imprecations are ultimately because "a single Man in England [George III], who happens to love Blood and to hate Americans," hired German mercenaries "to destroy in a continued Course of bloody Years near 100,000 human Creatures . . . of useful Talents, Virtues and Abilities." Franklin's rage intensifies as he continues. "It is he who has furnished the Savages with Hatchets and Scalping Knives, and engages them to fall upon our defenceless Farmers and murder them with their Wives and Children, paying for their Scalps." It is this, perhaps, that has led colonialists to "kill all Indians that fall into their Hands without Distinction." So George's crimes are compounded, and while innocents fall around him he "lives, enjoys all the good Things this World can afford, and is surrounded by Flatterers, who keep even his Conscience quiet by telling him he is the best of Princes!" Although ripped apart by such apparent injustice, Franklin ends his letter by reaffirming his faith in providence. But his protestation sounds thin and somewhat

forced: "I cannot . . . part with the comfortable Belief of a Divine Providence. . . . In this Faith let you & I, my dear Friend, comfort ourselves; it is the only Comfort, in the present dark Scene of Things, that is allow'd us." Franklin's religious ambivalence speaks loudly here. His head sees blatant injustice that his heart cannot accept.

Years earlier, in 1755, Franklin had likewise expressed concern for Indians in a letter to James Read when he advised him to keep firearms away from hot-tempered men who might "rashly hurt our Friends with them." *Papers,* vol. 6, p. 234. And in 1764 he wrote a scathing indictment of the Lancaster, Pennsylvania, massacre of Indian men, women, and children by the so-called Paxton Boys, declaring that "THE BLOOD OF THE INNOCENT WILL CRY TO HEAVEN FOR VENGEANCE." "A Narrative of the Late Massacres," *Papers,* vol. 11, p. 53.

38. Letter to Jean-Baptiste Le Roy, 18 April 1787, *Writings,* vol. 9, p. 572. Similarly, Franklin laments in another late letter that our hopes for a healthy and happy old age are frequently dashed by hard reality. "But what signifies our Wishing? Things happen, after all, as they will happen." In his case, for example, "three Contraries have befallen me, being subject to the Gout and the Stone, and not being yet Master of all my Passions." In spite of all his hopes, he is "like the proud Girl . . . Who wished and resolv'd not to marry a Parson, nor a Presbyterian, nor an Irishman; and at length found herself married to an Irish Presbyterian Parson." Letter to George Whatley, 23 May 1785, *Writings,* vol. 9, p. 333.

39. Letter to George Whitefield, [prior to] 2 September 1769, *Papers,* vol. 16, p. 192. Franklin's words reflected his growing alarm over the deteriorating relations between Britain and America. The editors of the *Papers* write that it is unclear whether Franklin's comments about providence here were intended "to tease his friend [Whitefield] into annoyance." But as I read the letter, there is not a trace of jocularity or playfulness in it, only heartfelt pain and bewilderment.

40. Ibid.

41. Two additional examples of Franklin's ambivalence about providence are instructive. In 1753 he cautions against an overzealous redressing of poverty by warning that God may have "appointed Want and Misery as the proper Punishments for, and Cautions against as well as necessary consequences of Idleness & Extravagance." He then warns that if "we attempt to mend the scheme of Providence and to interfere in the Government of the World, we had need to be very circumspect lest we do more harm than Good." Letter to Peter Collinson, 9 May 1753, *Papers,* vol. 4, p. 480. This is a strangely passive, almost fatalistic statement for an Enlightenment figure, particularly one as enthusiastic for public works and self-improvement as Franklin. In *Poor Richard* for 1757, Franklin speculates whether the anticipated Halley's comet will "strike the Earth" and "instantly beat it to Pieces." In prose whose piety would have pleased the Mathers, he then writes: "But our Comfort is, the same great Power that made the Universe, governs it by his Providence. And such terrible Catastrophes will not happen till 'tis best they should." *Papers,* vol. 7, p. 91.

42. Almost, but not quite. A strange little piece written in 1778 suggests that Franklin despaired at times over the likelihood of a general providence. The essay, published

originally as "Lettre à Madame B[rillon]" but better known as "The Ephemera," is a sad reflection on the fleetingness and vanity of human endeavor. Pretending to overhear the lecture of an aged "Ephemere," a fly that normally lives but one day, Franklin recounts the insect's melancholy ruminations: "What now avails all my Toil and Labour in amassing Honey-Dew on this Leaf, which I cannot live to enjoy! What the political Struggles I have been engag'd in for the Good of my *Compatriotes* . . . ; or my philosophical Studies for the Benefit of our Race in general! . . . Our present Race of Ephemeres will in a Course of Minutes, become corrupt . . . And in Philosophy how small our Progress! . . . And what will become of all History, . . . When the World itself, even the whole Moulin Joli, shall come to its End, and be buried in universal Ruin?" *Papers,* vol. 27, pp. 434–35. How seriously should this little fable be taken as a reflection of Franklin's views? It's not clear. The gloom of this piece, if genuine, may be more expressive of a passing mood than a lifelong conviction—although it is worth pointing out that it is perfectly in keeping with Franklin's Calvinist background. But Franklin could also have written the piece to play on the sympathies of the much younger Madame Brillon, whom he was quite unsuccessfully trying to seduce. For more on Franklin and Madame Brillon, see chap. 6.

43. Letter to Jane Mecom, 17 July 1771, *Papers,* vol. 18, p. 185. Franklin adds that he has "perhaps as much Trust in God as the most pious Christian." Franklin earlier (1 March 1766) expressed a similar view to Jane when he wrote that "the World is a pretty good sort of a World." *Papers,* vol. 13, p. 188. Leo Lemay also attributes to him a "Parody of and Reply to a melancholy religious Meditation" (*Pennsylvania Gazette* 8 [August 1734]: 203), in which a similar sentiment is defended. See J. A. Leo Lemay, *The Canon of Benjamin Franklin, 1722–1776: New Attributions and Reconsiderations* (Newark: University of Delaware Press, 1986), p. 86. See also Franklin's letter to Montandouin, 17 March 1779, *Papers,* vol. 29, p. 143.

44. To the Editor of the Federal Gazette (1788), "A Comparison of the Conduct of the Ancient Jews and of the Anti-Federalists in the United States of America," *Writings,* vol. 9, pp. 702–3.

45. Motion for Prayers in the Convention, 28 June 1787, ibid., p. 601. For an interesting treatment of this episode, see William G. Carr, *The Oldest Delegate: Franklin in the Constitutional Convention* (Newark: University of Delaware Press, 1990), pp. 96–101. Compare Franklin's motion with his reflections on the American defeat of the British: "Do not imagine that I am vain enough to ascribe our Success to any superiority. . . . I am too well acquainted with all the Springs and Levers of our Machine, not to see, that our human means were unequal to our undertaking, and that, if it had not been for the Justice of our Cause, and the consequent Interposition of Providence, in which we had Faith, we must have been ruined. If I had ever before been an Atheist, I should now have been convinced of the Being and Government of a Deity!" Letter to William Strahan, 19 August 1784, *Writings,* vol. 9, p. 262.

46. Letter to George Whitefield, 19 June 1764, *Papers,* vol. 11, pp. 231–32.

47. Ibid., p. 232. Just a week later (25 June 1764) Franklin expressed similar sentiments to William Strahan (*Papers,* vol. 11, p. 241): "God has been very good to you, from whence I think you may be *assured* that he loves you, and that he will take at least as good Care

of your future Happiness as he has done of your present. What Assurance of the *Future* can be better founded, than that which is built on Experience of the *Past?*" Franklin concludes with a line that points to his perspectival endorsement of useful religious fictions: "If you had Christian Faith, quantum suff[icit]. This might not be necessary: But as Matters are, *it may be of Use*" (my emphasis).

48. Letter to George Whatley, 23 May 1785, *Writings*, vol. 9, pp. 333–34. Franklin says the following at one point in this long letter: "You see I have some reason to wish, that, in a future State, I may not only be *as well as I was,* but a little better. And I hope it; for I . . . *trust in God.* And when I observe, that there is great Frugality, as well as Wisdom, in his Works, since he has been evidently sparing both of Labour and Materials; for by the various wonderful Inventions of Propagation, he has provided for the continual peopling of his World with Plants and Animals, without being at the Trouble of repeated new Creations; and by the natural Reduction of compound Substances to their original Elements, capable of being employ'd in new Compositions, he has prevented the Necessity of creating new Matter; so that the Earth, Water, Air, and perhaps Fire, which being compounded from Wood, do, when the Wood is dissolved, return, and again become Air, Earth, Fire, and Water; I say, that, when I see nothing annihilated, and not even a Drop of Water wasted, I cannot suspect the Annihilation of Souls, or believe, that he will suffer the daily Waste of Millions of Minds ready made that now exist, and put himself to the continual Trouble of making new ones. Thus finding myself to exist in the World, I believe I shall, in some Shape or other, always exist; and with all the inconveniences human Life is liable to, I shall not object to a new Edition of mine; hoping, however, that the *Errata* of the last may be corrected."

49. Letter to James Hutton, 7 July 1782, ibid., vol. 8, p. 562.

50. Letter to Ezra Stiles, 9 March 1790, ibid., vol. 10, p. 84. See also the (possibly just conventional) assurances of an afterlife Franklin offers to a grieving Catherine Greene on 15 February 1764 (*Papers*, vol. 11, p. 79) and to his sister Jane Mecom on the loss of her daughter Sarah Flagg (ibid., p. 253).

On at least one occasion Franklin speculated about divine providence and the afterlife in strongly Calvinist terms. If, he says, heaven is a state of happiness that is infinite in degree and eternal in duration, there is no action that a finite human being can perform to "deserve such rewards." Consequently, it is divine grace, not good works, that pave the road to paradise: "Even the mix'd imperfect Pleasures we enjoy in this World, are rather from God's goodness than our Merit; how much more such Happiness from Heaven. For my own part I have not the Vanity to think I deserve it, the Folly to expect it, nor the ambition to desire it; but content myself in submitting to the Will and Disposal of . . . God." Letter to Joseph Huey, 6 June 1753, *Papers*, vol. 4, p. 505.

51. Letter to James Hutton, 7 July 1782, ibid., vol. 8, pp. 561, 562.

Chapter 5: Taming Wolves

1. *Autobiography*, p. 106.

2. *Papers*, vol. 1, pp. 99–100. The spirit of self-creation behind these words is reminiscent of Nietzsche's famous injunction to "make one's life a work of art!"

3. *Autobiography,* pp. 95–106.

4. Ibid., p. 106.

5. Ibid., p. 58. Years later, Franklin would reminisce fondly about both Cotton Mather and his father, Increase. He met both of them as a youth in Boston and once heard Increase preach. In 1723, while visiting Cotton, Franklin brained himself on a low beam in the clergyman's study. Cotton, ever on the lookout for opportunities for instruction, instantly moralized: "Let this be a Caution to you not always to hold your Head so high; Stoop, young Man, stoop—as you go through the World—and you'll miss many hard thumps." Franklin good-humoredly adds that this was such an effectual way of "hammering Instruction into one's Head" that he never forgot it. Letter to Samuel Mather, 7 July 1773, *Papers,* vol. 20, pp. 286–87.

6. Daniel Defoe, *An Essay Upon Projects* (1697); reissued as *Essays upon Several Projects: Effectual Ways for Advancing the Interests of the Nation* (London, 1702), p. 1. For background on the *Essay,* see Michael Shinagel, *Daniel Defoe and Middle-Class Gentility* (Cambridge, Mass.: Harvard University Press, 1968), chap. 4, and James Sutherland, *Defoe* (London: Methuen, 1937), pp. 55–59. For an analysis of Defoe's influence on Franklin that also discusses Franklin's admiration for Defoe's fiction, see Gilbert D. McEwan, "'A Turn of Thinking': Benjamin Franklin, Cotton Mather, and Daniel Defoe on 'Doing Good,'" in *The Dress of Words: Essays on Restoration and Eighteenth-Century Literature in Honor of Richmond P. Bond,* ed. Robert B. White Jr. (Lawrence: University of Kansas Libraries, 1978), pp. 53–65.

7. Cotton Mather, *Bonifacius,* p. 17. Levin's introduction (pp. vii–xxviii) to his edition of *Bonifacius* is excellent. Phyllis Franklin's *Show Thyself a Man: A Comparison of Benjamin Franklin and Cotton Mather* (The Hague: Mouton, 1969) is worth consulting, as is chap. 2 of Mitchell Robert Breitwieser's *Cotton Mather and Benjamin Franklin: The Price of Representative Personality* (Cambridge: Cambridge University Press, 1984). A broader treatment of Mather on virtue is found in Richard F. Lovelace, *The American Pietism of Cotton Mather: Origins of American Evangelicalism* (Grand Rapids, Mich.: Christian University Press, 1979), chaps. 5 and 6.

8. Cotton Mather, *Bonifacius,* p. 30.

9. Ibid., p. 41.

10. Ibid., pp. 11–12.

11. *Autobiography,* p. 58. There is, of course, a great deal of debate over just how much Franklin's Puritan background influenced his moral thought. I have argued throughout these pages for a pervasive influence, thus parting company, for example, with Norman S. Fiering, who, in his "Benjamin Franklin and the Way to Virtue" (*American Quarterly* 30 [Summer 1978]: 199–223), argues that "it makes little sense to relate Franklin's moral thought to Puritanism" (p. 219), and that Franklin is best viewed as a proto-utilitarian (an equally incorrect assessment, in my view). For an analysis that carefully shows the Puritan influence on Franklin's moral thought, see William Pencak, "Benjamin Franklin's *Autobiography,* Cotton Mather, and a Puritan God," *Pennsylvania History* 53 (January 1986): 1–25.

12. Cotton Mather, *Bonifacius,* p. 143.

13. The theme of inevitable social and individual progress is, of course, characteristic of the Enlightenment (although there were a few dissenters, such as Rousseau and Hammann). Helpful discussions of it include John Baillie, *The Belief in Progress* (New York: Scribner, 1951), pp. 88–119; Carl Becker, *The Heavenly City of the Eighteenth-Century Philosophers* (New Haven: Yale University Press, 1933), especially pp. 71–118; J. B. Bury, *The Idea of Progress: An Inquiry into Its Origin and Growth* (New York: Macmillan, 1932), pp. 98–237; Ernst Cassirer, *The Philosophy of the Enlightenment,* trans. Fritz C. A. Koelln and James P. Pettegrove (Princeton: Princeton University Press, 1951); Ulrich Im Hof, *The Enlightenment,* trans. William E. Yuill (Oxford: Blackwell, 1994), pp. 157–253; Theodore Olson, *Millennialism, Utopianism, and Progress* (Toronto: University of Toronto Press, 1982), pp. 191–218; John Passmore, *The Perfectibility of Man* (London: Duckworth, 1970), pp. 149–213; and R. V. Sampson's excellent *Progress in the Age of Reason: The Seventeenth Century to the Present Day* (Cambridge, Mass.: Harvard University Press, 1956), pp. 1–157.

14. This point is brilliantly made by Ronald A. Bosco, "'He that best understands the World, least likes it': The Dark Side of Benjamin Franklin," *Pennsylvania Magazine of History and Biography* 111 (October 1987): 525–54. This is one of the finest essays ever written on Franklin. As I have argued here, much of Franklin's darker side comes from the residue of his childhood Calvinism. But part of his cynicism about human goodness may also stem from his London acquaintance with Bernard de Mandeville, who argues in his *Fable of the Bees* that most individuals act throughout their lives from essentially selfish motives.

This is not to say, however, that Franklin's perspective was thoroughgoingly pessimistic. In addition to the writings discussed in the text, see also three additional pieces that Leo Lemay ascribes to Franklin: "The Trial and Reprieve of Prouse and Mitchel" (1729), "'Y.Z.' on the Benevolence as well as Selfishness of Man" (1722), and "Pennsylvanus on brave Men at Fires" (1733). Lemay, *Canon of Benjamin Franklin,* pp. 40–41, 74–75, 81–82, respectively. Even if Lemay is correct about the canonicity of these pieces—and I am inclined to think he is—it is important to keep in mind that they were written for the popular press, and Franklin never allowed himself public expressions of his deep-seated pessimism. To do so would have violated his socially conservative conviction that the masses were in need of edifying (and pacifying) moral and religious beliefs.

15. Letter to Joseph Priestley, 8 February 1780, *Papers,* vol. 31, p. 455. As Franklin says, "We may perhaps learn to deprive large Masses of their Gravity, & give them absolute Levity, for the sake of easy Transport. Agriculture may diminish its Labour and double its Produce; all Diseases may by sure means be prevented or cured, not excepting even that of Old Age, and our Lives lengthened at pleasure even beyond the antediluvian Standard."

16. Ibid. In a letter written two days earlier to Richard Price, Franklin voiced similar concerns: "We make daily great Improvements in *Nature*—There is one I wish to see in Moral Philosophy; the Discovery of a Plan; that would induce & oblige Nations to settle their Disputes without first Cutting one anothers Throats. When will human Reason be sufficiently improv'd to see the Advantage of this! When will Men be convinc'd that even successful Wars do at length become Misfortunes to those who unjustly

commenc'd them." Letter to Richard Price, 6 February 1780, *Papers,* vol. 31, p. 453. Franklin's doubts about virtue keeping up with science are especially striking in light of the fact that he considered the former more important than the latter. As he says in midlife, long after securing his international reputation as a scientist, "The Knowledge of Nature may be ornamental, and it may be useful, but if to attain an Eminence in that, we neglect the Knowledge and Practice of essential Duties, we deserve Reprehension. For there is no Rank in Natural Knowledge of equal Dignity and Importance with that of being a good Parent, a good Child, a good Husband, or Wife, a good Neighbour or Friend, a good Subject or Citizen, that is, in short, a good Christian." Letter to Mary Stevenson, 11 June 1760, ibid., vol. 9, p. 121.

17. *A Defence of the Rev. Mr. Hemphill's Observations* (1735), *Papers,* vol. 2, p. 114.

18. Letter to James Logan, 1737 [?], *Papers,* vol. 2, p. 185.

19. Letter to Abbé de la Roche, April 1786, *Writings,* vol. 9, p. 506. "I sometimes wonder that all good Men and Women are not by Providence kept free from Pain and Disease. In the best of all Possible Worlds, I should suppose it must be so; and I am piously inclin'd to believe that this World's not being better made was owing merely to the Badness of the Materials."

20. Letter to Peter Collinson, 9 May 1753, *Papers,* vol. 4, p. 481. Franklin speaks particularly of Indians here, but his remarks are clearly not intended to be limited to "heathens."

21. *Autobiography,* p. 161. Also see Franklin's observation later on in the *Autobiography* (p. 212) that statesmen put forth public Measures "seldom . . . *From previous Wisdom,*" but usually because they find themselves "*forced by the Occasion.*" The passage quoted in the text is from a manuscript Franklin included in his memoirs entitled "Observations on my Reading History in Library, May 9, 1731." In it Franklin laments that history shows politics to be a self-interested, unvirtuous enterprise, and he proposes the formation of a "united Party for Virtue" to rectify the situation. This proposal is frequently interpreted as evidence of Enlightenment optimism on Franklin's part, but this is a misreading. Franklin makes it clear that the men who would constitute this body will be "govern'd by suitable good and wise Rules" (p. 162). This suggests, as I argue in the text, that Franklin sees a program of habituation to virtue as a necessary corrective to our corrupt natural inclinations. It is not a question of "perfecting" human nature so much as finding a method to hold it in check.

22. "The Busybody," no. 2, 11 February 1728/29, *Papers,* vol. 1, p. 121. Franklin concludes that "*Virtue alone is sufficient to make a Man Great, Glorious and Happy.*"

23. "A Man of Sense," 1734/35, *Papers,* vol. 2, pp. 15–17. In this little dialogue, written for the Junto, Franklin argues that a "Science of Virtue" is necessary for both human happiness and wisdom. Without it, regardless of how educated persons are, they remain fools, dunces, blockheads.

24. Letter to Thomas Cushing, 10 June 1771, *Papers,* vol. 18, p. 124; letter to John Fothergill, 14 March 1764, ibid., vol. 11, p. 185. The Fothergill letter is of some interest, because it suggests the ambivalence in Franklin's attitude toward human nature that he often tried to ameliorate through humor. Franklin asks Fothergill when he intends

to retire and then teasingly tells him that he ought not remain in medical practice because of the illusion that his ministrations do any good. "Half the Lives you save are not worth saving, as being useless; and almost the other Half ought not to be sav'd, as being mischievous. Does your Conscience never hint to you the Impiety of being in constant Warfare against the Plans of Providence? Disease was intended as the Punishment of Intemperance, Sloth, and other Vices; and the Example of that Punishment was intended to promote and strengthen the opposite Virtues. But here you step in officiously with your Art, disappoint those wise Intentions of Nature, and make Men safe in their Excesses." Now, on one level Franklin is having a bit of fun with his physician friend, not only complimenting his medical skill in a humorous, backhanded fashion, but also taking a shot or two at the Calvinist notion of special providences. But when one reads this passage against the gloomy pronouncements on human nature sprinkled throughout Franklin's writings, not to mention, as we saw in chapter 4, his sometimes desperate need to believe in providence in order to assure himself of ultimate justice for human wickedness, then his apparently light-hearted quips here about "Intemperance, Sloth, and other Vices" take on a darker tone.

25. *Autobiography*, p. 160. Franklin goes on to remark that the reader of his memoirs will perhaps see traces of pride throughout. "For even if I could conceive that I had compleatly overcome it, I should probably [be] proud of my Humility."

26. Letter to Joseph Priestley, 7 June 1782, *Writings*, vol. 9, pp. 451–52. In a bagatelle ("The Whistle") written for Madame Brillon in late 1779, Franklin claims that a "great Part of the Miseries of Mankind, were brought upon them by the false Estimates they had made of the Value of Things." His list of idolatrous pleasures would have made his Presbyterian forebears proud: lust for public recognition and popularity, opulence, revelry, vanity, and so on. The implication, again very Calvinistic, is that there is a dark side to human nature that drives individuals toward these ultimately unfulfilling goals. Letter to Madame Brillon, 16 November 1779, *Papers*, vol. 31, pp. 69–77. Nine years earlier, Franklin discussed a book by one Jacob Ilive, published in 1730, which argued that the world in fact was hell, a place of punishment for those who had transgressed in earlier lives. Although Franklin obviously thinks the thesis quaint, he concedes that it strikes an intuitive chord because humans "are devils to one another; so that, on the established doctrine of the goodness and justice of the great Creator, this apparent state of general and systematical mischief seemed to demand some such supposition." But then, ever ambivalent, Franklin retreats: "But our reasoning powers, when employed about what may have been before our existence here, or shall be after it, cannot go far." Letter to Jane Mecom, 30 December, *Papers*, vol. 17, pp. 315–16.

27. Thomas Jefferson was to share this enthusiasm. This is one of the reasons Jefferson was an adherent of the "moral faculty" theory defended by Shaftesbury, among others. As he wrote to his nephew Peter Carr (10 August 1787), "This sense is as much a part of [man's] nature, as the sense of hearing, seeing, feeling; it is the true foundation of morality. . . . The moral sense, or conscience, is as much a part of man as his leg or arm. It is given to all humans in a stronger or weaker degree, as force of members is given them in a greater or less degree. It may be strengthened by exercise, as may any par-

ticular limb of the body. This sense is submitted, indeed, in some degree, to the guidance of reason; but it is a small stock which is required for this: even a less one than what we call common sense. State a moral case to a ploughman and a professor. The former will decide it as well, and often better than the latter, because he has not been led astray by artificial rules." *The Writings of Thomas Jefferson,* ed. Albert Ellery Bergh (Washington, D.C.: Thomas Jefferson Memorial Association, 1903), vol. 6, pp. 257–58. See also Jefferson's letter to Thomas Law, ibid., vol. 14, pp. 141–44. Jefferson's practical fear of basing virtue on reason was that it could legitimize an elitism in which intellectuals are ethically privileged. The natural aristocracy was to be groomed for leadership, not autocracy. For discussions of Jefferson on the moral faculty, see Adrienne Koch, *The Philosophy of Thomas Jefferson* (Chicago: Quadrangle Books, 1943), pp. 9–22; Charles B. Sanford, *The Religious Life of Thomas Jefferson* (Charlottesville: University Press of Virginia, 1984), pp. 43–54; and my *Rational Infidels,* chap. 5.

28. *Autobiography,* p. 63. One is reminded here of the Old Testament story of Shadrach, Meshach, and Abednego (Daniel 1), who refused to eat the meat dishes of their Babylonian captors and thrived on a diet of vegetables and water. A boy raised in a piously dissenting way undoubtedly would have known the story.

29. Ibid., pp. 87, 88.

30. Ibid., pp. 155–56.

31. Ibid., p. 156. Robert Middlekauf's *Benjamin Franklin and His Enemies* (Berkeley: University of California Press, 1996) is a disturbing but penetrating reminder that Franklin was not immune to moral irrationalities and lapses of integrity. He may not have been as corrupt as John Adams always insisted he was. But, as Middlekauf says, "neither was he simple and innocent" (p. 211).

32. *Autobiography,* p. 114. At least one Franklin scholar, Leo Lemay, argues that a short piece published in *General Magazine* 1 (March 1741), which defends a determinism very much like that of the *Dissertation,* was penned by Franklin. The article, "Letter from Theophilus, Relating to the Divine Prescience," argues that if God is not the principal efficient cause of every action, then some actions would be independent of God. But this is absurd, violating as it does the doctrine of divine prescience or foreknowledge. Consequently, God is the efficient cause of every action. This implies a necessitarianism that denies free will. It also means that God is directly responsible for the world's evil.

Both the terse, syllogistic style of argumentation (the characteristically Franklinian reductio ad absurdum) and the concordance of its denial of free will with the *Dissertation*'s conclusion point to Franklin's authorship. The question then arises: how is it that just a few years after his "conversion" and the writing of the "Articles" he reverts to the deterministic nihilism of his *Dissertation*? Several responses come to mind. One, as Lemay suggests, is that Franklin wanted a controversial piece in the *Magazine* to raise interest and boost circulation. Another is that Franklin penned a controversial piece that he himself intended (pseudonomously) to take apart in future issues. But a third is that the denial of free will is one of those doctrines he considered true though not very useful. The head acknowledged it, the heart cried against it. See Lemay, *Canon of Benjamin Franklin,* pp. 103–4.

33. *Autobiography,* p. 114.

34. Franklin proclaims in the "Articles," for example, that the God above gods is good and "abhorrest in thy Creatures Treachery and Deceit, Malice, Revenge, Intemperance and every other hurtful Vice; but Thou art a lover of Justice and Sincerity, of Friendship, Benevolence, and every Virtue." *Papers,* vol. 1, p. 105. He prays for a "VIRTUOUS and HOLY Life" and promises "continual Endeavours and Resolutions" to eschew vice and embrace virtue (p. 107). In a long recitation of duty, he vows humbleness, charity, integrity, compassion, and so on, and concludes by asking God's help to become "Truly Virtuous and Magnanimous" (p. 109).

35. *Autobiography,* p. 148.

36. As Aristotle says in the *Nicomachean Ethics* (book 2, i), virtue is "a result of habit." Humans acquire virtues "by first exercising them, as also happens in the case of the arts as well. For the things we have to learn before we can do them, we learn by doing them, e.g. men become builders by building and lyre-players by playing the lyre; so too we become just by doing just acts, temperate by doing brave acts. . . . It makes no small difference, then, whether we form habits of one kind or another from our very youth; it makes a very great difference, or rather *all* the difference." Trans. David Ross, revised by J. L. Ackrill and J. O. Urmson (Oxford: Oxford University Press, 1986), pp. 28–29. Aristotle makes a similar point in his *Eudemian Ethics,* trans. Michael Woods (Oxford: Clarendon Press, 1982), book 2, i–ii.

37. Letter to Mary Stevenson, 28 October 1768, *Papers,* vol. 15, p. 244.

38. "A Letter from Father Abraham, to His Beloved Son," 1758 [?], *Papers,* vol. 8, pp. 124–25. This document appeared in the first (of only three) issues of the *New-England Magazine* (August 1758), edited by Benjamin Mecom, Franklin's nephew. It is not entirely clear that the piece was written by Franklin, but there are so many parallels between its advice for cultivating virtue and the *Autobiography*'s description of Franklin's plan for moral self-improvement that his authorship is probable. For a fuller discussion see Jack C. Barnes, "A Moral Epistle: A Probable Addition to the Franklin Canon," *New England Quarterly* 30 (1957): 73–84.

39. "Letter from Father Abraham," *Papers,* vol. 8, p. 125. At the beginning of chapter 2 of *Bonifacius,* for example, Mather says, "Every man upon Earth may find in himself something that wants mending; and the work of *repentance* is to inquire, not only *what we have done,* but also, *what we have to do?* Frequent SELF-EXAMINATION, is the duty and the prudence, of all that would *know themselves,* or would not *lose themselves.* The great intention of SELF-EXAMINATION is, to find out, the points, wherein we are to *amend our ways*" (p. 35, Levin edition). Mather then goes on to prescribe regular times for self-examination, preferably in the evenings, just as Franklin does.

40. "Letter from Father Abraham," *Papers,* vol. 8, p. 128. One is reminded here of Locke's plan in his *Essay Concerning Human Understanding* to search for the "original, certainty, and extent of *human knowledge*" (I, 1). See chap. 1 on Locke.

41. "Letter from Father Abraham," vol. 8, p. 128.

42. Some of the best analyses are Herbert W. Schneider, "The Significance of Benjamin Franklin's Moral Philosophy," *Studies in the History of Ideas* 2 (New York: Colum-

bia University Press, 1925), pp. 293–312; Campbell Tathan, "Benjamin Franklin, Cotton Mather, and the Outward State," *Early American Literature* 6 (Winter 1971–72): 223–33; David Larson, "Franklin on the Nature of Man and the Possibility of Virtue," *Early American Literature* 10 (Fall 1975): 111–20; and Fiering, "Benjamin Franklin and the Way to Virtue."

43. *Autobiography,* p. 149. Franklin's virtues were temperance, silence, order, resolution, frugality, industry, sincerity, justice, moderation, cleanliness, tranquility, chastity, and humility ("imitate Jesus and Socrates"). Ibid., pp. 149–50.

44. Ibid., p. 151. For Franklin, small daily victories such as he battled for in his plan of self-improvement were the heart of both morality and happiness. Few persons will ever perform heroic, self-sacrificial deeds; nor need they do so. As Dorothy Day, cofounder of the Catholic Worker Movement, would later insist, moral improvement and the attainment of happiness is accomplished "by little and by little." Franklin echoes this sentiment in a 1768 letter to Lord Kames: "I have long been of an Opinion . . . that . . . Happiness consists more in Small Conveniences or Pleasures that occur every day, than in great Pieces of good Fortune that happen but seldom to a Man in the Course of his Life." *Papers,* vol. 15, pp. 60–61.

45. *Autobiography,* p. 152.

46. Ibid., p. 148. In virtue as well as religion, Franklin the experimentalist always valued works over mere words. One of his more memorable expressions of this is in a letter to Jane Mecom, 16 September 1758, *Papers,* vol. 8, p. 155. In it, Franklin refers to the children's verse "A Man of Words and not of Deeds / Is like a Garden full of Weeds." This is his gloss:

> 'Tis a pity that *Good Works* among some sorts of People are so little Valued, and *Good Words* admired in their Stead: I mean seemingly *pious Discourses,* instead of *Humane Benevolent Actions.* These they almost put out of countenance, by calling Morality *rotten Morality,* Righteousness *ragged Righteousness* and even *filthy Rags;* and when you mention *Virtue,* they pucker up their Noses as if they smelt a Stink; at the same time that they eagerly snuff up an empty canting Harangue, as if it was a Posie of the Choicest Flowers. So they have inverted the good Old Verse, and say now,
>
> A Man of Deeds and not of Words
> Is like a Garden full of ______.
>
> I have forgot the Rhime, but remember 'tis something the very Reverse of a Perfume. So much by Way of Commentary.

Franklin's most obvious target here is the shallowly pious Calvinist who discounts human attempts at virtue on the grounds of utter moral depravity, and who would rather listen to long-winded sermons on the futility of human works than actually dirty his hands by engaging in them. But by implication his scorn stretches to armchair moralists of any or no sectarian persuasion.

47. Never one to miss an opportunity to instruct in virtue, Franklin even argued that chess could serve as a moral monitor. In his 1779 bagatelle "The MORALS OF CHESS,"

he argues that, when played properly, the game cultivates intellectual and moral virtues such as foresight, circumspection, caution, preservation of resources, hope, a regard for equality, and civility. *Papers,* vol. 29, pp. 750–57. This is one instance, however, in which Franklin seems not to have followed his own intuition that one becomes good by doing good. According to all accounts, he was an impatient and testy chess player who was not above noisily drumming his fingers to distract his opponent or rearranging the board pieces if his opponent momentarily left the table. For more on "The MORALS OF CHESS," see *Papers,* vol. 30, pp. 18, 19–20.

48. Perry Miller agrees with Lawrence, as does Randall Stewart. Miller sees Franklin's morality as a justification for economic exploitation (*Jonathan Edwards* [New York: William Sloan Associates, 1949], pp. 116–17); Stewart even more harshly thunders that the values Franklin defended "started us on the road which has led to a gadgeteers' paradise" but, more significantly, a human nightmare (*American Literature and Christian Doctrine* [Baton Rouge: Louisiana State University Press, 1958], p. 34).

49. Letter to Joseph Priestley, 19 September 1772, *Papers,* vol. 19, p. 300. See also *Papers,* vol. 20, pp. 336–38; vol. 29, pp. 283–84, 318–19, 445; vol. 31, p. 456. Franklin was properly rebutted on one occasion in which he recommended his moral algebra. In an 8 April 1779 letter he advised Jonathan Williams Jr. to weigh the pros and cons of the marriage he was contemplating. *Papers,* vol. 29, pp. 283–84. A week later Williams replied: "I have used [the algebraic calculus] already in one or two Instances with some Success, but in the matrimonial way I a little differ from your Opinion, & instead of my never beeing married if I don't 'use it' I am afraid I shall never be married if I do, for the negative Column seems in this Instance the weightiest. Before a Man is married he must *fall* in love and this seems to be as involuntary an act as *falling* into a Well—which requires something more than algebra to get out of." Letter to Franklin, 13 April 1779, *Papers,* vol. 29, pp. 318–19. Franklin must have smiled at this good-natured and entirely appropriate reminder that sometimes important life decisions cannot be solved algebraically. Given his theistic perspectivism, it is a conclusion with which he clearly sympathized.

50. *Autobiography,* p. 156.

51. Ibid. As was frequently his custom in his self-descriptions, Franklin uses printer's language to make his point here: "I was by the Endeavour a better and happier Man than I otherwise should have been, if I had not attempted it; As those who aim at perfect Writing by imitating the engraved Copies, tho' they never reach the wish'd for Excellence of those Copies, their Hand is mended by the Endeavour, and is tolerable while it continues fair and legible." See also his repeated references (e.g., pp. 70, 86, 96, 99, 122, 129) to moral lapses as "errata," along with the occasionally stated hope for the opportunity of a second edition of his life so that he may edit out the errata. In addition, the epitaph he wrote for himself (p. 44n) utilizes the same imagery.

52. Ibid., pp. 157–58.

53. Letter to Lord Kames, 3 May 1760, *Papers,* vol. 9, pp. 103–6. In this letter, Franklin repeats his intention that the *Art of Virtue* will not be based on religious belief: "Christians are directed to have *Faith in Christ,* as the effectual Means of obtaining the Change they desire. It may, when sufficiently strong, be effectual with many. A full Opinion that

a Teacher is infinitely wise, good, and powerful, and that he will certainly reward and punish the Obedient and Disobedient, must give great Weight to his Precepts, and make them much more attended to by his Disciples. But all Men cannot have Faith in Christ; and many have it in so weak a Degree, that it does not produce the Effect. Our *Art of Virtue* may therefore be of great Service to those who have not Faith, and come in Aid of the weak Faith of others. . . . It is, in short, to be adapted for universal Use" (p. 105). See also Franklin's letters to Lord Kames, 21 October 1761, *Papers,* vol. 9, p. 375; 2 June 1765, ibid., vol. 12, p. 162; and 25 February 1767, ibid., vol. 14, p. 71, which convey his excitement about the project. Sometime around 1774, Franklin told David Williams that there "was not much to be done" in the composition of his "little moral work." Letter to David Williams, 4 September 1778, ibid., vol. 27, p. 355. Since no fragments of Franklin's "little moral work" have come down to us, either he exaggerated in the letter to Williams, or the manuscript has been lost. I suspect the former.

Franklin probably intended the *Art of Virtue* to be "of great Service" to youngsters as well. In all his curricular plans for the education of youth, he emphasized the importance of moral instruction. This is best done, he thought, in the teaching of history, where "Observations on the Causes of the Rise or Fall of any Man's Character, Fortune, Power, Ec." can serve as object lessons, fixing "in the Minds of Youth deep Impressions of the Beauty and Usefulness of Virtue of all Kinds." *Papers,* vol. 3, pp. 412, 418. See also vol. 4, p. 325. If virtue is a matter of habituation, it only stands to reason that Franklin advocated early formal training. As he says in a printer's preface to *Cato's Moral Distichs Englished in Couplets* (Philadelphia, 1735), "such excellent Precepts of Morality, contain'd in such short and easily-remember'd Sentences, may to Youth particularly be very serviceable in the Conduct of Life." *Papers,* vol. 2, p. 130.

54. There are few currents in the American Enlightenment less understood than deism's account of reason. Part of the responsibility for this must rest with the frequently confused and abbreviated discussions of it written by the deists themselves. A major study is badly needed. I have attempted a few sorties in *Elihu Palmer's Principles of Nature: Text and Commentary* (Wolfeboro, N.H.: Longwood Academic, 1990), *The American Deists,* and *Rational Infidels.*

55. Elihu Palmer (1764–1806) was the major figure in late eighteenth-century American militant deism. His reflections on the "double despotism" of church and state are primarily found in his 1800/1801 *Principles of Nature; or, A Development of the Moral Causes of Happiness and Misery among the Human Species.* See my *Elihu Palmer's Principles of Nature.* Selections from Palmer's other writings are included in my *The American Deists.* Secondary commentary is scarce, but see Roderick S. French's fine "Elihu Palmer, Radical Deist, Radical Republican: A Reconsideration of American Freethought," in *Studies in Eighteenth-Century Culture,* vol. 8 (Madison: University of Wisconsin Press, 1979); the introduction to my critical edition of *Principles of Nature;* chap. 6 of my *Rational Infidels;* and my "Elihu Palmer's Crusade for Rational Religion," *Religious Humanism* 24 (Summer 1990): 113–29, 146.

56. Like Shaftesbury, Hume was a proponent of moral sense theory. Actions, he argued, are the consequences of passions, and "reason of itself is utterly impotent in this

particular," being concerned exclusively with truth and falsehood. Obviously, then, reason is an unreliable guide in the ethical arena. See *A Treatise of Human Nature* (London, 1740), especially book 3.

57. "Self-Denial Not the Essence of Virtue" (18 February 1734/35), *Papers,* vol. 2, p. 21. In a similar vein, Franklin suggests in his "A Turkish Tale" (1779[?]) that ascetic self-denial runs the risk of encouraging vanity. *Papers,* vol. 31, pp. 310–11.

58. *Autobiography,* p. 157. See also Franklin's letter to Lord Kames, 3 May 1760, n. 53, above.

59. *Autobiography,* p. 147: "not a single moral Principle was inculcated or enforc'd, their Aim seeming to be rather to make us Presbyterians than good Citizens."

60. See *Papers,* vol. 6, pp. 320, 363; vol. 7, p. 89; vol. 8, p. 154.

61. Letter to John Huey, 6 June 1753, *Papers,* vol. 4, pp. 505–6. The passage in which this line appears is worth quoting, because it underscores Franklin's concern for good works and also sheds some light on his attitude to the figure of Jesus. "Your great Master tho't much less of these outward Appearances and Professions than many of his modern Disciples. He prefer'd the *Doers* of the Word, to the meer *Hearers;* the Son that seemingly refus'd to obey his Father, and yet perform'd his Commands, to him that profess'd his Readiness, but neglected the Work; the heretical but charitable Samaritan, to the uncharitable tho' orthodox Priest and sanctified Levite; & those who gave Food to the hungry, Drink to the Thirsty, Raiment to the Naked, Entertainment to the Stranger, and Relief to the Sick, tho' they never heard of his Name, he declares shall in the last Day be accepted, when those who cry Lord! Lord! Who value themselves on their Faith, tho' great enough to perform Miracles, but have neglected good Works, shall be rejected." Franklin's letter is rather harsh in tone, prompted, perhaps, by his exasperation with Huey, whom he elsewhere described as a "zealous Religionist." Five years later, Frankin makes a similar point in a letter to his sister Jane Mecom. In it, he discusses the Christian virtues of faith, hope, and charity, and like Paul concludes that the last is greatest: "Improvement in Religion, is called *Building Up,* and *Edification. Faith* is then the Ground-floor, *Hope* is up one Pair of Stairs. My dearly beloved Jenny, don't delight so much to dwell in these lower Rooms, but get as fast as you can into the Garret; for in truth the best Room in the House is *Charity.*" Letter to Jane Mecom, 16 September 1758, *Papers,* vol. 8, p. 154.

62. Letter to Thomas Coombe Jr., 22 July 1774, *Papers,* vol. 21, p. 246. Elsewhere, Franklin remarks that any religious sect that teaches virtues such as frugality and industry is to be commended because of its utility. "On the Increase of Mankind," 1751, *Papers,* vol. 4, p. 232. In another place, he argues that Christians would be better examples to the "Heathen" than the "vicious and abandoned Wretches" who typically trade with the Indians. Letter to George Whitefield, 2 July 1756, *Papers,* vol. 6, p. 469. He even urges his wife, Deborah, to "go oftener to Church," although whether for moral improvement or to satisfy social expectations is not clear. *Papers,* vol. 10, p. 291. See also vol. 6, p. 320, and vol. 7, p. 78. Finally, one of the reasons Franklin so admired Whitefield was that "His Integrities, Disinterestedness, and indefatigable *Zeal in prosecuting every good work* [my emphasis] I have never seen equalled, I shall never see exceeded." Letter to Noble Wim-

berly Jones, 5 March 1771, *Papers,* vol. 18, p. 53. For more on Franklin's admiration for Whitefield, see chap. 6.

63. Letter to [?], 3 July 1786 [?], *Papers,* vol. 7, pp. 294, 295; 3 July 1757 [?], *Writings,* vol. 9, p. 533.

64. "An Inquiry concerning Virtue and Merit," I, 3, p. 76, in *Characteristics.*

65. This is Page Smith's quite accurate summation of Adams's evaluation of Franklin. See his magisterial *John Adams* (New York: Doubleday, 1962), vol. 1, p. 548. Adams's acidic comments on Franklin's character are legion. See, for example, Butterfield, *Diary and Autobiography of John Adams,* vol. 2, pp. 367, 392; vol. 3, pp. 38–39; vol. 4, pp. 69, 87–88. Two studies that clearly point out that Franklin was not merely a theoretical moralist are Thomas P. Haviland, "Of Franklin, Whitefield, and the Orphans," *Georgia Historical Quarterly* 29 (December 1945): 211–16, and William E. Juhnke, "Benjamin Franklin's View of the Negro and Slavery," *Pennsylvania History* 12 (October 1974): 375–88.

Chapter 6: Sugar and Paper

1. Letter to Elizabeth Partridge, 11 October 1779, *Papers,* vol. 30, p. 514; letter to Comtesse d'Houdetot, 16 February 1788, collection of Vicomte Foy, quoted in Claude-Anne Lopez, *Mon Cher Papa: Franklin and the Ladies of Paris* (New Haven: Yale University Press, 1967), p. 308. The letter to Madame d'Houdetot is not included in *Writings,* but the letter to Michel-Guillaume Jean de Crèvecoeur, in which Franklin enclosed it, does appear there. *Writings,* vol. 9, p. 636.

2. Adams complains in his diary (27 May 1778) that after observing Franklin's dissolute ways he decided that "the Business of our Commission would never be done, unless I did it." Franklin, he asserts, rose late and breakfasted later, occupied his day by entertaining slavish admirers in one or another Parisian salon, and dined out almost every night. Afterward he played at games or listened in company to music, and "came home at all hours from Nine to twelve O Clock at night." Given this schedule, Adams claims, it was impossible to catch Franklin except to secure an occasional quick signature. Such an easy schedule, Adams caustically concludes, was agreeable to Franklin, and no doubt contributed to his health and long life. As for Adams, he conscientiously (and rather priggishly) declined all dinner invitations, stayed at home, and occupied himself with commission business or serious reading. Butterfield, *Diary and Autobiography of John Adams,* vol. 4, p. 118.

3. As Franklin candidly admitted late in life, "For sixty years, now, masculine and feminine things—and I am not talking about modes and tenses—have been giving me a lot of trouble. I used to hope that at the age of 80 I would be free of all that. But here I am, four times 19, which is mighty close to 80, and those French feminines are still bothering me." Quoted by Lopez, *Mon Cher Papa,* p. 25.

4. Letter to Elizabeth Partridge, 11 October 1779, *Papers,* vol. 30, p. 514.

5. Charles Burney, *An Eighteenth-Century Musical Tour in France and Italy,* ed. Percy A. Scholes (New York: Oxford University Press, 1959), vol. 1, p. 27.

6. Unhappily, there is little secondary literature on Madame Brillon. The fullest account is found in Lopez, *Mon Cher Papa,* pp. 29–122. But as Lopez admits, Brillon is a

"most elusive figure" who remains "hidden in the private archives of her descendants" (p. 350). A handful of her musical compositions have been published in Gilbert Chinard, "Music Enjoyed by Franklin," *Proceedings of the American Philosophical Society* 100 (1956): 331–37.

7. For details on the fascinating story of Franklin's courtship and later fatherly affection for Madame Brillon, see Lopez, *Mon Cher Papa,* pp. 29–88.

8. Letter to Madame Brillon, April 1781, *Writings,* vol. 10, p. 418. Franklin also assures the Brillons that "J'aime, moi, tout la Famille sans exception" and that he especially has a "tres bonne Opinion" of "cette admirable" Cunegonde.

9. Ibid., p. 419; translation mine. Franklin had used the simile before. A young Thomas Coombe Jr., who traveled to England in 1768 for ordination in the Church of England, reports a version of it. In a letter to his father (8 October 1770) in which he enthusiastically describes dinner conversation with "Dr. Franklin," Coombe recalls, "He told me some time ago, that Christians did not debate about the Essentials, but about *the Paper and Packthread of Religion.*" *Papers,* vol. 17, p. 241.

10. Letter to Madame Brillon, April 1781, *Writings,* vol. 10, p. 419. These *choses essentielles* are substantially the same as those enumerated by Franklin as early as his "Doctrine to be Preached" (1731) and as late as his letter to Ezra Stiles (1790) outlining his religious beliefs.

11. Ibid. Ever wary of religious dogmatism, Franklin curiously goes on to undercut his own case: "C'est avec ces Pensées que je m'ai satisfait sur cette Sujet. Mais comme les mêmes Raisonnement ne sont bons pour tout le Monde, je ne pretend pas que les miens doivent etre bons pour vous, & pour M. Brillon."

12. Franklin came by his high regard for freedom of conscience naturally. His maternal grandfather, Peter Folger (1617–90), wrote a verse defense in 1675 of religious toleration. Franklin's description of it in his memoirs suggests it was a jeremiad with an interesting spin. It argued that "many Judgments of God" had fallen upon England because of its persecution of "Sectaries" such as Baptists and Quakers. "The whole," adds Franklin, who had read the poem "many Years since . . . appear'd to me as written with a good deal of Decent Plainness and manly Freedom." *Autobiography,* pp. 51–52.

For treatments of Franklin's high regard for religious toleration, see Henry Cohen, *The Religion of Benjamin Franklin* (New York: Jewish Forum, 1957); Leonard W. Labaree, "Franklin and the Presbyterians," *Journal of the Presbyterian Historical Society* 35 (December 1957): 217–28; Melvin H. Buxbaum's authoritative *Benjamin Franklin and the Zealous Presbyterians* (University Park: Pennsylvania State University Press, 1975); and Alfred Owen Aldridge, "Franklin's Experimental Religion," in *Meet Dr. Franklin,* ed. Roy N. Lokken (Philadelphia: Franklin Institute, 1981), pp. 101–23.

13. "Toleration in Old and New England," June 1772, *Papers,* vol. 19, p. 164. Toward the end of his life, Franklin rejoiced over the legal act that mandated religious freedom for non-Catholics in France because he saw it as a "good step" toward that open-mindedness that leads to an end to persecution. Letter to M. Le Veillard, 8 June 1788, *Writings,* vol. 9, p. 657.

14. The quotations are taken from a draft of an apparently unsent response Franklin wrote to his parents. The letter he eventually mailed them is less peremptory and more

accommodating. Given the impatient tone of the draft, one surmises that Josiah and Abiah's concern (and possible chastisement) hit a raw nerve. Both the draft and the final version are in *Papers,* vol. 2, pp. 202–4. Franklin's parents may have sensed they had crossed over the line with their son. Their response to his letter was both swift and conciliatory, as suggested by a letter from Franklin to his father in May 1738 in which he writes, "it gave me great Pleasure when [Abiah] declar'd in her next to me that she approv'd of my letter and was now satisfy'd with me." Ibid., p. 206. My guess is that Abiah in fact was far from satisfied.

15. Ibid., p. 203.

16. For example: "We have justly deny'd the Infallibility of the Pope and his Councils and Synods in their Interpretations of Scripture, and can we modestly claim *Infallibility* for our selves or our Synods in our way of Interpreting? . . . it little becomes poor Fallible Man to be positive and dogmatical in his Opinions." "Dialogue between Two Presbyterians" (1735), *Papers,* vol. 2, p. 33. In the same work, Franklin rhetorically asks: "do you think that the Reformation was of a sudden perfect, and that the first Reformers knew at once all that was right or wrong in Religion[?]" Ibid., p. 31. Franklin also opines, "A Pretence to Infallibility is absurd," in his pamphlet *A Letter to a Friend in the Country* (1735). *Papers,* vol. 2, p. 78. In a *Pennsylvania Gazette* (27 March 1735) piece entitled "Veridicus on a pertinacious Obstinacy in Opinion," attributed to Franklin by Leo Lemay, Franklin writes, "in our present fallible Condition . . . a Love of Truth and Goodness is not more essential to an honest Man than a readiness to change his Mind and Practice, upon Conviction that he is in the wrong." Lemay, *Canon of Benjamin Franklin,* p. 89. In a letter to Mary Stevenson (1759): "All our Knowledge is so imperfect, and we are from a thousand Causes so perpetually subject to Mistake and Error, that Positiveness can scarce ever become even the most Knowing." *Papers,* vol. 8, p. 456. In responding to a critic of his involvement in the Hutchinson letters affair, Franklin writes, "I am sensible there is a good deal of Truth in the Adage, that *our Sins and our Debts are always more than we take them to be;* and tho' I cannot at present on Examination of my Conscience charge myself with any Immorality of that kind, it becomes me to suspect that what has *long appeared* to you may have some Foundation." Letter to Josiah Tucker (26 February 1774), *Papers,* vol. 21, pp. 127–28. And in a speech to the Constitutional Convention delivered on 17 September 1787, Franklin humorously congratulates the delegates on their willingness to consider dissenting perspectives: "Most men, indeed, as well as most sects in religion, think themselves in possession of all truth, and that wherever others differ from them, it is so far error. Steele, a Protestant, in a dedication, tells the Pope, that the only difference between our two churches in their opinions of the certainty of their doctrine, is, the Romish Church is *infallible,* and the Church of England is *never in the wrong.* But, though many private Persons think almost as highly of their own infallibility as of that of their Sect, few express it so naturally as a certain French lady, who, in a little dispute with her sister, said, 'But I meet with nobody but myself that is *always* in the right.'" *Writings,* vol. 9, p. 607.

17. Letter to Mary Stevenson, 2 September 1769, *Papers,* vol. 16, p. 193. Franklin goes on to claim that a life regulated by reason has no need for the "imaginary Pains and

Mortifications" of religious zealotry and that Mary, therefore, "ought not to wish [herself] an Enthusiast."

18. Letter to Jane Mecom, 23 February 1769, *Papers,* vol. 16, p. 51. Religious quarrels have become so ugly, writes Franklin, that Christians, who from the earliest days of the church were associated with love, are now inextricably associated in the minds of many with hatred. Franklin so deplored sectarian hatred that he took a last shot at it toward the end of his life. In a letter (25 November 1788) to Elizabeth Partridge, he writes "with regard to future Bliss I cannot help imagining, that Multitudes of the zealously Orthodox of different Sects, who at the last Day may flock together, in hopes of seeing [mutilated] damn'd, will be disappointed, and oblig'd to rest content with their own Salvation." *Writings,* vol. 9, p. 683.

19. See chap. 3 for a discussion of the possibility of "ironic commitment." Franklin once advised a young Mason Weems (who would later write hagiographies of both Franklin and Washington) that it made little difference whether he was ordained by bishops from the Church of England or the Church of Ireland. One was as good as the other; the manner of ordination was perfectly contingent. What mattered were core beliefs, not ritualisms. Letter to Mason Weems and Edward Gant, 18 July 1784, *Writings,* vol. 9, p. 239.

20. So much so that Franklin saw no reason to devote more than two short paragraphs to it in his memoirs. See *Autobiography,* pp. 167–68.

21. In fact Andrews, who had preached in Philadelphia since 1698, played a key role in organizing the synod in 1717. See Merton A. Christensen, "Franklin on the Hemphill Trial: Deism Versus Presbyterian Orthodoxy," *William and Mary Quarterly,* 3d ser., 10 (1953): 422–40.

22. Apparently, however, his personal life did. Andrews was suspended from the ministry in 1744 on moral charges but shortly thereafter reinstated. See Christensen, "Franklin on the Hemphill Trial," p. 426, and Aldridge, *Benjamin Franklin and Nature's God,* p. 98.

23. *Autobiography,* pp. 147–48.

24. Ibid., p. 167. Hemphill's emphasis on virtue as the heart of religious belief perfectly accorded, or course, with Franklin's own convictions. In his first apology for Hemphill, "Dialogue between Two Presbyterians," Franklin asserts that morality "made the principal Part" of the original apostles' preaching and was the primary point of Jesus' Sermon on the Mount. A bit later, he claims that religious faith without morality leads to a "Want of Charity" and "notorious . . . Heart-burnings and Bickerings." *Papers,* vol. 2, pp. 29, 31.

25. Hemphill was actually accused of eight separate breaches of orthodoxy. See *Papers,* vol. 2, pp. 41–43. Andrews's charge that Hemphill's sermons appealed to "freethinkers, Deists, nothings" is in a letter to Benjamin Colman, 14 June 1735, cited in Christensen, "Franklin on the Hemphill Trial," p. 436.

26. In his *Autobiography* (p. 167), Franklin recalls writing "two or three Pamphlets, and one Piece in the Gazette of April 1735" in defense of Hemphill. His memory was good. The first piece, written before the trial began, was "Dialogue between Two Presbyteri-

ans." It appeared in the *Pennsylvania Gazette* on 10 April 1735. The next three items were pamphlets: *Observations on the Proceedings against Mr. Hemphill* (July 1735); *A Letter to a Friend in the Country* (September 1735); and *A Defence of the Rev. Mr. Hemphill's Observations* (October 1735), which was a reply to Jonathan Dickinson's *A Vindication of the Reverend Commission of the Synod,* published a month earlier. See *Papers,* vol. 2, pp. 27–33, 37–65, 65–88, 90–126. Franklin's authorship of anything more in *A Letter to a Friend* than its preface has not been definitively established. But as Melvin H. Buxbaum points out, there are no stylistic or substantive reasons to doubt that the pamphlet is either entirely or mostly Franklin's. See his *Benjamin Franklin and the Zealous Presbyterians,* p. 234.

27. Hemphill's case was probably irredeemably damaged by the discovery during his trial that his wonderful sermons, supposedly delivered extemporaneously, in fact were plagiarisms. After he was found out, Hemphill, who was a "poor Writer" at best, confessed to Franklin that his prodigious memory allowed him "to retain and repeat any Sermon after one Reading only." The disclosure of Hemphill's deception only underscored in the minds of many his moral unworthiness to function as a man of the cloth. In Hemphill's defense, two points may be made. The first was offered by Franklin: "I rather approv'd his giving us good Sermons compos'd by others, than bad ones of his own Manufacture." *Autobiography,* p. 160. The second is that harried clerics' plagiarizing of sermons was not unusual. The protagonist in George MacDonald's novel *Thomas Wingfield, Curate* (1875), for example, regularly and guiltlessly passes on his late uncle's sermons as his own. MacDonald ultimately condemns the practice, but his raising of it to make a moral point suggests that the strategy was a popular one in his day.

28. *A Defence of the Rev. Mr. Hemphill's Observations,* pp. 113, 121.

29. Ibid., pp. 114, 115. This characterization of the clergy is reminiscent of Franklin's famous Dogood letter (no. 4) on Harvard divinity students. *Papers,* vol. 1, pp. 14–18. See chap. 1 for a discussion of this letter.

30. *A Defence of the Rev. Mr. Hemphill's Observations,* pp. 59, 49; *A Letter to a Friend in the Country,* p. 71.

31. *A Letter to a Friend in the Country,* p. 78.

32. Ibid., p. 80.

33. Ibid.

34. Ibid., pp. 83–84.

35. See, for example, chap. 5 for a discussion of Franklin's 1786 [?] letter to an unknown correspondent where he voices his fears about popular infidelity.

36. W. B. Yeats, "The Second Coming," in *Collected Poems,* ed. Richard J. Finneran (New York: Collier, 1989), p. 187.

37. *A Letter to a Friend in the Country,* pp. 83, 84, 85. According to his grandson, Franklin once told Samuel Johnson, president of King's (Columbia) College, that the more churches built, the better: "to build a new church in a growing place, is not properly *dividing,* but *multiplying,* and will really be a means of increasing the number of those who worship God in that way." Pluralism was no threat to religion. W. T. Franklin, *Memoirs of the Life and Writings of Benjamin Franklin,* vol. 2, p. 299.

38. *A Defence of the Rev. Mr. Hemphill's Observations,* p. 104. In his earlier *Letter,* Franklin referred to the Golden Rule as the "grand Law of Christianity," p. 78. See also *Observations on the Proceedings, Papers,* vol. 2, pp. 58–59.

39. *A Letter to a Friend in the Country,* pp. 78, 76.

40. One of Franklin's most pungent witticisms is associated with his attendance at Philadelphia's Anglican Christ Church. In June 1730 someone stole Deborah Franklin's prayer book out of the family pew. In a subsequent note in the *Pennsylvania Gazette,* Franklin asked that "the Person who took it, is desir'd to open it and read the *Eighth* Commandment, and afterwards return it to the same Pew again." *Papers,* vol. 2, p. 188. This is more than an illustration of Franklin's wit. It also underscores the high premium he placed on virtue in religion.

41. *A Defence of the Rev. Mr. Hemphill's Observations,* p. 103. Two of Franklin's later allusions to Presbyterians illustrate the extent of his animosity. Both are drawn from letters to his sister Jane Mecom. In the earlier letter (28 June 1756), Franklin humorously recalls "the Story of the Member of Parliament, who began one of his Speeches with saying, he thank'd God he was born and bred a Presbyterian; on which another took leave to observe, that the Gentleman must needs be of a most grateful Disposition, since he was thankful for such very small Matters." *Papers,* vol. 6, p. 463. In the later letter (9 January 1760), Franklin famously refers to "we zealous Presbyterians" who are "too apt to think ourselves alone in the right, and that besides all the Heathens, Mahometans and Papists, whom we give to Satan in a Lump, other Sects of Christian Protestants that do not agree with us, will hardly escape Perdition." Ibid., vol. 9, pp. 17–18.

42. For more on the bickering that arose from Franklin's defense of Hemphill, see Buxbaum, *Benjamin Franklin and the Zealous Presbyterians,* pp. 104–15.

43. *Papers,* vol. 2, p. 138.

44. *Pennsylvania Gazette,* 15 November 1739, *Papers,* vol. 2, p. 242.

45. Ibid., pp. 242–44.

46. Ibid., 29 November 1739, *Papers,* vol. 2, p. 244.

47. Buxbaum, *Benjamin Franklin and the Zealous Presbyterians,* pp. 141–46.

48. And it was generally effective, too. In his *Autobiography* (p. 177), Franklin admits that even a hardheaded listener like himself was moved to empty his pockets, first of copper, then silver, then gold, when Whitefield called for donations after one of his sermons. For a magisterial analysis of Whitefield's pulpit theatricality, see Harry S. Stout's *The Divine Dramatist: George Whitefield and the Rise of Modern Evangelicalism* (Grand Rapids, Mich.: William B. Eerdmans, 1991). Stout also discusses the friendship between Franklin and Whitefield (pp. 220–33). Frank Lambert's *"Pedlar in Divinity": George Whitefield and the Transatlantic Revivals, 1737–1770* (Princeton: Princeton University Press, 1994) is also worth consulting, particularly pp. 134–68.

49. Letter to Thomas Hopkinson [?], 16 October 1746, *Papers,* vol. 3, p. 88.

50. *Autobiography,* p. 178; letter to Jane Mecom, 7[–9] November 1770, *Papers,* vol. 17, p. 284.

51. Truth to tell, Franklin was probably also delighted that Whitefield increasingly angered a good percentage of orthodox Presbyterian divines by stirring up their con-

gregations in his revivalist sorties and disrupting the religious status quo. I suspect that Franklin, still angered about the Hemphill affair, was gratified by any exposure of Presbyterian cant. For more on the acquaintanceship between the two men, see David T. Morgan, "A Most Unlikely Friendship: Benjamin Franklin and George Whitefield," *The Historian* 47 (February 1985): 208–18.

52. *A Letter to the Inhabitants of Maryland, Virginia, and North and South Carolina Concerning their Negroes,* in *The Works of the Reverend George Whitefield, M.A.* (London: Edward and Charles Dilly, 1771), vol. 4, pp. 38, 37. The passage in which Whitefield compares slaves to household pets is quite eloquent: "Your dogs are caressed and fondled at your tables; but your slaves, who are frequently stated dogs or beasts, have not an equal privilege: they are scarce permitted to pick up the crumbs which fall from their masters tables; nay, some, as I have been informed by an eye-witness, have been, upon the most trifling provocation, cut with knives, and have had forks thrown into their flesh: not to mention what numbers have been given up to the inhuman usage of cruel taskmasters, who by their unrelenting scourges have plowed upon their backs, and made long furrows, and at length brought them even to death itself" (p. 38).

53. Letter to John Wesley, 25 August 1724, in *The Works of the Reverend George Whitefield, M.A.,* vol. 1, p. 205.

54. Letter to Noble Wimberly Jones, 5 March 1771, *Papers,* vol. 18, p. 53. Obviously Franklin was willing to exempt zeal for good works from his usual condemnation of zealotry.

55. At one point Franklin helped raise funds to build a general meetinghouse in Philadelphia that he envisioned as a gathering place "for the Use of any Preacher of any religious Persuasion who might desire to say something to the People of Philadelphia" about his sect. Even a missionary sent from the Moslem "Mufti of Constantinople" should "find a Pulpit at his Service." This echoes a sentiment in "Dialogue between Two Presbyterians," where Franklin asked, "And if the Turks, believing us in the wrong, as we think them, should out of the same charitable Disposition, send a Missionary to preach Mahometanism to us, ought we not in the same manner to give him free Liberty of preaching his Doctrine?" *Papers,* vol. 2, p. 32. Whitefield, on the other hand, had a quite different idea about how the meetinghouse should be used. In his judgment, only "orthodox experimental ministers" should be given access to its pulpit. Quoted in Walter Herbert Stowe, *Life and Letters of Bishop William White* (New York: King's Crown Press, 1937), p. 11.

56. Quoted in Aldridge, *Benjamin Franklin and Nature's God,* p. 115. No original citation given.

57. Ibid. John Adams relates a version of the sermon in a letter to Thomas Jefferson: "[Whitefield] began; 'Father Abraham'! With his hands and Eyes gracefully directed to the Heavens as I have more than once seen him; 'Father Abraham,' 'who have you there with you?' [']have you Catholicks?' No. 'Have you Protestants.' No. 'Have you Churchmen.' No. 'Have you Dissenters.' No. 'Have you Presbyterians?' No. 'Quakers?' No. [']Anabaptists?' No. 'Who have you then?' 'Are you alone?' No.

'My Brethren,! You have the Answer to all these questions in the Words of my Text, 'He who feareth God and worketh Righteousness, shall be accepted of him.'" Adams concludes by saying that if Whitefield really said as much, there is no philosopher, theologian, or moralist, "ancient of modern," more profound. Letter to Thomas Jefferson, 3 December 1813, *The Adams-Jefferson Letters,* ed. Lester J. Cappon (Chapel Hill: University of North Carolina Press, 1988), p. 406.

58. "*Conte,*" *Writings,* vol. 10, p. 123.

59. It is not entirely clear when Franklin wrote his version of the Lord's Prayer. Scholarly estimates span half a century, even though it is most likely that the revision was written between late 1768 and 1773. See *Papers,* vol. 15, p. 299.

60. *Papers,* vol. 15, p. 301.

61. Ibid., p. 302.

62. Ibid., vol. 20, pp. 346, 351, 347.

63. Letter to Granville Sharp, 5 July 1785, *Writings,* vol. 9, p. 358. In this letter Franklin admits that the edited prayer book was so "retrenched" that "approbation could hardly be expected" and acknowledges that perhaps a more moderate abridgement would have made his and Le Despencer's work more palatable.

64. *Papers,* vol. 20, p. 350. Franklin was convinced that long and elaborate liturgies and prayers bored rather than edified. In a 13 January 1772 letter to Ezra Stiles, for example, he criticizes Hinduism because of its overabundance of complicated ceremonies and prayers, and notes that a similar hypertrophic growth can be found in the "Romish Church." Ibid., vol. 19, pp. 30–31. In the "Preface" to the revised prayer book, Franklin notes that Jesus himself set a "short prayer as an example," and he asserts that "Morning and Evening Service," which are "so long, and filled with so many repetitions, that the continued attention suitable to so serious a duty becomes impracticable, the mind wanders, and the fervency of devotion is slackened," could profit from following that early exemplar. Ibid., vol. 20, p. 346.

65. "A Parable on Brotherly Love," *Papers,* vol. 6, p. 127. As with so many of Franklin's parables, the date of this one is unclear. Probably the best estimate is 1774–75. In this parable, Franklin tells the story of the ancient Israelite Reuben, who selfishly refuses the loan of an iron ax to three needy neighbors. Reuben's ax falls into a river and is lost. He goes to each of his three neighbors, who by this time have purchased their own axes, and requests help. One of them refuses: "Thou wouldst not lend me thine Ax, therefore will I not lend thee mine." One shames Reuben: "Thou wouldst not lend me thine when I desired it, but I will be better than thee, and will lend thee mine." But the third gladly shares his ax, saying, as indicated in the text, that all men are brothers. On the most obvious level, the parable is a tale of moral instruction. But it also suggests that tribal and sectarian differences ought not blanket over the more substantial spiritual connections between persons.

66. *Autobiography,* p. 146.

67. Ibid. See also Franklin's remarks in a letter to Henry Bouquet that Christendom is "torn to Pieces by Factions religious and civil." *Papers,* vol. 11, p. 367.

68. Letter to Cadwallader Colden, 14 May 1752. *Papers,* vol. 4, p. 311. In a "Statement of Editorial Policy" published in the 24 July 1740 edition of *The Pennsylvania Gazette* (ibid., vol. 6, p. 260), Franklin made a similar point: "It is a Principle among Printers, that when Truth has fair Play, it will always prevail over Falshood; . . . if what is thus

publish'd be good, Mankind has the Benefit of it: If it be bad . . . The more 'tis made publick, the more its Weakness is expos'd, and the greater Disgrace falls upon the Author, whoever he be; who is at the same Time depriv'd of an Advantage he would otherwise without fail make use of, viz. of Complaining *that Truth is suppress'd, and that he could say* MIGHTY MATTERS, *had he but the Opportunity of being heard.*"

It should be noted here, however, that Franklin's ambivalence breaks through even his passionate championing of the free marketplace of religious ideas. Some religious ideas, it seems, are too incendiary to allow on the market. In his *Autobiography* (pp. 73–74), he mentions a Dr. John Browne, of Burlington, New Jersey, who was "much of an Unbeliever, and wickedly undertook . . . to travesty the Bible in doggrel Verse." The parody was never published, much to the relief of Franklin, who concludes that it might have hurt "weak minds." See also *Papers,* vol. 7, pp. 294–95.

69. Letter to Cadwallader Colden, 23 April 1752. *Papers,* vol. 4, p. 301. In this letter, Franklin has been discussing issues in natural philosophy. But in an aside to Colden, he hints at the religious implications of their epistolary discussion of physics: "'Tis well we are not, as poor Galileo was, subject to the Inquisition for Philosophical Heresy. My Whispers against the orthodox Doctrine in private letters, would be dangerous; your Writing and Printing would be highly criminal."

Toward the end of his life, in referring to his old friend Joseph Priestley as an "honest heretic," Franklin reflected on his admiration of religious heresy: "I think all the heretics I have known have been virtuous men. They have the virtue of fortitude, or they would not venture to own their heresy; and they cannot afford to be deficient in any of the other virtues, as that would give advantage to their many enemies; and they have not, like orthodox sinners, such a number of friends to excuse or justify them." Letter to Benjamin Vaughan, 24 October 1788, *Writings,* vol. 9, p. 677.

70. In a letter to Richard Price (9 October 1780), Franklin writes that if eighteenth-century Christian preachers truly followed in the footsteps of Christ and the apostles, they would neither accept salaries nor insist on religious tests. Such tests, which are historically of late origin, are designed to secure "Emoluments" more than religion. Moreover, their presence points to a spiritual corruption within the tradition itself. *Writings,* vol. 6, p. 154.

71. Franklin had as little patience for Christian intolerance of non-Christians as for intra-Christian squabbling. He writes, for example, that Moslem missionaries should have as much liberty to proselytize as Christian ones (*Autobiography,* p. 176; *Papers,* vol. 2, p. 32), and in quoting a long passage from Vattel's *Le Droit des Gens,* he edits out an anti-Semitic line. Letter to Count Andreas Peter von Bernstorff, 22 December 1779, *Papers,* vol. 31, p. 264, n. 5.

72. "A Narrative of the Massacres," *Papers,* vol. 11, pp. 55–56. Franklin's words were prompted by his disgust at the 1764 slaughter of Indian men, women, and children by the notorious Paxton Boys. His denunciation of this racially motivated murder intentionally gestures at the equal outrage of religious persecution: "It is well known that Indians are of different Tribes, Nations and Languages, as well as the White People. In

Europe, if the French, who are White-People, should injure the Dutch, are they to revenge it on the English, because they too are White People? The only Crime of these poor Wretches seems to have been, that they had a reddish brown Skin, and black Hair; and some People of that Sort, it seems, had murdered some of our Relations. If it be right to kill Men for such a Reason, then, should any Man, with a freckled Face and red Hair, kill a Wife or Child of mine, it would be right for me to revenge it, by killing all the freckled red-haired Men, Women and Children, I could afterwards any where meet with." Ibid., p. 55.

73. Franklin's notes on "Documents on the Hearing of William Smith's Petition," 27 April 1758, *Papers,* vol. 8, p. 42. Franklin concludes that the religious toleration practiced by the Quakers "induc'd great Numbers of different Religions and Nations to remove into Pensilvania with their Families and Effects, thereby encreasing the Strength and Commerce of this Kingdom." Always practical, Franklin not only viewed religious freedom as ethically right; he also valued it for its pragmatic consequence of strengthening commerce. Three years earlier, in "A Dialogue between X, Y, & Z," Franklin had praised Quaker toleration along similar lines. *Papers,* vol. 6, pp. 301–2.

74. *Autobiography,* p. 190.

75. Ibid., pp. 190–91.

76. Letter to Ezra Stiles, 19 January 1790, *Writings,* vol. 10, p. 85. Franklin somewhat disingenuously adds "Without reflecting on them for those that appeared to me unsupportable and even absurd. All sects here, and we have a great Variety, have experienced my good will in assisting them with Subscriptions for building their new Places of Worship; and, as I have never opposed any of their Doctrines, I hope to go out of the World in Peace with them all." The Stiles letter is interesting because it provides a succinct statement of Franklin's religious beliefs (or at least those he was willing to share) at the close of his life. Particularly revealing are his remarks about Jesus. Franklin disclaims belief in his divinity but asserts that "it is a question I do not dogmatize upon, having never studied it, and I think it needless to busy myself with it now, when I expect soon an Opportunity of knowing the Truth with less Trouble." Characteristically, Franklin adds that there is no harm in the belief of Jesus' divinity if it has the "good Consequence" of making his moral teachings "more respected and better observed" (p. 84). Earlier, in a letter to Mary Stevenson, Franklin appears to have argued that the three wilderness temptations of Jesus were "visionary" rather than actual. This seems Franklin's general way of interpreting scriptural accounts of miracles. Letter to Mary Stevenson, 1760–62, *Papers,* vol. 9, p. 266. For more of Franklin's reflections on Jesus, see chap. 5.

77. *The Works of John Adams,* ed. Charles Francis Adams (Boston: Charles C. Little and James Brown, 1851), vol. 1, p. 661. Adams concludes by writing, "Indeed, all sects considered him, and I believe justly, a friend to unlimited toleration in matters of religion." Given Adams's general disapproval of Franklin, it is more than likely he intended more than one meaning here.

78. "The Levee," 1779 [?], *Writings,* vol. 7, p. 431.

79. "The Captivity of William Henry," 1768, *Papers,* vol. 15, p. 157.

Index

KERRY S. WALTERS, a specialist in early American philosophy and philosophy of religion, is Distinguished Teaching Professor in the Humanities and Professor of Philosophy at Gettysburg College. He is the author of a number of books, including *The American Deists: Voices of Reason and Dissent in the Early Republic* and *Rational Infidels: The American Deists.*

UNIVERSITY OF ILLINOIS PRESS
1325 SOUTH OAK STREET
CHAMPAIGN, ILLINOIS 61820-6903
WWW.PRESS.UILLINOIS.EDU